Narrative and Its Discontents

Narrative and Its Discontents

Problems of Closure in the Traditional Novel

by
D. A. Miller

PRINCETON UNIVERSITY PRESS
PRINCETON, NEW JERSEY

First Princeton Paperback printing, 1989

Publication of this book has been aided by a grant from the
Paul Mellon Fund of Princeton University Press

This book has been composed in Linotype Janson

Clothbound editions of Princeton University Press books
are printed on acid-free paper, and binding materials are
chosen for strength and durability

Printed in the United States of America by Princeton
University Press, Princeton, New Jersey

For H.M. and I.M.M.

Contents

see p 273 for Balzac

[vii]

Preface

—Il y avait un Pharaon. Il avait un collège de magi-
ciens attachés à sa personne.
—Pauvre homme . . .
—Survient Moise.
—Je l'admets. Si rien ne survenait, il n'y aurait pas
d'histoire.
—Très juste. On pourrait en faire une théorie du
roman.[1]

IT IS TOO BAD that Valéry never went on to give the
"theory of the novel" whose prospect he facetiously raises
in this passage. Ideally, it would have been no less than a
theory of the conditions that make narrative possible. To use
one of his own terms, it could have described the "implex"
of the novel—the cluster of latent potentialities that permit
a narrative to unfold. While such a theory will not be developed in the study that follows, I have taken its possibility
as a charter for my readings of three nineteenth-century
novelists: Jane Austen, George Eliot, and Stendhal. These
will focus not so much on narrative as on what I shall be
calling the "narratable": the instances of disequilibrium,
suspense, and general insufficiency from which a given narrative appears to arise. The term is meant to cover the various incitements to narrative, as well as the dynamic ensuing
from such incitements, and it is thus opposed to the "nonnarratable" state of quiescence assumed by a novel before the
beginning and supposedly recovered by it at the end. It is
my hope that the shift of emphasis—from narrative to its
underlying impulsions in the narratable—will better allow

[1] Paul Valéry, *L'Idée fixe* (Paris: Gallimard, 1938), pp. 140-41.

us to identify and account for a central tension in the traditional novelistic enterprise: namely, a discomfort with the processes and implications of narrative itself.

This discomfort represents a common ground on which three otherwise very dissimilar novelists meet. It is significant that all three orient their texts toward a "utopic" state that is radically at odds with the narrative means used to reach it. Jane Austen's novels, for example, are directed toward a state of absolute propriety: proper understanding expressed in proper erotic objects and proper social arrangements. Yet her narratives are generated precisely by an underlying instability of desire, language, and society, and as such, they are inevitably felt to threaten the very possibility of this definitive, "finalizing" state of affairs. Similarly, in *Middlemarch*, George Eliot directs her text toward a state of all-encompassing transcendence from which it is continually drawn back by the dispersive and fragmentary logic of the narrative itself. Similarly, too, the erotic excitement supremely cherished by Stendhal always gets misplaced as soon as it is committed to a "plot"—and in his case, the frustration remains even on apparently reaching the end of plot, "satisfaction." The project of these novelists seems curiously perverse, as though each had chosen the vehicle (narrative) least suited to its desired tenor (propriety, transcendence, erotic intensity). Their narratives stubbornly reach after what, as narratives, they seem intrinsically prevented from being. Accordingly, each novelist raises a problem far more radical than the specific problems furnished by the actual narrative: the problem of there being a narrative at all. In the case of Jane Austen and George Eliot, the novelist's implied ambition extends beyond resolving the particular issues of the story at hand to removing the very conditions under which a story is possible. In Stendhal, the impatience that he and his heroes display toward their narratives comes from a sense that the latter are always impoverishments of a richer (if only because less specified) order of possibilities. Whereas the novels of Jane Austen and George Eliot long to eliminate the narratable, those of Stendhal wish to preserve it, without committing or confining it to a particular narrative.

Each novelist, of course, motivates the narratable with different kinds of content, and these will need definition and analysis. In general, however, all the motivations refer us to two primary determinations: the drift of desire, continually wandering in a suggestible state of mediation, and the drift of the sign, producing other signs as it moves toward—or away from—a full and settled meaning. Whether in its erotic or semiotic dimension, the narratable inherently lacks finality. It may be suspended by a moral or ideological expendiency, but it can never be properly brought to term. The tendency of a narrative would therefore be *to keep going*, and a narrative closure would be, in Mallarmé's phrase, a "faire semblant." I should emphasize that the problematic of closure thus posed has nothing to do with the frequently evoked conflict between the closed form of art (as Henry James said, "all discrimination and selection") and the openness of life ("all inclusion and confusion"). The conflict that interests me here occurs not between the novel and its referent, but, within the novel, between the principles of production and the claims of closure to a resolved meaning.[2]

---

[2] In general, the word "closure" will be used instead of "ending" throughout this study. The former refers us better, I think, to the *functions* of an ending: to justify the cessation of narrative and to complete the meaning of what has gone before.

The term was first given currency in Anglo-American criticism by Barbara H. Smith, and her *Poetic Closure: A Study of How Poems End* remains a valuable introduction to the subject. Although she has little to say about narrative, the distinction she draws between "what keeps a poem going" and "what stops it from going" breaks the ground for a discussion of narrative in analogous terms. Ultimately, however, her general treatment of closure is limited by its purely descriptive and somewhat static character. She usefully catalogues closural themes and devices, but she never addresses the claim of closure to be offering a full or final meaning. As a result, not only is she unable to come to grips with the adequacy of closure, but she must also beg the question of its sheer possibility.

Substantial evidence of such a conflict is offered by all
three writers. Even in Jane Austen, whose novels are regulated by a comic marriage plot with an easily predictable
outcome, closure needs to be a moment of suppression,
where something is "a little disguised, or a little mistaken."
As we shall see, the ulterior object of this suppression is the
narrative dynamic itself, which can never be accommodated
in a final settlement. The closural scenes of *Middlemarch*,
seemingly set up to transcend the main sources of narrative
in the novel, are in fact the site of radical ambiguities, so
that it becomes doubtful whether transcendence has taken
place, or merely a deluded transcendence effect. In Stendhal,
either there seems to be no closure at all (as in *Lucien
Leuwen*), or it exists only to be subverted (much as Julien
Sorel gives himself a fate in order to enjoy the inconclusiveness of wondering what his fate may possibly mean).

I should indicate what I think the sheer existence of these
problems of closure implies for the theory of narrative. Although most of twentieth-century narratology pivots on the
priority of ending, or narrative closure, it also takes nothing
so much for granted. The accounts of traditional narrative
offered by the Russian Formalists, Jean-Paul Sartre, Frank
Kermode, Roland Barthes, Gérard Genette, Julia Kristeva,
and Charles Grivel have enormously varied ambitions, but
they all rely on the common assumption of an a priori "determination of means by the ends."[3] Sartre puts it in a nut-

[3] Gérard Genette, "Vraisemblance et motivation," *Figures II*, p. 94.
Similar postulations of end-determination are found in: Boris Tomashevsky, "Thematics," in Lee T. Lemon and Marian J. Reis, eds. and
trans., *Russian Formalist Criticism: Four Essays*, pp. 61-95; Jean-Paul
Sartre, *La Nausée*; Frank Kermode, *The Sense of an Ending*; Roland
Barthes, "Introduction à l'analyse structurale des récits"; Julia Kristeva, "Le texte clos," *Semiotike: Recherches pour une sémanalyse*, pp.
113-42; and Charles Grivel, *Production de l'intérêt romanesque*.
The best of these critics find ways to qualify the primacy of ending. Tomashevsky's concept of "free motifs" is one such qualification, and Kermode's emphasis on the moment of standing "in the
middest" is another. Sartre later modifies his theory of ending

shell in *La Nausée*: "Une chose commence pour finir." Everything in a narrative exists in view of the hidden necessity determined by its final configuration of event and meaning. While this assumption has given us several illuminating studies of the novel, which my own inquiry is happy to profit from, it has some clear limitations. Once the ending is enshrined as an all-embracing cause in which the elements of a narrative find their ultimate justification, it is difficult for analysis to assert anything short of total coherence. One is barred even from suspecting possible discontinuities between closure and the narrative movement preceding it, not to mention possible contradictions and ambiguities within closure itself.

The limitations of this perspective are precisely what enables Sartre, Barthes, or Grivel to go on to condemn the "récit classique." Whether condemnation takes the form of Sartre's charge of "bad faith," Barthes's censure of the "readerly," or Grivel's curse on "ideology," it is always based on the tyranny of a narrative so thoroughly predestined that it does nothing but produce spurious problems for a solution already in place. The danger of these anathemas, even coming from such sophisticated intelligences, is that they ultimately repeat the foreclosure of which they accuse the novel. When Grivel declares that a materialist literature must "abolish the novel," one is almost tempted to think that his militant recommendation merely serves to motivate the dead end reached by his theory. Once we can rest assured that all novels are completely legislated in advance, according to an identical general pattern, our serious interest is virtually forced to turn elsewhere.

I doubt whether we are in a position to take even the traditional novel thus for granted. If only to insist on our continuing need to *read* it, I shall be arguing that closure never

---

through the useful notion of "counterfinality," developed in "Question de méthode." Barthes, too, moves to a more flexible treatment of closure in *S/Z* and *Le Plaisir du texte*.

has the totalizing powers of organization that these critics claim for it. I have doubtless countered the one-sidedness of cases for end-determination with a one-sided emphasis of my own, which may at times lead me into the appearance of suggesting that closure is a wholly arbitrary imposition on the novel. My real argument, of course, is not that novels do not "build" toward closure, but that they are never fully or finally governed by it. The nineteenth-century novel seemed to be the best ground for such an argument, precisely *because* it is a text of abundant restrictions and regulations. For the regulations would be unnecessary if nothing resisted them, and the restrictions come into force for a reason. The ultimate subject of this study is the uneasiness raised in the novel text by its *need* for controls, an uneasiness of which problems of closure would only be the most visible symptom.

There remains to remark that this uneasiness will by no means take the same form or have the same value in each case. Since the trouble is specifically textual, there can be no shortcut through the detailed process of reading the texts. In Jane Austen, for example, what motivates the narratability of a story coincides with what the novelist strongly disapproves of (waywardness, flirtation), and what motivates closure is associated with her most important official values (settlement, moral insight, and judgment). In George Eliot, these equations are both preserved and reversed. On one hand, the narratable is a similarly negative phenomenon, and closure would ideally transcend the processes by which the story has been produced. On the other hand, while the narratable may not be the good or the beautiful, it *is* the true: *Middlemarch* is largely a world of processes that can only be suspended by acts of "make-believe." Closure thus becomes an impossibility on principle, even as it urgently takes place. If Austen's representation cannot justify the narratable, Eliot's difficulties come in justifying a fully narrated state of affairs. Stendhal is the most devious case of all. His crucial values (freedom, spontaneity, being oneself) are located neither in the narrative proper (plot always presupposing a move from "red" to "black"), nor in closure (which even more radically falsifies his values), but in the failures of both. Elaborately set-up plots fall flat, get bungled or even abandoned, in a constantly reenacted recovery of open-endedness, that is, a blissful moment of release from the tyranny of narrative control.

I have always taken comfort in the doctrine of Henry James, who said, "It is in the *waste*—the waste of time, of passion, of curiosity, of contact, that the true initiation resides." I must therefore express my deepest thanks to Peter Brooks and Martin Price, who, as advisers of this study when it was a doctoral dissertation at Yale University, generously staked their time, passion, curiosity, contact on the chances of my wastefulness. I also wish to thank J. Hillis Miller, for his useful counsel and encouragement; and Frederick C. Crews, for the meticulous care with which he read the manuscript. I am much indebted to Jonathan Culler, Thomas Matrullo, Michael Stern, and Susan Winnett, who listened to my vagrant talk during the period of inception and were willing to talk back; and to Julian Boyd, Jonathan Crewe, David Damrosch, and Franco Moretti, who gave helpful advice on later matters of revision. I am also grateful for a research grant from the American Council of Learned Societies, which made it possible for me to bring this project to term. To Ann Bermingham Miller, my wife, I owe a debt too extensive to be easily specified. Let it, with the other best things, go without telling.

Narrative and Its Discontents

Chapter 1

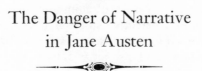

The Danger of Narrative
in Jane Austen

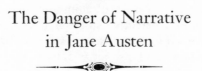

"Such a development of every thing most unwelcome"

> Que serait le récit du bonheur? Rien, que ce qui le pré-
> pare, puis ce qui le détruit, ne se raconte.[1]

THE NARRATIVE OF HAPPINESS is inevitably frustrated by the fact that only insufficiencies, defaults, defer-
rals, can be "told." Even when a narrative "prepares for"
happiness, it remains in this state of lack, which can only be
liquidated along with the narrative itself. Accordingly, the
narrative of happiness might be thought to exemplify the
unhappiness of narrative in general. Narrative proceeds toward, or regresses from, what it seeks or seems most to prize,
but it is never identical to it. To designate the presence of
what is sought or prized is to signal the termination of narrative—or at least, the displacement of narrative onto other
concerns.

It is clear that the category of the nonnarratable cannot
be limited to Gide's specification of it (as "le bonheur") in
my epigraph. What leaves a novelist speechless is not always
what makes him happiest, and there is a wide spectrum of
ways in which a novel may characterize the function of the

---

[1] André Gide, *L'Immoraliste*, in *Oeuvres complètes*, ed. L. Martin-
Chauffier, 15 vols. (Paris: Nouvelle Revue Française, 1932-39), 4: 70.

[3]

nonnarratable. In traditional fiction, marriage is a dominant form of this ne plus ultra, but death is another, and these are not the only ones. Narrative closure may coincide with the end of a quest, as in a story of ambition, or with the end of an inquest, as in a detective story. The closure, moreover, may be reinforced by other, secondary determinations, such as a proper transfer of property. But whatever the chosen privatives might be, it is evident that traditional narrative cannot dispense with the function that they motivate— namely, that of both constituting and abolishing the narrative movement. We might say, generally, that traditional narrative is a quest after that which will end questing; or that it is an interruption of what will be resumed; an expansion of what will be condensed, or a distortion of what will be made straight; a holding in suspense or a putting into question of what will be resolved or answered.[2]

What I have called the nonnarratable in a text should not be confused with what is merely unnarrated by it. In a broad sense, of course, every discourse is uttered against a background of all those things that it chooses, for one reason or another, not to say. Three subjects that Jane Austen's novels do not treat, for instance, are the Napoleonic wars, the sex lives of the characters, and the labor of the tenants who farm their estates. The first of these is only an unincluded subject of discourse; the second is an unincluded and also forbidden topic; the third is unincluded and perhaps (there are more than sexual taboos) forbidden as well. It is by no means a negligible fact that Jane Austen does not take up these subjects. To notice omissions of this order, however, seems to me mainly useful in establishing the level at which the novelistic representation is pitched (in Jane Austen's case, below the threshold of world history, above the threshold of primary biological functions and of work). This can help us to see the limits and lacunae of the novelis-

[2] See Roland Barthes, "Introduction à l'analyse structurale des récits," pp. 23-25; and Tzvetan Todorov, "Le secret du récit," *Poétique de la prose*, pp. 151-85.

tic representation, but it does not adequately account for the dynamics of the representation within the field so defined. Subjects like these have no place—not even the shadow of a place—in the novels, and the novels never invoke them to terminate their discourse. The marriage of the heroine in Jane Austen, on the other hand, does inhibit narrative productivity in this way. The "perfect union" of Emma and Mr. Knightley virtually *must* end the novel; otherwise, it would not be a "perfect" union. It would be brought back to the state of insufficiency and lack that has characterized the novelistic movement. What I am calling the nonnarratable elements of a text are precisely those that (like Emma's marriage) serve to supply the specified narrative lack, or to answer the specified narrative question. It is not the case that such elements cannot be designated by the text's language, or that they literally cannot be mentioned. The nonnarratable is not the unspeakable. What defines a nonnarratable element is its incapacity to generate a story. Properly or intrinsically, it has no narrative future—unless, of course, its nonnarratable status is undermined (by happiness destroyed, an incorrect solution, a choice that must be remade).

I want to begin, in the case of Jane Austen, by characterizing the eminently narratable states of affairs in her novels in relation to complementary nonnarratable states of affairs. Which kinds of character, or situation, or language seem inherently to lend themselves to the narrative production, and which to the narrative closure? Or, if one prefers to stress the difference between the representation and the construction, with which characters, situations, and languages does the narrative discourse motivate its productivity and its closure?

Harriet Smith has "business at Ford's," the principal shop in Highbury. "Tempted by every thing and swayed by half a word," she is "always very long at a purchase." Emma has left her "hanging over muslins and changing her mind," and returns to find her no further advanced. She tries, with all the force of her mind, to convince her that if she wanted a plain muslin it was of no use to look at figured; and that a blue ribbon, be it ever so beautiful, would still never match her yellow pattern. At last it was all settled, even to the destination of the parcel.

"Should I send it to Mrs. Goddard's, ma'am?" asked Mrs. Ford. "Yes—no—yes, to Mrs. Goddard's. Only my pattern gown is at Hartfield. No, you shall send it to Hartfield, if you please. But then, Mrs. Goddard will want to see it. —And I could take the pattern gown home any day. But I shall want the ribbon directly—so it had better go to Hartfield—at least the ribbon. You could make it into two parcels, Mrs. Ford, could not you?"

"It is not worth while, Harriet, to give Mrs. Ford the trouble of two parcels."

"No more it is."

"No trouble in the world, ma'am," said the obliging Mrs. Ford.

"Oh! but indeed I would much rather have it only in one. Then, if you please, you shall send it all to Mrs. Goddard's—I do not know—No, I think, Miss Woodhouse, I may just as well have it sent to Hartfield, and take it home with me at night. What do you advise?"

"That you do not give another half-second to the subject. To Hartfield, if you please, Mrs. Ford."

"Aye, that will be much best," said Harriet, quite satisfied, "I should not at all like to have it sent to Mrs. Goddard's."[3]

---

[3] *Emma*, in *The Novels of Jane Austen*, ed. R. W. Chapman, 5 vols. (London: Oxford University, 1932-34), 4: 235. I have used Chapman's edition for all the novels, as well as his edition of the *Minor Works* (London: Oxford University, 1954). Hereafter, references will be made in the text according to the following abbreviations:

SS   *Sense and Sensibility* (vol. 1)
PP   *Pride and Prejudice* (vol. 2)
MP   *Mansfield Park* (vol. 3)
E   *Emma* (vol. 4)

The episode is hardly crucial to an understanding of *Emma*. The ribbon and the gown never reappear to become significant items in a later development of plot. And what the episode tells the reader about Harriet's character is redundant: he knows it already and will be told it again. Yet in the playful quasi-gratuitousness of the episode, one might see a teasing and trivialized allegory of the mechanisms of textual production and closure. Silly and unimportant as it is, Harriet's indecision has the power to motivate a narrative episode. "Yes—no—yes" is a structure of insufficiency, allowing for the articulation of a potentially endless series of oscillations. It is a basically open structure, infinitely expandable, and one could imagine even greater play given to it than the text is in fact willing to tolerate. Moreover, so perfectly balanced a seesaw provides no principle with which to arrest its own play. Harriet might remain at "the interesting counter" forever.

In an obvious sense, not much is at stake—the state of hesitant insufficiency that motivates the episode does not substantially engage Jane Austen's deeper concerns. She can afford to let us enjoy the narratable state of deferred disclosure, without exacting anguish. In another sense, however, one might say that Harriet's indecision spells a clear and present danger to the text's ideal of legibility. Like Emma, so to speak, the novelist has no wish to stand at the interesting counter all day. Boredom impends and (what is behind boredom) inconclusiveness, a loss of intelligibility. What does Harriet mean to say in her wavering discourse? Like a stammer, her language refuses to form a complete sentence. Her endless retraction (it is a kind of blind irony, if that is conceivable) keeps meaning in an inchoate, unfinished state. Jane Austen's tolerance for this sort of textual

[handwritten marginal note: also ← woman responding to male sexual advances ?]

P   *Persuasion* (vol. 5)
MW   *Minor Works*

A page number without accompanying letters indicates the last work specified in preceding references.

stammering—like the patience Emma displays toward Harriet's behavior—is a limited one. The priority of making sense must be reinstated.

What is required is an intervention, based on different principles. Emma does not bother to weigh the pros and cons of Hartfield versus Mrs. Goddard's as possible destinations for Harriet's parcel. She merely invokes the closural force of choice—not this choice rather than that, but any choice rather than none. Emma forces disclosure to take place, and by so doing, she closes off the episode and leaves nothing to tell. The episode can now stand as a completed whole, coherently organized according to beginning, middle, and end. The whole process involves a number of paradoxical reversals. Harriet is weak and soft-minded, and Emma is strong and (here, at least) sensible; but Harriet's weakness is strong enough to generate an episode, which Emma's good sense can only put an end to. Common sense —meaning—a legible communication—these are all of the essence for Jane Austen; but it is an indispensable requirement of the episode's taking place that this essence be missing. And what is in its place—Harriet's wavering—becomes (from the viewpoint of Emma's intervention) deprived of any necessary reason for being. What the narrative values is, paradoxically, what reduces its own movement to a largely gratuitous, or inessential, middle; what it mocks, criticizes, or even loathes is precisely what it cannot do without.

In its full portrayal of Harriet, the novel elaborates the indecision that she betrays at Ford's into a more comprehensive and consequential structure of narratability. When Mr. Knightley tells Emma that Harriet's "character depends upon those she is with, but in good hands she will turn out a valuable woman" (58), he implicitly formulates both the risk (of an unclosed narratability) that Harriet's character runs and the refuge (of a nonnarratable closure) in which it will be safeguarded. The narratable risk is posed by the essentially docile nature of Harriet's desire, "only desiring to be guided by any one she looked up to" (26). Without much sense of what is at stake (since what is at stake is partly herself), Emma takes early notice of "Harriet's habits of dependence and imitation" (88); and she is relieved after the revelation of Mr. Elton's real intentions that "Harriet's nature should not be of that superior sort in which the feelings are most acute and retentive" (138). Emma can comfortably predict that Mr. Elton "might be superseded by another—he certainly would, indeed! nothing could be clearer" (183), much as she will affirm about Harriet's later attachment that "in time, of course, Mr. Knightley would be forgotten, that is, supplanted" (450). Harriet's unretentive and imitative desire responds only to what those she is guided by present as desirable. To put it in contemporary terms, we might say that Harriet's is a purely mediated *the code of* desire, directing itself only according to the directives of *female desire* others.[4] *generally*

What makes such a desire narratable, that is, capable of producing the waverings and variations that will make up a story line, is in part the plurality of mediators in the world *Girard* she inhabits. Two worlds of mediation, presided over by Emma and Mrs. Goddard respectively, propagate radically different faiths, and Harriet sometimes shows an ingenuous willingness to respond to their incompatible directives in a single fluctuating movement:

> Had it been allowable entertainment, had there been no pain to her friend, or reproach to herself, in the waverings of Harriet's mind, Emma would have been amused by its variations. Sometimes Mr. Elton predominated, sometimes the Martins; and each was occasionally useful as a check to the other. (184)

Moreover, Emma herself is an equivocal mediatrix. With so *because she is* little sense of her own desires, she points Harriet's in unpro- *female?*

---

[4] René Girard, *Mensonge romantique et vérité romanesque.*

ductive, potentially disastrous directions, almost as though by unwittingly frustrating Harriet's love life she meant to mirror the intrinsically blocked nature of her own.

It is hardly for reasons of mere economy that Jane Austen has the erotic education of both Harriet and Emma center on the same three men—Elton, Churchill, and Knightley. (Robert Martin is the only bachelor in the novel whom the two women do not in some way or other share, and it is he, significantly, who will save Harriet.) In a sort of vicarious promiscuity, Emma defines her own degree of response to the eligible men in the novel as part of a process of assigning them to "her own particular little friend" (219). This diminutively projected friend (Emma's "Harriet" versus Harriet's "Miss Woodhouse") is an ideal vicaress to act out Emma's own diminutive and strictly limited responses. In the scene of Mr. Elton's unwelcome addresses, for instance, the novelist's deepest irony turns on the underlying sense in which they are really appropriate. Emma's matchmaking has after all allowed her to acknowledge Mr. Elton's charms as much as, of course, their limited appeal. His manners— "good-humoured, cheerful, obliging and gentle" (34)— genuinely please her and make him worthy of being loved; but "a want of elegance of feature which she could not dispense with" (35) makes him only worthy of being loved *by another*, whose attachment Emma can sample at once intimately and at a safe distance. In a similar pattern, Emma sponsors Harriet's presumed attachment to Frank Churchill. Here is her perusal of the letter that Frank has written to Mrs. Weston after his first visit:

> The charm of her own name was not wanting. *Miss Woodhouse* appeared more than once, and never without a something of pleasing connection, either a compliment to her taste, or a remembrance of what she had said; and in the very last time of its meeting her eyes, unadorned as it was by any such broad wreath of gallantry, she could yet discern the effect of her influence and acknowledge

the greatest compliment perhaps of all conveyed. Compressed into the very lowest vacant corner were these
words—"I had not a spare moment of Tuesday, as you
know, for Miss Woodhouse's beautiful little friend. Pray
make my excuses and adieus to her." This, Emma could
not doubt, was all for herself. Harriet was remembered
only from being *her* friend. (266)

Emma's preliminary assimilation of Harriet's beauty to her
own appeal prepares us to understand her next step:

Gratifying, however, and stimulative as was the letter
in the material part, its sentiments, she yet found, when it
was folded up and returned to Mrs. Weston, that it had
not added any lasting warmth, that she could still do without the writer, and that he must learn to do without her.
Her intentions were unchanged. Her resolution of refusal
only grew more interesting by the addition of a scheme
for his subsequent consolation and happiness. His recollection of Harriet, and the words which clothed it, the
"beautiful little friend," suggested to her the idea of Harriet's succeeding her in his affections. (266)

And now can come the decisive revelation:

"When [Frank Churchill and I] cease to care for each
other as we do now, it will be the means of confirming us
in that sort of true disinterested friendship which I can
already look forward to with pleasure." (267)

A match between Frank and Harriet would institutionalize
the right degree of relationship between Frank and Emma:
close enough for the game of a standing flirtation, far enough
from the earnest of a courtship.

The novelist's best stroke comes when Emma unwittingly
directs Harriet's desire onto the one man whom she is able
to love without need of reservation. In a brilliant intuition
(which, if it is an exception to her general want of clever-
ness, is perfectly of a piece with the mimetic nature of her

desire), Harriet knows how to imitate Emma's ultimate conception of the desirable even before Emma has formulated it to herself. Harriet's infatuation with Mr. Knightley, to be sure, does not so much produce Emma's desire as it permits her to recognize it: its intrinsic rightness, we feel, transcends the kind of mediation to which the attachments of a Harriet Smith can be so entirely given over. Still, the unplanned rivalry between Emma and Harriet suggests a limited sense in which the mediation is mutual. Emma may mediate Harriet's desires, but Harriet's desires are in turn the means whereby she defines and comes to acknowledge her own.

How can Harriet, so at the mercy of the suggestions of others, be safely settled in life? Or, to put the question in another way, how can her narratability ever be brought to a close? In contrast to the examples of mediated desire discussed by René Girard, Harriet's incorrigible stupidity puts a "conversion" out of the question. If it is a hopeless task to reform her character, however, the world in which her character moves must be reorganized instead. In Mr. Knightley's words, she must be placed "in good hands": taken from a world where competing mediators issue an endless series of fresh directives and relocated in a world where "any one she looks up to" will point her desire toward a single object on which it may effectively fix. The contention between Hartfield and Mrs. Goddard's school must be dissolved, and Emma must no longer want (or need) to use Harriet as a stalking horse for her own half-felt fancies. To settle Harriet with Robert Martin, and in a home that includes two very partial sisters and a loving mother (all pointing desire on Robert alone), meets these requirements exactly. Harriet "would be placed in the midst of those who loved her, and who had better sense than herself; *retired enough for safety, and occupied enough for cheerfulness. She would never be led into temptation, nor left for it to find her out*" (482, my italics).

It is already apparent that Harriet's narratable "habits of dependence and imitation" imitate and depend upon a more

fundamental source of the narratable in *Emma*: Emma's own
prolonged inability to give her fancy its proper direction.
Before he knows his own feelings, Mr. Knightley tells Mrs.
Weston, "There is a curiosity, an anxiety in what one feels
for Emma. I wonder what will become of her!" (40). He
wonders, of course, because one *can* wonder. Emma repeatedly appropriates people and projects, and relinquishes them
painlessly. She untiringly fabricates "interesting" situations
without much caring whether reality can, or ought to, sustain them. In both its erotic and inventive senses, "that very
dear part of Emma, her fancy" (214) is at once the scandal
and the sine qua non of the novelistic production: scandalous
because it is without inherent resolution or ending, and indispensable because it supplies the compositional resource
behind most of the novel.

One might describe Emma's textual productivity in two
different (if ultimately coextensive) ways: as a psychology
of narcissism, and as a narrative without purposiveness. An
early notice of *Emma* in the *Literary Panorama* summarized
the novel in terms that are surely congenial to some of its
main concerns: "*Emma* presents the history of a young lady,
who, after allowing her imagination to wander towards several gentlemen, and almost to mislead her affections, fixes
them, at last, on the proper object."[5] Until her reformation,
Emma is unable to "fix" her "affections" on "the proper
object," much as, *mutatis mutandis*, a Freudian narcissist cannot "cathect" his "libido" onto an external "object choice."[6]

[5] Unsigned notice in the *Literary Panorama*, 6 (June 1816): 418;
rpt. in B. C. Southam, ed., *Jane Austen: The Critical Heritage*, p. 70.

[6] Freud also suggests that sexual maturity (in "its final normal
shape," after the changes of puberty) comes at the level of object
choice, when autoeroticism is relinquished. See the third of his *Three
Essays on the Theory of Sexuality*, 7: 207-30. For Freud on narcissism,
see "On Narcissism: An Introduction," and "Mourning and Melancholia." These and all further references to Freud are from *The
Standard Edition of the Complete Psychological Works of Sigmund
Freud*, ed. James Strachey, 24 vols. (London: The Hogarth Press and
the Institute of Psycho-Analysis, 1953-74).

The narrator broadly characterizes Emma's narcissism as her "power of having too much her own way" and her "disposition to think a little too well of herself" (5). Emma herself breezily observes to Harriet,

> "I have never been in love; it is not my way or my nature; and I do not think I ever shall. . . . I believe few married women are half as much mistress of their husband's house as I am of Hartfield; and never, never could I expect to be so truly beloved and important, so always first and always right in any man's eyes, as I am in my father's." (84)

The novelist takes it casually for granted that an overattachment to her doting father maintains Emma's self-love. Yet a further turn of the screw is needed if Emma's narcissism is to become a structure of narratability, rather than remaining a quasi-iconic pose. Narcissus, one remembers, merely stared at himself—his kind of narcissism has no real temporal or narrative dynamic. One might say that Emma's narcissism, by contrast, is deprived of its mirror. Mr. Woodhouse's admiration is too self-absorbed and undiscriminating to reflect all that Emma dotes on in herself. What her father leaves to be desired, of course, her Miss Taylor had once perfectly supplied:

> It had been a friend and companion such as few possessed, intelligent, well-informed, useful, gentle, knowing all the ways of the family, interested in all its concerns, and peculiarly interested in herself, in every pleasure, every scheme of her's;—one to whom she could speak every thought as it arose, and who had such an affection for her as could never find fault. (6)

Poor Miss Taylor, however, has become Mrs. Weston, and "great must be the difference between a Mrs. Weston only half a mile from them, and a Miss Taylor in the house" (7).

A narcissism no longer sufficiently provisioned, then, sends Emma's affections into the "world," where she acts out her fantasies of omnipotent manipulation in a blinded search for mirror substitutes. This enterprise of relocating a blocked narcissism in the outside world accounts for Emma's narratability. It also threatens to produce an interminable narrative, since what defines the narcissist is this very failure to organize his libidinal energies at the site of an external object choice. Recognition such as Emma seeks to exact can never be fully forthcoming if she only half wants it, or wants it under a condition of nonreciprocity that makes it untenable in an adult world. Emma's desire must seem nonobjectal, giving itself only apparent and transitory objects in a movement that continually surpasses them. Harriet is only a way of loving herself ("Nobody is equal to you!—I care for nobody as I do for you!"[268]); Frank Churchill is only an occasion for the display whose real principle of satisfaction is independent of any one of its pretexts. If uncorrected, the narrative of Emma's desire would turn the text into what might be called a radical picaresque: an endless flirtation with a potentially infinite parade of possibilities.

Moreover, an essentially novelistic power of invention significantly determines Emma's fancy. Her "genius for foretelling and guessing" and her "art of giving pictures in a few words" (38, 250) display a mind that works rather by means of novelistic scenes than by conceptual formulations: not in the assertive mode of established facts and fixed principles, but in the dramatizing mode of fiction. "It was much easier to chat than to study; much pleasanter to let her imagination range and work at Harriet's fortune, than to be labouring to enlarge her comprehension or exercise it on sober facts" (69). To persuade Harriet of Mr. Elton's attachment, for instance, Emma evokes the following scene:

> "At this moment, perhaps, Mr. Elton is shewing your picture to his mother and sisters, telling how much more beautiful is the original, and after being asked for it five or six times, allowing them to hear your name, your own dear name."

"My picture!—But he has left my picture in Bond-street."

"Has he so!—Then I know nothing of Mr. Elton. No, my dear little modest Harriet, depend upon it the picture will not be in Bond-street till just before he mounts his horse to-morrow. It is his companion all this evening, his solace, his delight. It opens his designs to his family, it introduces you among them, it diffuses through the party those pleasantest feelings of our nature, eager curiosity and warm prepossession. How cheerful, how animated, how suspicious, how busy their imaginations all are!" (56)

Her refutation of Mrs. Weston's theory about Mr. Knightley and Jane Fairfax produces a satiric sketch:

"If it would be good to her, I am sure it would be evil to himself; a very shameful and degrading connection. How would he bear to have Miss Bates belonging to him? —To have her haunting the Abbey, and thanking him all day long for his great kindness in marrying Jane?—'So very kind and obliging!—But he always had been such a very kind neighbour!' And then fly off, through half a sentence, to her mother's old petticoat. 'Not that it was such a very old petticoat either—for still it would last a great while—and, indeed, she must thankfully say that their petticoats were all very strong.' " (225)

And when Mrs. Elton would offer her the patronage of a Mrs. Partridge of Bath, Emma is instantly ready with a characterization: "probably some vulgar, dashing widow, who, with the help of a boarder, just made a shift to live!" (275-76). We have no way of verifying these projections absolutely, but Miss Bates's flighty garrulity and Mrs. Elton's thoroughgoing vulgarity suggest that Emma has hit the mark in both cases. It may even be the case that Mr. Elton took Emma's portrait of Harriet home with him, with different views, of course, from those Emma envisions. Her least worthy and most wrongheaded piece of novelizing, of course, comes when she invents a forbidden liaison between Jane Fairfax and Mr. Dixon; but it too bears a relation, be it only that of travesty, to the actual truth. Jane's reserve, her intercepted smiles and guilty blushes are proven to sustain the meaningfulness, if not the meaning, that Emma finds in them.

"A mind lively and at ease, can do with seeing nothing, and can see nothing that does not answer" (233). Although the context in which this is said makes it a positive tribute to Emma's ability to animate the *temps morts* of her life, we see her elsewhere exercising the same ability in less tempered ways. On an obvious level, she fabricates the attachment between Harriet and Mr. Elton, or between Jane Fairfax and Mr. Dixon, out of nothing, and sees nothing that does not answer to her fabrication. So pure a novelistic imagination cannot go unchallenged by the more scrupulous characters in the novel, on both moral and cognitive grounds. Mrs. Weston replies to Emma's satire on Miss Bates, "For shame, Emma! Do not mimic her. You divert me against my conscience" (225). When Emma and Mr. Knightley discuss Frank Churchill's failure to visit his father, Emma characteristically defends him by an appeal to human probabilities and the force of circumstance: "Oh! the difference of situation and habit! I wish you would try to understand what an amiable young man may be likely to feel in directly opposing those, whom as child and boy he has been looking up to all his life" (148). In telling contrast, Knightley speaks a resolute language of duty and principle that allows and indeed calls for moral judgment:

> "Your amiable young man is a very weak young man, if this be the first occasion of his carrying through a resolution to do right against the will of others. It *ought to have been* an habit with him by this time, of following his duty, instead of consulting expediency. I can allow for the fears of the child, but not of the man. As he became rational, he *ought to have* roused himself and shaken off

all that was unworthy in their authority. He *ought to have* opposed the first attempt on their side to make him slight his father. *Had he begun as he ought, there would have been no difficulty now.*" (148, my italics)

Emma entertains the same undisciplined "novelism" that Mary Crawford displays in *Mansfield Park.* "You have given us an amusing sketch," Edmund Bertram tells her at Sotherton, "and human nature cannot say it was not so" (MP 87). Like Mary's more radically tainted sketches, Emma's lack a moral control, and are based on no more exacting a conception of truth than that of generalized human probabilities. Emma's pictures *might* be such as she paints them, but she is less concerned than Jane Austen likes whether they *are*, or *ought to be* so.

Even when the issues of morality and truth are put aside, moreover, Emma's willingness to invest virtually everything with a novelistic aura would make a real novel, such as Jane Austen conceives it, impossible. It is true that, far from merely "allowing her imagination to wander," Emma actively plots out its course of error. However, Emma's articulation of her own aimlessness produces a narrative that is no narrative at all: only a suite of local, fragmentary, unincremental scenes and sequences. Her imagination is a kind of portmanteau of novelistic effects and details, unordered by an overall coherent structure. One recalls again Henry James's invidious comparison between life and art, "life being all inclusion and confusion, and art being all discrimination and selection." Without needing to turn Jane Austen's kind of novel into Henry James's, one can recognize in both the traditional novelist's obligation to bind his form together into what can strike us as a completed unity. If "the *whole* of anything is never told; you can only take what groups together," then the novelist needs a principle of grouping; if "really, universally, relations stop nowhere," then he needs a geometry whereby "they shall happily *ap-*

pear to do so."[7] Jane Austen's fiction gives no very ample
play to the principle of the "pourrait être continué" that
Gide would formulate. It is rigorously designed in terms of a
resolution that leaves no residue or excess remaining to be
told, and all the imaginative energies raised by the development are fully cathected onto the final configuration of
event and meaning. By contrast, Emma's novelizing imagination never would seem able to bind its energies in end-
oriented plots. It only stylizes its free-floating release by
throwing off little novel fragments that are at once unpro-
ductive and much too fertile. They cannot really *go* anywhere in a reality to which they rarely adhere, and by the
same token, released from the claims of the real, the moral,
and the true, they can really go *anywhere*.

Once again, an intervention of sorts—proceeding according to a different rule—is demanded for closure. It is a
measure of how inherently inconclusive Emma's fancy is
that it must undergo a radical reconstruction before it can
fix on what will end its vagrancy.

> Her own conduct, as well as her own heart, was before
> her in the same few minutes. She saw it all with a clearness
> which had never blessed her before. How improperly had
> she been acting by Harriet! How inconsiderate, how in-
> delicate, how irrational, how unfeeling, had been her con-
> duct! What blindness, what madness, had led her on! It
> struck her with dreadful force, and she was ready to give
> it every bad name in the world. (E 408)

In the series of reflections that make up her decisive *prise de
conscience*, Emma's language and her priorities differ dramatically from what they have been. Stress is now laid on
common sense and principled comprehension. "But with

[7] Henry James, "Notebook Entry on *The Portrait of a Lady*," rpt.
in an edition of that novel, ed. Leon Edel (Boston: Houghton Mifflin,
1963), p. 487; "Preface to *Roderick Hudson*," rpt. in *The Art of the
Novel*, p. 5.

common sense, I am afraid I have had little to do." "How to
understand it all! How to understand the deceptions she had
been thus practising on herself and living under!—The
blunders, the blindness of her own head and heart!" "To
understand, thoroughly understand, her own heart, was the
first endeavour" (402, 411-12, 412). Emma's language is now
organized according to Jane Austen's most prestigious an-
titheses: blindness versus understanding, ignorance versus
knowledge, error versus truth. Whenever it is a matter of
articulating the cognitive, moral, or erotic ideology of her
texts, Jane Austen invariably brings such language forward:
an infallible sign that we are in the presence of the novel's
truth. Only such language will sponsor the definitive nominations of narrative closure, and it is no accident that its use
here coincides with Emma's "cure." Indeed, the fact that
Emma now is able to use this language is our main guarantee
that a cure has taken place. And Emma's cure, like the psy-
choanalytic one, is worked out by means of replacements or
exchanges. In place of nonobjectal desire, there is put an object choice; in place of the symptomatic language of error,
there is put a language that can designate and disclose error;
and in place of the picaresque narrative constituted by wandering desire and errant language, there are put a sense of
the novel's true itinerary and the ending to which it was always directed.

Emma's basically healthy mind is strong enough to work
its own cure, and even Harriet, *faute de mieux*, can be placed
in a sanatorium where her disease will remain latent. Emma's
cure would seem internally produced and deep-psychologi-
cal in nature, and Harriet's only externally manipulated and
behavioristic; but both kinds of therapy effectively extin-
guish any alarming symptoms of narratability. How does
the novelist treat a case of narratability that cannot be cured
or quarantined in these ways? Henry Crawford in *Mansfield
Park* presents an exemplary instance of what might be called
"interminable analysis."

"To any thing like a permanence of abode, or limitation

of society, Henry Crawford had, unluckily, a great dislike"
(MP 41), and a similar mobility governs the placement of
his affections. His sister calls him "the most horrible flirt
than can be imagined," and Henry himself considers "the
blessing of a wife as most justly described in those discreet
lines of the poet, 'Heaven's *last* best gift' " (43). Marriage is
indeed the last best gift in Jane Austen's novels, but Henry
Crawford's narratability comes from his systematic deferral
of a gift whose finality he prefers to stress over its superiority. He begins by treating the Miss Bertrams much in the
way that Emma initially treats Frank Churchill:

> Mr. Crawford did not mean to be in any danger; the Miss
> Bertrams were worth pleasing, and were ready to be
> pleased; and he began with no object but of making them
> like him. He did not want them to die of love; but with
> sense and temper which ought to have made him judge
> and feel better, he allowed himself great latitude on such
> points. (45)

To flirt for Henry Crawford means to cultivate a suspense
in relationships: to hesitate between meaning, and not meaning, the gestures to which flirtation gives rise. In its teasing
approach to meaning and its avoidance of definitive nomination, flirtation is well qualified to motivate the moment of
narratability. What it threatens most directly in the novel is
the possibility of fixing sexual attraction in love and marriage, but it is able to threaten this only on the basis of a
semiological equivocation: its signs refuse to point straight.
Generating and preserving a state of half-meaning, it tends
to frustrate the text's attempt to resolve itself in a decisive
configuration of character and even in a final disclosure of
significance.

Here is Henry's telling recollection of the Mansfield theatricals:

> "It is as a dream, a pleasant dream!" he exclaimed,
> breaking forth after few minutes musing. "I shall always

look back on our theatricals with exquisite pleasure. There was such an interest, such an animation, such a spirit diffused! Everybody felt it. We were all alive. There was employment, hope, solicitude, bustle, for every hour of the day. Always some little objection, some little doubt, some little anxiety to be got over. I never was happier." (225)

Let a Mr. Yates look back on the theatricals and feel all the disappointment of a suspended spectacle; when a Henry Crawford looks back, he feels only the fascination of a spectacle of suspense. The threatricals offer him an image of vitality ("We were all alive") in direct proportion to their state of incompletion and uncertainty ("always some little anxiety to be got over"). There are, we know, less exhilarated responses to the theatricals in the novel. In her own observation of them, Fanny Price found "every body requiring something they had not, and giving occasion of discontent to the others" (165). What fascinates Henry and appalls Fanny is, under different aspects, the same moment of narratability. Henry prizes the narratable, which makes Fanny uncomfortable. Henry's "unsettled affections, wavering with his vanity" (441) actively motivate the plot of *Mansfield Park* and also prove irredeemable, while the deserving Fanny (as one critic has put it) "triumphs by doing nothing."[8] What keeps Henry from reforming is nothing but his unrelenting pursuit of the narratable moment: a moment in which meaning is postponed ("there was hope, solicitude"), or scattered along the ground of various possibilities ("such a spirit diffused!").

It was never chance that attracted him to Maria Bertram rather than Julia. Aside from the bare mechanism of flirtation itself, there was nothing in Julia's case to generate an incipient attachment and preserve it as such. Maria's engagement ensured the noncommittal nature of the flirtation by

[8] Tony Tanner, in his introduction to *Mansfield Park*, p. 8.

setting boundaries to it, boundaries that could then be subject to doubtful transgressions. Maria better answered the need of "some little objection, some little doubt, some little anxiety to be got over." The same need stands behind the remarkable insistence (even Edmund wonders at it) of Henry's pursuit of Fanny.

> He was in love, very much in love; and it was a love which, operating on an active, sanguine spirit, of more warmth than delicacy, made her affection appear of greater consequence, because it was withheld, and determined him to have the glory, as well as the felicity, of forcing her to love him. (326)

And, in a more pointed echo of his enchanted remembrance of the theatricals, we are told that

> he had so much delight in the idea of obliging her to love him in a very short time, that her not loving him now was scarcely regretted. A little difficulty to be overcome, was no evil to Henry Crawford. He rather derived spirits from it. He had been apt to gain hearts too easily. His situation was new and animating. (327)

There is no reason to deny Henry other, better motives (such as his "moral taste" and "sense") for falling in love with Fanny.[9] If these fail to impose themselves, however, it is because his attachment has needed to thrive on "a little difficulty to be overcome." Fanny's resistance is not really the superably spirited kind such as most deeply commands his interest. Her refusal "to be overcome" frustrates the clichéd pattern that Henry has brought to the relationship out of his compulsion to repeat it. It is easy to see why, in spite of his best intentions, he finally goes elsewhere: to a

[9] An interesting case for these better motives is made by Martin Price, "Manners, Morals, and Jane Austen," pp. 274-75. Price also cites Gilbert Ryle, "Jane Austen and the Moralists," in B.C. Southam, ed., *Critical Essays on Jane Austen*, pp. 106-22.

situation that better motivates what he requires. What else is to be overcome, but Mrs. Rushworth's proud "display of resentment" (468)? The narrator insists, of course, that "would he have persevered, and uprightly, Fanny must have been his reward" (467). If Henry doesn't persevere, however, it is because he wants to evade his reward—under its aspect, at least, of "a permanence of abode," an irrevocable ending. Fanny is his reformation, his closure—"this is the end of [idle designs]," he tells Mary (292). One feels that it is the end of idle designs, as such, that inspires the latitudinal slippage into extended narratability, much as his approaching marriage may inspire a bachelor's "last fling." The supreme act of flirtation is to flirt with what might bring it to an end.

Always "just stopping short" of "consistence" and "steadiness," Henry Crawford's wavering affections cannot by themselves issue in a closure (115). Maria Rushworth may trap him into an elopement, but he will abandon her to survive in a world where the penalty for his share of the offense "is less equal than could be wished" (468). Indeed, his sister Mary seems scarcely willing to consider the Crawford's continued participation in the world of Mansfield Park—even after the elopement—at an end. In his own terms, Henry will always be an unknown quantity, for these terms do not allow a real knowledge to be constituted. "He was too little accustomed to serious reflection to know [good principles in a wife] by their proper name" (294). Henry Crawford never can live in Jane Austen's closural world of proper names, categories, feelings, and relationships. "He allowed himself great latitude on such points." "Unused to make any sacrifice to right," his conduct cherishes the equivocal situation, much as his sister's vocabulary prizes the double meaning and the "something between" word (467, 287). An incurable (and hence interminable) narratability traverses him. "We will cure you . . . Mansfield shall cure you . . . Stay with us and we will cure you," Mrs. Grant promises Henry and Mary; and the narrator drily resumes, "The Crawfords,

without wanting to be cured, were very willing to stay"
(47).

If Henry Crawford won't be cured, however, the novelist
will not let him stay. Jane Austen always will have her closure, and if a character does not provide himself the means
to bring it about, it will take place without him: elsewhere,
along other lines, and according to different principles. Here
the principles are those of moral-ideological fiat. Fanny, Edmund, and Sir Thomas expel Henry permanently from their
world on the basis of a peremptory moral judgment, whose
unquestionable rightness the novelist's own prestigious voice
comes to reinforce. This moral judgment imposes the right
names and relationships, and makes a "sacrifice to right" of
the wrong ones. It makes way, moreover, for the match between Fanny and Edmund, which overlays the ideological
dismissal with a practical one. All the open slots have been
filled, and there is no longer even a place toward which the
Crawfords can flirtingly delay their approach. The novelist's
expulsion of Henry is indispensably sustained by a moral
decorum, much as Sir Thomas's refusal to readmit Maria to
Mansfield Park is based on moral and social propriety. "He
would never have offered so great an insult to the neighbourhood, as to expect it to notice her" (465). Such notice could
indeed be given; but to promote it would be an "insult" to
the neighborhood's integrity, as well as to Sir Thomas's own
self-esteem. Analogously, one might say, Henry Crawford's
continuing narratability could in fact be narrated; but his
actions have placed him beyond the reach of the novelist's
"therapy," which is implicitly Jane Austen's only moral justification for engaging the narratable at all. Having frustrated, as it were, her curative powers, Henry has forfeited his
right to her continuing notice and to that of her presumed
readers. If he will not bring his continuing story to a proper
end, she will make it unworthy of being continued, and will
focus on the endings of those who deserve to matter.

Henry Crawford's wavering affections, along with the
extended narratability they suppose, cannot be absorbed into

a closural pattern directly; but they can be taken into account, obliquely, as that which the pattern leaves out. Henry's career is "closed" at least insofar as it continues in the wings of a closural spectacle in which he has no part but that of a significant absence. The novel fixes its own meanings by banishing him, and among the meanings thus fixed is included the meaning of Henry Crawford. He may still be a narratable character at the end of *Mansfield Park*, but the ending of the novel irrevocably changes the status of his narratability. Whether explicitly or not, closure in Jane Austen provides a complete set of nominations for all that needs to be named. If the novel cannot "cure" Henry, it does come to know and name him. The equivocal signification that he has sponsored becomes, upon closure, the unequivocal sign of his character in a wholly intelligible world. Earlier in the novel, one had been allowed to feel, like Mr. Knightley in the case of Emma, some curiosity about what would become of him. Now one knows (to put it in terms akin to the novel's ideology of improvement) that Henry Crawford will never amount to anything. His character had seemed problematical, because it made its own outcome a matter of suspense, delay, teasing possibility. Once the novel has instituted the language of disclosure, resolution, and understanding, however, Henry's semiological hesitation can be designated as a pathetic inadequacy, an irresponsible evasion. His significance is that he will never signify. Fanny, "the woman whom he had rationally, as well as passionately loved" (469), is lost to him forever, and the "vexation" from which under other circumstances he might have derived spirits is now coupled with "regret." His regret only changes the mode of his insufficiency: once eagerly cultivated, now irreversibly imposed. As in the Dantesque *contrappasso*, Henry is simply forced to be what he willingly has been. The shift of emphasis—from choice to necessity—makes his ongoing narratability a fraudulent show. It is easily condensed under what E. H. Gombrich has called "the etc principle," that is, "the assumption we tend to make that to see a few members of a series is to see them all."[10] The continuing story of Henry Crawford need not be told, since the pattern that it will merely extend is essentially already known.

The "diffused intimacies" (273) of the Crawfords take a more purely linguistic form in the case of Mary. Whereas Henry's "latitude" produces an important series of actions in the novel, one remembers his sister less for what she does than for what she says. If one sometimes feels that one could go on listening to Mary Crawford's witty talk forever, one has implicitly acknowledged its main principle of construction: the perpetual promise and deferral of knowledge and right nomination. Despite an apparent preference for the set piece and the epigram, Mary's talk presents itself less as finished language, putting matters into definitive form, than as fragmentary evidence of an untiring and interminable fund of discourse that suspends and resumes its own saying and unsaying at will. It is not exactly that Mary calls things by their wrong names (although this is how it must look when the novel's moral ideology is imposed). Simply, her kind of talk doesn't recognize there being right names. The distinctions between proper and improper designations, knowledge and corrupt ambiguity, talk licensed by principle and licentious talk, are not those that it intrinsically draws. Mary's repeated inability to give things their proper name has been admirably discussed and documented by Stuart Tave.[11] What needs recognition is only the productivity of this inability. In a discourse that inherently refuses to name, there are no stopping points or resting places whereby to arrest its dilations or give them an object. The principle of Mary's talk—its refusal of definitive nomination—is precisely what makes it so eminently discursive. In contrast to the principled Fanny's comparative muteness, she can scarcely open her mouth without an ample "speech" coming out.

[10] E. H. Gombrich, *Art and Illusion*, p. 220.
[11] Stuart M. Tave, *Some Words of Jane Austen*, pp. 26-28.

Strictly speaking, we may not want to see Mary's language as an instance of narratability, since it does not directly or obviously issue in plot sequences. Even as mere discursiveness, however, it can profitably be placed in the same framework of discussion. It offers similar resources to the textual production, and poses similar threats to the textual closure. Jane Austen imposes an exemplary closure on Mary Crawford, which I shall want to discuss in detail later when I take up the novelist's closural procedures. Here I am concerned only to establish the fundamental evasiveness of her discourse in relation to what is being evaded. A single example of Mary's language, although uncharacteristically brief, will yield the structure that allows for its more typical expansions. Mary is reviewing the respective merits of the Bertram brothers and finds Thomas her favorite:

> *He* had been much in London, and had more liveliness and gallantry than Edmund, and must, therefore, be preferred; and, indeed, his being the eldest was another strong claim. She had felt an early presentiment that she *should* like the eldest best. She knew it was her way. (47)

If one defines indirect discourse as a device whereby the narrator reorganizes a primary discourse into a secondary framework deconstructing it, then a passage of indirect discourse might seem the least likely place to want to characterize Mary Crawford on her own terms. We are certainly invited to read its first sentence under the assumptions of indirect discourse as conventionally practiced. We assume, for instance, that it is the narrator who emphasizes the quasirational nature of Mary's reflections ("he must, therefore, be preferred," "his being the eldest was another strong claim"), in order to interpret it in ways that are not available to Mary. A narratorial inflection of Mary's discourse would seem to disclose what she herself cannot see or will not confess—namely, that she is rationalizing baser motives. In the last two sentences of the passage, however, Mary's discourse overthrows this structure of our reading, as well as the distinction between the narrator's truth and the character's error that is maintained by it. In a typical gesture of *forestalling* ("but I forestall you; remember I have forestalled you"[94]), Mary disarms our superior judgment by taking it playfully for granted. Not only has she seen the blind spots that the narrator seemed to be revealing despite her, she can even tease herself about them with some amusement. "She had felt an early presentiment that she *should* like the eldest best. She knew it was her way." On the perspective now opened up, the emphasized rationality of her language (which had seemed a sign of the narrator's secondary revision of it) would instead signify her self-irony, as though Mary had been wittily catering all along to a view of her own bad faith. To an important extent, Mary disqualifies the indirect discourse practiced on her in what may be the only possible way: by practicing it on herself.

The traditional practice of indirect discourse puts the narrator at a distance from a character's thoughts and feelings, a privilege that the character's intimate relation to them tends to deny him. In this way it at once asserts the narrator's superior claims to understanding and the character's inferior ones. The novelist might simply have written, "Mary thought to herself, she *should* like the eldest best. It was her way." We should have been presented with a spontaneous thought and its simultaneous undercutting. Instead, the novelist's implicit "Mary thought to herself:" is reduplicated within the structure of Mary's thinking. We might elaborate the actual text as follows: "Mary thought to herself, *she had felt a presentiment that* she should like the eldest best. *She knew that* it was her way." Mary Crawford holds off from the discourse of which she is also the subject, so that the primary discourse appropriated by the narrator is already an indirect one. " 'She' had a presentiment that 'she' should like the eldest best," but the two shes do not coincide, and they represent Mary's correspondingly double "I."

A noumenal I (who has presentiments and who knows) be-holds another, phenomenal I (whose way it is to like, and to hide its motives for liking, the eldest best).

"She knew it was her way" seems Mary's obvious private joke on the economic construction that might be put on her predilection for heirs. With a self-consciously false naiveté, she pretends that her choice of Thomas Bertram is more mysteriously determined and more irretrievably idio-syncratic than it plausibly can be. She invites herself to recognize a logic in the choice that transcends the coyly puz-zled stance she takes toward it, and turns its asserted mysteri-ousness into a wholly coherent and intelligible motivation. At the same time, this coherence is itself never fully revindi-cated. If Mary isn't really saying, "How curious that my choice has fallen upon the heir, just as I had a hunch that it might," neither is she saying, "I want Thomas Bertram for his money and his consequence—my strategy has always been based on these." Her ironic formulation stops just short of a Satanic assumption of motive, or if one prefers, it goes suggestively beyond it, insinuating that this perspective too is hedged with ironic qualifications. An indirect statement apparently alludes to a direct one, but its very indirection keeps the direct statement (as its "true" construction) in doubt. Indirection casts a shadow that it obliges to remain shadowy. The ironic switchword, of course, is "way": a decided course of action, or blind habit? a stratagem or an idiosyncrasy? Mary will not clarify her motivation either into the benign self-mockery of an Elizabeth Bennet, tracing her change of heart toward Darcy from her first sight of Pemberley, or into the artful hypocrisy of a Lady Susan, unscrupulously angling for the recognition of her every desire. Nor is Mary a mixture of Elizabeth and Lady Susan, if this means that she lends herself to being sorted out ac-cording to good and bad properties. The way that Mary actually takes preserves both possible meanings of the word, by suggesting that neither decisively grasps a self that can play them off one another in so adroit a fashion. Her way

is really (to bring up a third meaning) her *style*: of saying
things in such a way that they are also unsaid, of suspending
self-knowledge in structures of teasing uncertainty.

Mary's language lays claim both to her blindness and to
her ironical purchase on her blindness. Yet the nature of this
purchase is hard to specify, unless we take its sheer occulta-
tion for the sign, par excellence, of its ironical mode. Mary's
way might be compared to the practice of indirect discourse
in Flaubert, whose narrator seems to affirm that there is a
superior perspective to that of his characters and simultaneously dares us to find it and place ourselves comfortably
within it.[12] Or, to change comparisons, we might consider
Mary a puppet who is also her own ventriloquist. Our
awareness of the ventriloquist's obliquely operated control
prevents us from taking the puppet's engaging chatter with
full seriousness, but the ventriloquist remains evidently mute
for all that. One must hesitate to identify Mary's apparent
meaning with her "real" one; and although one can say
what her meaning is *not* (or not quite), it is difficult to put
it into a positive or definite form. Mary closes one of her
letters to Fanny with a telling phrase: "but—but—but"
(416). We might make it stand for the sly nature of her
irony: insisting upon a qualification, but failing to tell us
what exactly it might be. "She knew it was her way." We
can't begin to characterize what Mary knows except as this:
a way of staying unknown, impermeable to the categories of
right knowledge. Her assumption of irony coincides with
her refusal of knowledge, as a stable and fixed truth. Her
lively mind "can hardly be serious even on serious subjects"
(87), and it evades the earnestness of the others by "turning
the subject" (89, 290). She undermines proper measure,
whether (in a literal sense) the distance she and Edmund
have walked in the wilderness, or the accepted boundaries
of diction. Even her famous pun—"Of *Rears*, and *Vices*, I
saw enough" (60)—invites more speculation about its mean-

---

[12] See the discussion of Flaubertian irony in Jonathan Culler, *Flaubert: The Uses of Uncertainty*, pp. 185-207.

ing than puns normally do.[13] Operating in the suspense generated by the absence of fixed points of reference, Mary's discourse can always find something to say, or unsay. Her ambiguities and ironies do not conspicuously extend the narrative (into further articulations of plot), but they may be said to deepen unwholesomely the narrative language. They disturb the clarity of the textual surface with evidence of a language that does not mean what it says, or say what it means.

I have somewhat overstated the case for Mary's ironical threat; but this seems inevitable if one is to state it at all. We are never allowed to pursue Mary's irony so thoroughly as she. Throughout the novel, it is inserted into a moral-ideological context which reorganizes its uncertainties according

[13] Does she pun merely on vice admirals (plausibly introduced into a context set up by the mention of rear admirals) and vices? or on rear admirals and rear ends, too? Would not this acceptance of "Rears" give similarly anatomical overtones to "Vices"? A vice was a screw as well as a bad habit in Jane Austen's day. Is the *vitium* the *vis*, in its vulgar metaphorical sense? One might further wonder whether Mary's pun is mainly a clever piece of wordplay or she has really witnessed a "scene" such as the pun might imply. What sort of scene might the pun—even considered as mere wordplay—be seen to evoke? Mary's pun opens up a range of possible constructions, from the more or less ladylike to the more or less licentious, in a mode that might be wittily fabulous or coyly referential. Moreover, Mary denies even having made a pun ("Now, do not be suspecting me of a pun, I entreat"), literally insisting on the literalness of her language. In the face of the emphasis that she gives to her words (*"Rears* and *Vices"*), one doubts the asserted innocence of her language; but neither is one sure to what extent her language is *not* innocent. Mary's irony merely invites—and does no more than invite—an ironic reading. She lets her auditors (or, in another dimension, her readers) take responsibility for interpreting her language, without telling them —even if the fact of a pun be taken for granted—which construction is the one meant and which are illegitimate inferences. How far we wish to go with her statement, where we choose to stop in our speculation (which is always embarrassed and often arrested by the question, "Could a character in Jane Austen ever mean *this*?"), is our business, she would imply, not hers.

to a different rule. Its subversion of nomination can itself
be named, and its indiscriminate liveliness can be sorted out
into good and bad moral properties. We are invited to notice, for instance, that the ironic inflection Mary gives to her
choice of Bertram does not keep her from making that
choice. The closural system of *Mansfield Park* disposes of a
moral ideology that makes Mary's irony always seem a mode
of bad faith: a way of preserving a morally dubious choice
by anticipating the perspectives that might trouble it. We
need not—we cannot, even were there a need—deprive the
novel of its moral ideology. Yet if we try to imagine what
Mary's discourse would be like without it, we shall have an
idea of what the moral ideology (with its insistence on "fixing" feeling and assuming the proper name for conduct) is
meant to defend against: not only a character who refuses
to synthesize herself once for all, but also a language that
refuses to abstract a "transcendent signified" from the production and play of its signifiers.

If Mary Crawford's language wittingly evades definitive
disclosure, its "poor relations" might be the blinded languages that bungle disclosure, or trivialize it, or unfastidi-
ously level down its essential discriminations: languages of
chatter, such as uttered by Miss Diana Parker in *Sanditon*
or Miss Bates in *Emma*.

Here is Diana Parker's "explanation" of her arrival in
Sanditon:

> "Well—now for the explanation of my being here.—I told
> you in my Letter, of the two considerable Families, I was
> hoping to secure for you—the West Indians & the Semi-
> nary.—" Here Mr P. drew his Chair still nearer to his Sis-
> ter, & took her hand again most affectionately as he an-
> swered "Yes, Yes;—How active & how kind you have
> been!"—"The West-Indians, she continued, whom I
> look upon as the *most* desirable of the two—as the Best of
> the Good—prove to be a Mrs Griffiths & her family. I
> know them only through others.—You must have heard

me mention Miss Capper, the particular friend of *my* very
particular friend Fanny Noyce;—now, Miss Capper is extremely intimate with a Mrs Darling, who is on terms of
constant correspondence with Mrs Griffiths herself.—
Only a *short* chain, you see, between us, & not a Link
wanting. Mrs G. meant to go to the Sea, for her Young
People's benefit—had fixed on the Coast of Sussex, but
was undecided as to the where, wanted something Private, & wrote to ask the opinion of her friend Mrs Darling.
—Miss Capper happened to be staying with Mrs D. when
Mrs G.'s Letter arrived, & was consulted on the question;
she wrote the same day to Fanny Noyce and mentioned
it to her—& Fanny all alive for *us*, instantly took up her
pen & forwarded the circumstance to me—except as to
Names—which have but lately transpired.—There was
but *one* thing for *me* to do.—I answered Fanny's letter by
the same Post & pressed for the recommendation of Sanditon. Fanny had feared your having no house large enough
to receive such a Family.—But I seem to be spinning out
my story to an endless length.—You see how it was all
managed. I had the pleasure of hearing soon afterwards by
the same simple link of connection that Sanditon *had been*
recommended by Mrs Darling, & that the West-Indians
were very much disposed to go thither.—This was the
state of the case when I wrote to you;—but two days ago;
—yes, the day before yesterday—I heard again from
Fanny Noyce, saying that *she* had heard from Miss Capper, who by a Letter from Mrs Darling understood that
Mrs G.—has expressed herself in a letter to Mrs D. more
doubtingly on the subject of Sanditon.—Am I clear?—I
would be anything rather than not clear."—"Oh! perfectly, perfectly. Well?"—"The reason of this hesitation, was her having no connections in the place, &
no means of ascertaining that she should have good ac-
commodations on arriving there;—and she was particularly careful & scrupulous on all those matters more on
account of a certain Miss Lambe a young Lady (probably

a Neice) under her care, than on her own account or her Daughters.—Miss Lambe has an immense fortune—richer than all the rest—& very delicate health.—One sees clearly enough by all this, the *sort* of Woman Mrs G. must be—as helpless & indolent, as Wealth & a Hot Climate are apt to make us. But we are not all born to equal Energy.—What was to be done?—I had a few moments indecision; —Whether to offer to write to *you*,—or to Mrs Whitby to secure them a House?—but neither pleased me.—I hate to employ others, when I am equal to act myself—and my conscience told me that this was an occasion which called for me. Here was a family of helpless Invalides whom I might essentially serve.—I sounded Susan—the same Thought had occurred to her.—Arthur made no difficulties—our plan was arranged immediately, we were off yesterday morn^g at 6—, left Chichester at the same hour today—& here we are.—" (MW 408-409)

I would regret the expense of a quotation so full and so inevitably out of proportion to my commentary on it, if it didn't point to a defining characteristic of chatter: namely, its excess—its constant overproduction in relation to that which it can be said to communicate. "I seem to be spinning out my story to an endless length." The technique of Diana Parker's spinning out is hypotaxis. The humor of "only a *short* chain, you see, between us, & not a Link wanting" comes from our opposite sense that her language has more links than it really wants, just as it tells of more complications than really prove the case. We soon discover that "the Family from Surry & the Family from Camberwell were one & the same" (420). What is threatened in Diana's discourse is perfectly clear ("Am I clear?—I would be anything rather than not clear"): clarity and—what clarity is a necessary condition of in Jane Austen—truth. This excessive and excessively differentiated language would seem basically a response to a lack of provision for discourse. It is a kind of linguistic hypochondria. Much as Diana fills her abundant leisure with the motions of bustle (mainly, only an active form of inefficaciousness), her language supplies its meager and trivial matter by overarticulating it, as though there were all too much to tell.

A related kind of chatter is the epistolary style of Lady Bertram in *Mansfield Park*. She has formed for herself "a very creditable, common-place, amplifying style, so that a very little matter was enough for her," though of course "she could not do entirely without any." Blessed with "such a capital piece of Mansfield news, as the certainty of the Grants going to Bath," she had wished to spread it "over the largest part of a page" in a letter to Fanny; but Edmund has already treated it ("as concisely as possible") at the end of his own letter to his cousin. "Being so soon to lose all the benefit of Dr. Grant's gouty symptoms and Mrs. Grant's morning calls, it was very hard upon her to be deprived of one of the last epistolary uses she could put them to" (MP 425). Like Diana Parker's speech, Lady Bertram's writing is generally out of all proportion to its matter. Diana Parker industriously exaggerates the complication of her communications; the less energetic Lady Bertram merely lines her own with polite boilerplate. Her "diffuse style" consists largely of a "medley of trusts, hopes, and fears, all following and producing each other at hap-hazard" (427).

When the matter becomes her own son's illness, Lady Bertram's style begins to outrage not only the text's cognitive ideals of clarity and concision, but also its moral conception of topical proprieties.

> "This distressing intelligence, as you may suppose," observed her Ladyship, after giving the substance of it, "has agitated us exceedingly, and we cannot prevent ourselves from being greatly alarmed, and apprehensive for the poor invalid, whose state Sir Thomas fears may be very critical; and Edmund kindly proposes attending his brother immediately, but I am happy to add, that Sir Thomas will not leave me on this distressing occasion, as it would be

too trying for me. We shall greatly miss Edmund in our small circle, but I trust and hope he will find the poor invalid in a less alarming state than might be apprehended, and that he will be able to bring him to Mansfield shortly, which Sir Thomas proposes should be done, and thinks best on every account, and I flatter myself, the poor sufferer will soon be able to bear the removal without material inconvenience or injury. As I have little doubt of your feeling for us, my dear Fanny, under these distressing circumstances, I will write again very soon." (426)

Her amplifying rhetoric only trivializes the life-or-death issue at stake. This is plainly not the style in which a mother ought to report her son's serious illness; but its deficiencies precisely reveal the limited range of emotions that has characterized Lady Bertram throughout the novel.

It is Miss Bates, of course, who pursues the logic of chatter to its most radical extreme. In contrast to Diana Parker's compensatory hypotaxis, Miss Bates's language has almost no use for syntax at all. An ill-sorted clutter of names and half-sentences, it never comes to the point. It is an incipient aphasia, determined to pull an endless and would-be totalizing discourse out of the silence closing in on it. Miss Bates displays an "impatience to say everything" (E 455), and never keeps a secret (239, 329). This "great talker on little matters, full of trivial communications and harmless gossip" (21) observes the want of proportion characteristic of chatter. Her speech is typically a "medley" (237) of heterogeneous items, submitting only to the minimal organization of its obsessive themes. (It is not difficult to desentimentalize these: to see in her constant gratitude an altruistic inversion of *ressentiment*, or in her boisterous praise of Jane Fairfax a displaced aggressivity.) The stylish Emma seems most affronted by Miss Bates's conversational style: "If I thought I should ever be like Miss Bates! so silly—so satisfied—so smiling—so prosing—so undistinguishing and unfastidious—and so apt to tell every thing relative to every body about me, I would marry to-morrow" (84-85). Undistinguishing, unfastidious, likely to tell everything relative to everybody about her, Miss Bates gives scandal to the unities of elegant conversation. She represents baroque extravagance in a classical order, and low-comic leveling of high-comic nuances. Her talk resembles a radio wave that several stations are trying to appropriate all at once; and under cover of her "static," the finer discriminations, the more interesting encounters and disclosures, threaten to go unperceived. She is always forestalling or frustrating the communications of the others (172-73, 194, 329), and at the Westons' ball, not only Mrs. Elton's words, but "every body's words, were soon lost under the incessant flow of Miss Bates" (322). We rightly protest when Emma shuts her up at Box Hill, but to be charitable toward Miss Bates is only another, better way of acknowledging the fact that our charity is indeed exercised by her. Her generalized good will potentially undermines the subtler distinctions of the novelist (her "our dear Mrs. Elton," for instance). Nor is there a doubt that so superior a woman as Jane Fairfax must suffer in the continual society of an aunt "who never holds her tongue" (194). Mrs. Weston and Mr. Knightley both agree that "her aunt is a good creature, but as a constant companion must be very tiresome" (286), and no major character in *Emma* ever seeks —quite the contrary—to take her into his confidence. For all the respect canvassed on behalf of Miss Bates, the main business of the novel must be carried on elsewhere: in other languages than that of chatter.

The expansionist tendencies in Miss Bates's discourse are apparent enough, but they present no real difficulty to the novelist. Significantly, Jane Austen's chatterboxes are always minor characters whom a closural system is licensed to shunt off center stage at will. Under the traditional assumptions of novelistic form, the text-producing deficiencies of minor characters need not be cured, or completed in a destiny; an "etc principle" is always available to truncate the discourse that they sponsor. Yet it seems odd that a novelist whose

own language is in general highly disciplined (observing semantic shades of difference, topical propriety, and the standard of clear syntax) should give a conspicuous place to the
opposite language of chatter. The function of chatter, as that
language whose appearance in the text must always be under
restraint, serves some fundamental ambivalences in Jane
Austen.

The underdetermined language of chatter, exceeding its
task of communication, answers mainly to a sheer need to
talk—or perhaps better, a need not to stop talking. Roland
Barthes calls it "an unweaned language: imperative, automatic, unaffectionate, a minor disaster of static," whose motions are those of "an objectless sucking" and "an undifferen-
tiated orality."[14] On this perspective, Jane Austen would be
pointing, in her portrait of Miss Bates, to the undifferentiat-
ed source of energy on which her own more discriminating
and chastened language draws. If the novel's characteristic
tone, according to Mary McCarthy, is one of "gossip and
tittle tattle," one might well consider chatter such as Miss
Bates's to be the novel's primary language: the ground on
which its more significant structures are built.[15] The portrait of Miss Bates is Jane Austen's tribute to the gestation of
her text in the womb of trivial communications and unre-
served gossip. Not unusually, however, the parentage here
is a matter of some ambivalence, both lovingly idealized and
coolly disowned. One easily responds to the richness of Miss
Bates's static: she is a one-woman chorus, presenting a dimension of an entire society almost at a stroke. "Such a host
of friends! . . . Everything is so good!" (323). She idealizes
a community whose very static—however boring, trite, and
even ridiculous—contains no breath of evil. The novelist's

[14] Roland Barthes, *Le Plaisir du texte*, p. 12. I have followed the
translation of Richard Miller, *The Pleasure of the Text* (New York:
Hill and Wang, 1975), p. 5, except where he mitigates the force of
"une succion sans objet" by rendering it as "an ungratified sucking."

[15] Mary McCarthy, "The Fact in Fiction," *On the Contrary* (New
York: Farrar, Strauss and Cudahy, 1961), pp. 249-70.

full response to Miss Bates, however, includes more than love, as though Jane Austen could grasp the primal language only through antithetical meanings. While the moral sense of the novel protects Miss Bates, its sense of style condemns her. Indeed, it is difficult not to see the narrator's language as a "reaction formation" to Miss Bates's. The rigor of the one inverts the shapelessness of the other, and the capacity of the one to invest with seriousness is a reaction to the incapacity of the other to do anything but trivialize. Kinship with Miss Bates can be warmly acknowledged only when the traces of family resemblance have been practically effaced. The daughter's language needn't fear the mother tongue.

[margin handwritten: the mother tongue as uncontrollable chatter ??]

The portrait of Miss Bates also serves to disarm—if only locally—what will prove a far more consequential ambivalence in Jane Austen. In her "impatience to say everything," Miss Bates tells nothing much worth hearing; though she threatens an abundant text, it is a boring one. Her language has no reserves of secrecy, employs no processes of withholding, which alone make disclosure worthwhile or interesting. If her language is to be unsecretive and without feints, therefore, it is indispensable that it be stupid as well. For the more Miss Bates knew, the more she would tell, and the pleasures of the "novelistic" would be ruined.

Now as an ideologue, Jane Austen puts the highest value on transparent communication. Like Mr. Knightley, she officially upholds "truth and sincerity in all our dealings with each other," and condemns "Mystery" and "Finesse" as perversions of the understanding (446). Yet if all her characters behaved according to Mr. Knightley's principles—as, morally, Jane Austen thinks they should have—there would be no source of narratability. How can the novelist recognize the necessity of mystery and finesse without appearing to call into question the moral ideology of the text? The recognition can never be carried by morally ideal characters like Mr. Knightley or Elinor Dashwood. The novelistic dangers of a transparent, unsecretive language can only be admitted to in a version of it that is scaled down, trivialized, and voided of moral-ideological freight. Miss Bates meets the case. She is Jane Austen's object lesson in the fate of novelistic interest when it is in default of suspense or delay: boring, supererogatory prattle.

One easily moves from everlasting talkers like Miss Bates or Diana Parker to obsessive characters ("humor characters") like Sir Walter Elliot or Mrs. Elton, in whom an idiosyncrasy engrosses every opportunity for exhibition. This side of boredom, such characters are inexhaustible textual resources, on account of their refusal to develop: pure instances of Freudian repetition without Freudian working through. "Vanity was the beginning and end of Sir Walter Elliot's character" (P 4)—which is another way of saying that there will be no linear or sequential development of Sir Walter's character, and no inherent stopping place in his portrayal. Mrs. Elton is still running on—insisting, as it were, that she still *can* run on—in the penultimate sentence of *Emma*: "Very little white satin, very few lace veils; a most pitiful business!—Selina would stare when she heard of it" (E 484). The textual fertility of a situation in which two such psychic automata compete with one another to determine the conversational topic (Mr. Weston and Mrs. Elton [E 305 ff.]), or in which a character of good sense tries to exact information from a character bounded by obsessive themes (Elinor Dashwood and Mrs. Palmer [SS 114 ff.]), is partly responsible for the comedy of such scenes. The text of obsession or idiosyncrasy is intrinsically interminable; as it can never be properly concluded, it can only be arbitrarily abandoned. The peripheral status of humor characters in the novels exempts them from the closural exigencies of reconstruction. Provided the careers of the main characters are brought to an appropriate close, they can stay loose ends, embodying a persistent narratability. Closure occurring elsewhere allows the novelist not to realize this narratability, and the invocation of an "etc principle" disarms its persistence.

--·⊷{ *Chapter One* }⊶·--

The sources of narratability in Jane Austen are not always psychological kinks in her characters, though my discussion has tended to imply this. Because character is a dominant mode of organization in Jane Austen's novels, it has been possible to show how a certain psychology in the text doubles for a certain kind of narrative in it as well. There are, however, other sources of narratability that are independent of character.

For example, one might point to the probabilities of social intercourse in the novels, which open up a perspective with no real vanishing point. Think of the suite of episodes beginning *Pride and Prejudice*. There is first Mr. Bennet's visit to Mr. Bingley; then, Mr. Bingley's visit to Mr. Bennet; then, the assembly; the visits between Longbourn and Netherfield; the gathering at Sir William Lucas's; Jane's cold and the incidents in its train; the arrival of Mr. Collins at Longbourn and Mr. Wickham in Meryton; Mr. Bingley's ball, and so on. The only logic binding the events in the sequence together is that they are all highly probable activities in the social world chosen for representation: "3 or 4 Families" of a leisured middle class "in a Country Village." At first, only this grounding in a general social verisimilitude keeps Jane Austen's construction from appearing baldly episodic and picaresque. Manners motivate the production of episodes (now a visit, now a ball), but while manners may change, they never stop. There is no evident point at which the record of the daily round of intercourse among three or four families in a country village naturally comes to an end. In *Persuasion*, Anne Elliot waits out a series of contingent episodes of this order, and part of the pathos of her situation comes from one's sense that her wait might well have gone on virtually forever. Her reunion with Wentworth, of course, ultimately saves her from being a mere function in the narrative of social circumstance, but even at the moment of their reunion, the novelist offers an image of the persistency of that social world that the lovers have transcended. Much as Arthur and Amy Clennam, at the end of Dickens's

Little Dorrit, will go down into the "roaring streets" of London, where "the noisy and the eager, and the arrogant and the froward and the vain, fretted and chafed, and made their usual uproar,"[16] so Anne and Wentworth slowly pace the "gradual ascent" of a street in Bath, "heedless of every group around them, seeing neither sauntering politicians, bustling house-keepers, flirting girls, nor nursery-maids and children" (P 241).

We might say (in the words that Roland Barthes has applied to the text of prattle) that the narrative of manners or social circumstance is "a frigid text . . . until desire, until neurosis forms in it."[17] This is the function of the marriage plot in Jane Austen: to impose a desire and an object of desire on the "frigid" but far too fecund narrative of social circumstance. The relationship between the marriage plot and the narrative of circumstance can strike us sometimes as complementary, sometimes as antagonistic. At one level, the marriage plot would seem to form within the narrative of circumstance: a meaningful precipitate happily dropping out of an ongoing flux. At another level, the marriage plot, obliged to pass through the narrative of circumstance, seems to run the risk of losing its realization under the counteracting pressures of retardation and dispersion. In either case, the edge on the heroine's desire (as well as the readers') comes from the interaction of a direct objectal desire (Anne wants Wentworth) and a theoretically unending obstacle course.

The ending of the marriage plot disarms the threat of frustration and suspense, and the narrative of circumstance is concomitantly abridged under an "etc principle." We need not follow Emma and Mr. Knightley beyond the threshold of their "perfect union" through visits, balls, business, lyings-in (little Henry Knightley's claim to the Donwell estate has surely gone for good). If Jane Austen's

[16] Charles Dickens, *Little Dorrit* (London: Oxford University Press, 1953), p. 826.

[17] Barthes, *Le Plaisir du texte*, p. 12.

novels cannot quite bring us to a point at which time stops, they do bring us to a point where time lapses into benign repetition: where nature, along with "naturalized" social probabilities, will resume a predictable run.

I hope to have established how a narratability deferring closure matches up a closure correcting and abolishing it. Hesitation is matched by decision; nonobjectal desire by object choice; the cultivation of suspense by the culmen of moral judgment; irony by knowledge; chatter by an elsewhere of serious revelations; the course of social circumstance by the resolution of a marriage plot; et cetera. However incomplete the series, the heterogeneity of its items, on a rhetorical level, remains troubling. What do Harriet's indecision and Mary Crawford's irony have in common, as figures of novelistic speech? At the same level, what can Emma's choice of Mr. Knightley and the moral condemnation of Henry Crawford be said to share? And how are we to formulate the rhetorical interaction of narratable and closural elements?

What integrates narratable elements with closural elements seems to be a problematic of the name, such as Michel Foucault has discussed most impressively:

> One might say that it is the Name that organizes all Classical discourse; to speak or to write is not to say things or to express oneself, it is not a matter of playing with language, it is to make one's way towards the sovereign act of nomination, to move, through language, towards the place where things and words are conjoined in their common essence, and which makes it possible to give them a name. But once that name has been spoken, all the language that has led up to it, or that has been crossed in order to reach it, is reabsorbed into it and disappears. So that Classical discourse, in its profound essence, tends always towards this boundary; but, in surviving it, pushes the boundary further away. It continues on its way in the perpetually maintained suspension of the Name. . . . The figures

through which discourse passes act as a deterrent to the name, which then arrives at the last moment to fulfil and abolish them. The name is the *end* of discourse. And possibly all Classical literature resides in this space, in this striving to reach a name that remains always formidable because it exhausts, and thereby kills, the possibility of speech. . . .

All Classical literature resides in the movement that proceeds from the figure of the name to the name itself, passing from the task of naming the same thing yet again by means of new figures . . . to that of finding words that will at last name accurately that which has never been named before or that which has remained dormant in the enveloping folds of words too far removed from it.[18]

Not the least advantage of Foucault's perspective is that it gives us a fresh sense of what it means when we call Jane Austen a classical writer—that his conception of classical literature allows us to recognize much more than the elegant balance of her style. If the name is the end of classical discourse, then all the closural impositions that we have considered can be assimilated to "the sovereign act of nomination." The final marriage ceremony in which the heroine gets *renamed* is only the most obvious thematization of closure as an act of nomination. (*Emma* is a wryly intimate title. Emma who? The novel addresses, precisely, a question of identity: what will Emma's full name ultimately be?) Closural forces like decision and object choice can readily be seen to name desire once for all, and real knowledge of character can be taken for its irrevocable name. Moral ideology imposes a set of right names on feeling and conduct, and the resolution of plot names the ultimate direction or sense of a movement whose logic was hidden and dispersed. While the closural system of the novels works to impose

[18] Michel Foucault, *Les Mots et les choses*, pp. 133-34. The translation is from *The Order of Things* (London: Tavistock, 1970), pp. 117-18.

the name, moreover, the figures of narratability work to prolong a metonymical sliding: preserving and depending upon "the perpetually maintained suspension of the Name." Hesitation, flirtation, suspense all defer the sovereign act of nomination. In a different dimension, less bound by linear sequence, Mary Crawford's irony subverts the fixity of definitive formulations. (One recalls the fuss Edmund makes over her choice of words to describe the elopement of Henry and Maria—"no harsher name than folly given!" [MP 454]. Appropriately enough, since she is resisting the closure about to be imposed on her, Mary has replaced the right ideological name with a mere metonymy.) Similarly, the texts of babble, blind idiosyncrasy and obsession, and social circumstance all embody a language that never comes to the point—to the name and (what accompanies it) meaning and truth.

The coincidence of truth and closure in Jane Austen's novels, therefore, is far from fortuitous. "It is always a matter of placing in the perspective of the classical text," Roland Barthes argues, "a profound or final truth (profundity is what is discovered *at the end*)." The terminal position of a novel is assigned a completive function, most visibly operating at the levels of plot and mystery. Plot moves toward its ultimate issue, which implicitly stands for its "real" sense; and mystery is prolonged to the point at which it yields to that full explanation of events taken for their "true" solution. One might say, with Barthes, that "truth is that which completes, which closes": a mere effect of its terminal position in the text and the completive function there located. After all the delays, a presence; after all the lies and equivocations, the truth; at the end of a tentative process of naming, unnaming, and renaming, a peremptory final nomination: "the discovery and proffering of an irreversible word."[19]

While it is unlikely that Jane Austen worked in complete awareness of these matters, they were probably less foreign

[19] Roland Barthes, *S/Z*, pp. 172, 82, 216.

In Lilly—
Natalie has
the last word

How does
this work,
with Felix's
narrative +
Nat's response

to her conscious mind than might be supposed. "The Mystery," for instance, a comedy she wrote in adolescence, wittily parodies the excesses of retarding and occulting the act of definitive nomination.

Scene the 2ᵈ

A Parlour in HUMBUG's House

MRS HUMBUG & FANNY, *discovered at work.*

MRS HUM: You understand me my Love?

FANNY: Perfectly ma'am. Pray continue your narration.

MRS HUM: Alas! it is nearly concluded, for I have nothing more to say on the Subject.

FANNY: Ah! here's Daphne.

Enter DAPHNE.

DAPHNE: My dear Mrs Humbug how d'ye do? Oh! Fanny t'is all over.

FANNY: Is it indeed!

MRS HUM: I'm very sorry to hear it.

FANNY: Then t'was to no purpose that I. . . .

DAPHNE: None upon Earth.

MRS HUM: And what is to become of? . . .

DAPHNE: Oh! thats all settled. [*whispers* MRS HUMBUG]

FANNY: And how is it determined?

DAPHNE: I'll tell you. [*whispers* FANNY]

MRS HUM: And is he to? . . .

DAPHNE: I'll tell you all I know of the matter [*whispers* MRS HUMBUG & FANNY]

FANNY: Well! now I know everything about it, I'll go [and dress] away.

MRS HUM: ⎫
DAPHNE: ⎭ And so will I.

Exeunt

(MW 56)

The mystery here is exclusively a product of the characters talking in ellipses and whispers, and using pronouns for which no ghost of an antecedent has been provided. The mysteriousness depends entirely on the writer's sleight of hand in withholding information; and the comedy comes from the unwitting clumsiness of this sleight of hand, withholding information that there seem no reasons (besides the sheer structural exigencies of mystery writing) not to tell. Young Jane Austen, of course, is scoring the failure of mystery writers sufficiently to "naturalize" their mysteries —that is, to clothe them in a socially plausible secrecy. What on one view is a practical critique of mere ineptness, however, becomes on another a theoretical recognition of the necessity of structural casuistry in mystery writing. Jane Austen declares in the dedication that her comedy, "tho' an unfinished one, is I flatter myself as *complete* a *Mystery* as any of its kind" (55). The want of closural nomination may make "The Mystery" an unfinished piece, but it certainly also makes it a thoroughgoing mystery. To consummate "The Mystery" would be to consume its quintessential mysteriousness as well. Mystery, it might be said, is nothing more than that which has no full name. A conspicuously artificial avoidance of naming is fatal only to a realistic verisimilitude, not at all to the production of the mystery text. Whether naturalized or not, retardation and withholding are inevitably the means that produce our sense of mystery, and the "bad faith" of the form turns on its appearance of soliciting a name that in fact it is working to defer.

The equivocation of form which can be so blatantly displayed in a satire like "The Mystery" gets hidden in the mature novels, where the delay of final nomination is consistently motivated as an evil contingent on a lapse of right conduct. The "good" characters (Elinor, Fanny, Anne) anxiously pursue or attend the final settlement upon which the novelistic discourse expires, while the "bad" or inadequate ones (the Crawfords, Emma unreformed) postpone or fuddle it. The narrator of *Mansfield Park* characterizes herself as "impatient to restore every body, not greatly in fault themselves, to tolerable comfort, and to have done with all the rest" (461); but how are we to take an impatience that has been able to contain itself over almost three volumes? The double-dealing here might be suggestively compared to that of a competent mystery novel. There the detective typically proceeds toward the solution of the crime with all due haste; when other characters accuse him of "dragging his feet," this is only the genre's code language for saying the opposite, that his mind is secretly busy turning over a productive new hypothesis. Yet while the representation shows the detective hastening, the construction shows the novelist stalling. It is *he* who is dragging his feet, and this very drag generates the length of the form. Viktor Shklovsky recognized in the mystery novel the necessary moment of false solutions. "The manipulation of false and true solutions is what constitutes the method of organizing the mystery. The dénouement consists in shifting from one to the other."[20] This is what the mystery novel "knows," but can never representationally assert. Indeed, it must assert the exact opposite, that the crime is being solved as quickly as its complications permit, that all the delays and detours on the road to solution are accidents of the represented world. Implicitly, the mystery novelist is saying, "Theoretically, of course, it would have been possible for the case to be solved in the space, say, of a short story—if this clue had been noticed in time, or that bit of information extorted earlier. Unluckily, it has so happened in the case I have chanced to treat that this theoretical possibility, on account of various contingencies, could not be realized."

In a conventional mystery novel, of course, this equivoca-

[20] Viktor Shklovsky, "The Mystery Novel: Dickens's *Little Dorrit*," in Ladislav Matejka and Krystyna Pomorska, eds., *Readings in Russian Poetics: Formalist and Structuralist Views*, pp. 220-21.

tion is not much more than a playful rule of the game; in Jane Austen's fiction, however, it takes the more problematical form of an ideological ambivalence toward narrative itself. Foucault's remarks on the organization of classical discourse have already hinted at a primary ambivalence in its "striving to reach a name that remains always formidable because it exhausts, and thereby kills, the possibility of speech." It is as though what the classical text wanted most were to disappear, to get rid of its own excessive energies and deficient figures by an act of nomination that, once performed, would relieve them of a reason for being. The articulation of an ideology, in Jane Austen's text, serves to legalize, as it were, this primary ambivalence: to reinforce the primacy of the closural nomination, and at the same time to depreciate the status—even to occult the necessity—of narratable insufficiencies. Essentially, this ideology is one of settlement. Socially, it assumes that marriage is the permanent and proper means of recognition, the defining compact. Cognitively, it assumes that character can be known in all its essentials, and morally, that it can be pinned down on such knowledge. Linguistically, it assumes that adequate formulations are available to settle whatever needs to be formulated. It is evident that novelistic closure confirms each of these assumptions, instituting what is virtually an ideological paradise. Every mystery has been solved, every major lack liquidated and rift made good. Willoughby is really this, the Crawfords really that. These feelings are true love, those are only infatuation. Conversely, the deferral of settlement (that is, the narratable) is typically seen throughout the novels as a matter of unbearable "suspense and indecision," "doubt," "torment," "vexation," by either the narrator or the characters who best register her moral-ideological vision. William Elliot in *Persuasion* is called a "retarding weight" (P 241) for inspiring a presumption about Anne's destiny that has made Captain Wentworth timid to propose again; and retarding weights, in all Jane Austen's novels,

tend to be judged rather like William Elliot's "real character" (199): an unwelcome obtrusiveness threatening incal-
culable evil—"hollow and black!" (199).

Significantly, only characters like Lucy Steele or Mary
Crawford thrive on waiting games, and the characters like
Wickham or Frank Churchill who willfully engage in "mys-
tifications" are pointedly blamed for it. By contrast, the
novelist's most admirable heroines (Elinor, Fanny, Anne)
have practically to be abducted into narratable zones, almost
as though the excitement they exerted themselves to defend
against were part of a sexual advance. (Sometimes, indeed,
it is, as in Fanny's resistance to Henry Crawford.) Virtually
every event in the novelistic world represents to them some
loose, dangerously free-floating energy that must be bound.
"Let there be an end of this suspense" (MP 424). Every unsettled development needs somehow to be settled, even if
unfortunately, or only by a definitive observation of the
ambiguity or tentativeness of its meaning. Common to all
the heroines is a mania for explanation, an imperious desire
for settled answers, which will stabilize and fix their response to experience.

"That the Miss Lucases and the Miss Bennets should meet
to talk over a ball was absolutely necessary; and the morning after the assembly brought the former to Longbourn to
hear and to communicate" (PP 18). Even so commonplace
an occurrence as a ball needs to be screened: to what hopes,
dangers, did it give rise? what legitimate inferences does it
allow? what hazardous extrapolations does it not quite warrant? The novelist's joke here aside, we see how "absolutely
necessary" it is "to talk over" experience, if only to oneself,
being demonstrated throughout the novel. Elizabeth catches
the cool greeting exchanged between Darcy and Wickham:
"What could be the meaning of it?—It was impossible to
imagine; it was impossible not to long to know" (73). Later
she must engage Wickham in "a full discussion" (115) of
the reasons for his absence from Mr. Bingley's ball. And

after the first evening of her visit to Charlotte Collins ("spent chiefly in talking over Hertfordshire news, and telling again what had been already written"),

> Elizabeth in the solitude of her chamber had to meditate upon Charlotte's degree of contentment, to understand her address in guiding, and composure in bearing with her husband, and to acknowledge that it was all done very well. She had also to anticipate how her visit would pass, the quiet tenor of their usual employments, the vexatious interruptions of Mr. Collins, and the gaieties of their intercourse with Rosings. A lively imagination soon settled it all. (157-58)

When experience throws up so many provocative and often provoking mysteries, the typical response is to take some step, whether ratiocinative or imaginative, to settle them. "Till this moment, I never knew myself" (208), says Elizabeth, beginning to realize her true feelings for Darcy, and she has turned even her relationship to herself into a mystery that has now been solved. What are Emma Woodhouse's fantasies, in a sense, but a less reasoned and more freely inventive version of this same need to anticipate the narrative gaps in experience, to give speech to its muteness? Because Harriet's parentage is unknown, "Emma was obliged to fancy what she liked" (E 27); because there is a perceptible incoherence, however slight, in Jane Fairfax's behavior, Emma's fancy "received an amusing supply" (214).

Whether cautiously indulged or not, this obsessive need to settle it all arises in response to the imposition of its opposite: an uncomfortable suspension of settlement, an awkward silence of signification. With a confidence and an anxiety oddly belying one another, the heroines engage to do the work of closure, which is to make sense. Ignorance, incoherence, or ambiguity must never be enjoyed, but always submitted to as an enforced evil. (It is better, of course, to recognize this evil for what it is—like, *grosso modo*, Elinor and Fanny—than to liquidate it prematurely in the manner of Emma or Elizabeth.) To make sense is a right and proper task, but it is essential to the novelistic production that it be frustrated: undermined by the parodic endeavors of matchmakers like Mrs. Bennet and Mrs. Jennings; misled by the false representations of tricksters like Wickham and Frank Churchill; resisted by the confusingly various behavior of the Crawfords and the dogmatism of Marianne Dashwood; even simply deflected by the heroines' own blindness. If the novel is to be kept going, all the senses made excepting the last must be untrue, incomplete, or merely unconfirmed. The assertiveness of these may anticipate the closural act of nomination, but their inadequacy only validates its sovereignty as the moment of full, true explanation.

Jane Austen mobilizes a full range of pseudoclosures: mendacious or equivocating, suspended or only partial solutions.[21] Wickham gives Elizabeth a false account of Darcy's coolness toward him, which she mistakenly takes for true. The Dashwoods' servant unwittingly equivocates when he announces that Lucy Steele has become Mrs. Ferrars, for "Mrs. Ferrars" can be construed as either Mrs. *Edward* Ferrars or Mrs. *Robert* Ferrars. Emma suspends Frank Churchill's confession ("In short, Miss Woodhouse—I think you can hardly be quite without suspicion—"), erroneously believing that she already knows its purport (E 260). And the news of Willoughby's intended marriage to Miss Grey, a partial explanation of events, accounts for his cutting Marianne at the London party, but not for his initially amiable behavior toward her. These pseudoclosures make a nice instance of the way narratable and closural systems intersect in the text. Insofar as they fail to measure up to Jane Austen's rigorous ideal of a wholly and properly intelligible world, the wrongheaded, equivocal, interrupted, or scanted attempts at closure only promote further narrative. Yet inso-

---

[21] For a full discussion of "the structural tracks of the lie," see Barthes, *S/Z*, sections 42, 60, 62, 63, 69.

far as they implicitly or by contrast anticipate the form that closure will assume, they promote further narrative only in the direction of closural rectification or completion. The narratable lie postulates as its future a corresponding closural truth. A switchword is equivocal, but at least narrows the closural possibilities down to two, one of which will be chosen. And we know that a suspended solution will be resumed, much as an incomplete one will be completed.

It becomes clear, then, that Jane Austen's novels must proceed (in a rather literal sense) by trial and error, if they are to proceed at all. Only narratable errors can mark the "progress" toward an increasingly definitive closural truth. It might be argued, of course, that other novelists proceed in the very same way; but here, what might well be a common novelistic *modus operandi* goes patently against the drift of the novelist's highly unexperimental moral ideology, which is always suggesting that the knowledge of what one "ought to have done" is available to the conscience of characters from the start. The particular effects of this ambivalence would not occur, say, in George Eliot's fiction, where an ideology of process and becoming perfectly accounts for the narrative procedures. In Jane Austen, the ideology articulated in the representation can never fully rationalize the necessities of novelistic construction, except as lapses, that is, events that really need not have happened. From the standpoint of her moral ideology, Jane Austen's novel is always on the wrong track; according to the exigencies of her novelistic construction, however, it must be on the wrong track when it moves on a track at all. For the novelist's ideal—what she calls "the reality of reason and truth" (SS 361)—is a great good place where movement (unless already known and reduced to an iterative mode) is impossible.

What I have been discussing as the equivocation of Jane Austen's form—its tendency to disown at an ideological level what it embraces at a constructional one—shows up in miniature in the moral casuistry of the heroines, who limit the excitement they feel to fewer dimensions than their actual response often seems to warrant. Fanny Price's full response to the Mansfield theatricals, for instance, encompasses more shades of feeling than her conscience means to cope with:

> Fanny looked on and listened, not unamused to observe the selfishness which, more or less disguised, seemed to govern them all, and wondering how it would end. For her own gratification she could have wished that something might be acted, for she had never seen even half a play, but every thing of higher consequence was against it. (MP 131)

Later, when Mrs. Grant has accepted the part that Fanny has refused,

> Fanny was at first in some danger of envying her the character she had accepted. But reflection brought better feelings, and shewed her that Mrs. Grant was entitled to respect, which could never have belonged to *her*, and that had she received even the greatest, she could never have been easy in joining a scheme which, considering only her uncle, she must condemn altogether. (160)

The evident attraction in the idea of a play; the temptation, just barely budding, to act herself; the subtle resentment of her refusal ("Mrs. Grant was entitled to respect, which could never have belonged to *her*")—all of this gets flattened before "every thing of higher consequence" into a peremptory moral judgment. It is part of the complexity of Fanny's whole response that her moral judgment—real and respectable enough—serves more than merely her moral sense. Sir Thomas's presumed opinion provides a principle by which her conduct can be rightly guided, but also a pretext by which her richly motivated "shyness" can be protected. Fanny herself shows some awareness of this: "Was it not ill-nature—selfishness—and a fear of exposing herself? . . . It would be so horrible to her to act, that she was

inclined to suspect the truth and purity of her own scruples"
(153). Do these suspicions merely prove that there is nothing to suspect in so scrupulous a mind? Or do they in fact
invite us to suspect—to push our suspicions even beyond
Fanny's? Fanny's psychology of shyness exhibits neither ill-
nature nor selfishness, but this is not to say that it is innocent
of all unpretty motivations. If it were our main concern, one
could readily trace its relations, direct or tangential, to resentment, jealousy, rivalry, fear of sexual display, or even of
physical movement. Fanny's psychology works to counter-
act an underlying aggressivity of desire— is there any doubt,
for all her humility and reticence, how much she *wants* Edmund?—by inverting it into a shaming willingness to be
mistreated and misconstrued that constitutes a perverse demand for care and recognition. It would be well named (if
rather too simply judged) in Nietzsche's terms, as a strategy
of blinded *ressentiment*. What I wish mainly to stress here,
however, is how Fanny's moral judgment effectively preserves her full response—paradoxically—by refusing to take
it into account. Far from leading her to withdraw from all
participation in the rehearsals, it allows her—"sometimes as
prompter, sometimes as spectator"—to watch, assist, and
even enjoy them. The innocence of her enjoyment would
seem to be licensed by her original refusal to solicit it as well
as her moral disapproval. With these reservations securely
established, "Fanny believed herself to derive as much innocent enjoyment from the play as any of them" (165). The
line is wonderfully ambiguous. Most obviously, this is
Fanny's modesty speaking, and we are supposed to know
that her enjoyment alone is genuinely innocent. Yet to the
extent that a community of feeling obtains between Fanny
and the rest of the players (on the basis of a fascination with
playing, a fear of Sir Thomas, jealousies and minutely conducted scrutinies of one another), a more literal reading
opens up. "As much innocent enjoyment as any of them":
how much is that, when the innocence of their enjoyment
is very much in question?

Madame
de
Montsauf >

[56]

Fanny's use of moral judgment to resist the attractions exerted by the theatricals (so that they can be, in effect, reinstated in a less troubling mode of response) is a strategy common to both prudery and prudence, its good twin. We are probably all excited by the display of sin or scandal, but we may have to (or choose to) express our excitement in moral forms that tend not to acknowledge it: in shock, disbelief, disapproval, regret, even calmly detailed analysis. These are often valuable responses, and productive ones; to a crucial extent, the possibility of a moral life depends on them. However, under the pressure of converting the excitement of newly aroused desire, complicity, ambivalence, into units of moral currency, a full awareness of these feelings often gets scanted. It is terribly wrong when Henry Crawford runs off with Maria Rushworth. It is also exciting —as sex, as transgression, as an expressive piece of novelistic melodrama. For Fanny in particular, it is inevitably charged with the added excitement of a wish unexpectedly fulfilled (namely, of course, the dismissal of Mr. and Miss Crawford from the Mansfield circle). Fanny's morally exemplary response, however, is curiously blind to the sources of its own excitement:

> The horror of a mind like Fanny's, as it received the conviction of such guilt, and began to take in some part of the misery that must ensue, can hardly be described. At first, it was a sort of stupefaction; but every moment was quickening her perception of the horrible evil. She could not doubt; she dared not indulge a hope of the paragraph being false. Miss Crawford's letter, which she had read so often as to make every line her own, was in frightful conformity with it. Her eager defence of her brother, her hope of its being *hushed up*, her evident agitation, were all of a piece with something very bad; and if there was a woman of character in existence, who could treat as a trifle this sin of the first magnitude, who could try to gloss it over, and desire to have it unpunished, she could believe Miss

[57]

Crawford to be the woman! Now she could see her own
mistake as to *who* were gone—or *said* to be gone. It was
not Mr. and Mrs. Rushworth, it was Mrs. Rushworth and
Mr. Crawford.

Fanny seemed to herself never to have been shocked
before. There was no possibility of rest. The evening
passed, without a pause of misery, the night was totally
sleepless. She passed only from feelings of sickness to
shudderings of horror; and from hot fits of fever to cold.
The event was so shocking, that there were moments even
when her heart revolted from it as impossible—when she
thought it could not be. A woman married only six
months ago, a man professing himself devoted, even *engaged*, to another—that other her near relation—the
whole family, both families connected as they were by
tie upon tie, all friends, all intimate together!—It was too
horrible a confusion of guilt, too gross a complication of
evil, for human nature, not in a state of utter barbarism,
to be capable of!—yet her judgment told her it was so.
His unsettled affections, wavering with his vanity, *Maria's*
decided attachment, and no sufficient principle on either
side, gave it possibility—Miss Crawford's letter stampt it
a fact. (440-41)

In the world of *Mansfield Park*, the elopement of "a
woman married only six months" with "a man professing
himself devoted, even *engaged*, to another" presents no difficult case to judge. A moral condemnation by a moral character like Fanny Price is so very much in order that the disarray induced in her mind and even inscribed in her body
must seem extravagant. Her curious disbelief and excessive
disgust are inadequately served by the moral terms in which
they are accounted for. One willingly grants the obvious,
that Fanny's disbelief (despite Mary's letter, despite her own
judgment) comes from an innocence that can barely conceive so "gross a complication of evil." Yet one might notice
as well the unwitting flirtatiousness of this incredulity—how
it forces Fanny to go over the event just as she goes over and

over Mary's letter, how it indulges and perpetuates forbidden topics in the inverted mode of denial. The repetitions to which disbelief gives rise, however, serve a more urgent and creditable end than that of indulging a prude who says "I can't believe it!" and means "Tell me again." Fanny reads and rereads Mary's letter to master its contents ("to make every line her own"), and similarly, she rehearses the elopement to master the energy it releases in her. The nature of this energy is unambiguously pointed to by the other main dimension of her response—her physical disgust. Freud has taught us about the role of disgust and shame as resistances to sexual instinct.[22] Here, these resistances, in what is loosely the form of hysterical conversion, blindly and parodically reenact what they are meant to resist: the forbidden sexual act inferable from the elopement. Hot and cold fevers—at least since Petrarch, the traditional ailment of unrequited passion—are tellingly drafted into the service of Fanny's revulsion; and the sleepless night, the feelings of sickness, the shudderings of horror inevitably recall their obvious sexual counterparts. (Of course, to sexualize Fanny's response in this way is bound to seem crude, since one effect of the novelist's moral ideology is to infect—even to intimidate—our reading with its own good manners. Although we rightly tend to respect the novelist's tact, we may sometimes need to suspect it, lest our reading, inhibited by the safeguard of "good taste," become like Fanny's reading of her father's newspaper and Mary's letter, covertly including more than it can ever openly acknowledge.)

If Fanny's excitement retroactively masters the relationship she might have had with Henry Crawford by turning it into a torture, it also proleptically masters the relationship that is now possible with Edmund Bertram by turning the thought of it into a taboo. The passage continues,

> What would be the consequence? Whom would it not injure? Whose views might it not affect? Whose peace

[22] Especially in *Three Essays on the Theory of Sexuality*.

would it not cut up for ever? Miss Crawford herself—
Edmund; but it was dangerous, perhaps, to tread such
ground. She confined herself to the simple, indubitable
family-misery which must envelope all, if it were indeed
a matter of certified guilt and public exposure. The mother's sufferings, the father's—there, she paused. Julia's,
Tom's, Edmund's—there, a yet longer pause. They were
the two on whom it would fall most horribly. Sir Thomas's parental solicitude, and high sense of honour and decorum, Edmund's upright principles, unsuspicious temper, and genuine strength of feeling, made her think it
scarcely possible for them to support life and reason under such disgrace, and it appeared to her, that as far as this
world alone was concerned, the greatest blessing to every
one of kindred with Mrs. Rushworth would be instant
annihilation. (441-42)

Why is it "dangerous to tread such ground," when this
ground is obvious? Surely it is because the more Henry's
act is seen to open up a possible perspective of happiness for
Fanny, the more the purity of her moral response is brought
into question, the more her "terrors" seem a compensatory
defense against a "joy, senseless joy" such as Anne Elliot is
"ashamed to investigate" in *Persuasion* (MP 442, P 168). If
only even in part, Fanny is upset because her wish has been
fulfilled (albeit in what seems like a distorted way), and she
responds to the wish fulfillment hysterically to avoid facing
it as such.

The technique by which repressed material enters the
mind of a character on the condition that it be repudiated,
or that it make a forced entry for which the character cannot be blamed, is used frequently among Jane Austen's heroines. Much as the play acting in *Mansfield Park* is felt to
infect the real characters of the players, so the heroines display a reluctance to listen to reports of evil, as though to
listen to them were vicariously to act them out. (Think of
Elinor Dashwood's initial unwillingness to hear Willough-

by's confession.) The hypothesis of such threatened contagion, at least, would help account for the heroines' pointed need to express moral indignation at the end of every paragraph of disclosure. We need not, however, always think of the repressed material as sexual, in the narrow and obvious sense of the word. When Mrs. Smith reveals William Elliot's "real character" to Anne, and especially, when she shows her his letter to Mr. Smith, Anne's response works to stave off an essentially different kind of recognition.

At first, Anne's curiosity about Mr. Elliot is explicit ("I have a great curiosity to know what Mr. Elliot was as a very young man"), and we see her pumping Mrs. Smith every step of the way: "Why did Mr. Elliot draw back? . . . Mr. Elliot married, then, completely for money? . . . I am more curious to know why he should be so different now?" (P 198, 200, 201, 202). When it becomes a matter of her fetching the letter by which she will have proof of Mrs. Smith's assertions, however, the curiosity oddly disappears. "Anne, seeing her friend to be earnestly bent on it, did as she was desired" (202). A moment before eagerly soliciting information, Anne is now presented as politely *compelled* to hear it, in her customary role of one whose "convenience was always to give way" (5). What this shift prepares us for and protects Anne from becomes clear, when the letter proves to be such as "could not be read without putting Anne in a glow" (204). The "shock and mortification" of finding her father called a fool by his heir has to be, besides a mere affront, an unwelcome recognition. What else is Sir Walter but a fool? How else has Jane Austen presented him? Most important, how can Anne prevent herself from seeing that William Elliot says precisely what she has always needed all her goodness *not* to say? Without contest the most perceptive character in the novel, she has "a knowledge, which she often wished less, of her father's character" (34). Whether she sighs in despair over his inflated delight with his place in Bath, or observes with amusement that Mrs. Clay's freckles, despite his claims, have not diminished, Anne is perfectly aware of the appropriateness of William Elliot's charge. A buried sense that William's response to her father is only a less suppressed double of her own may account for her quick willingness to excuse the letter, "to recollect that her seeing the letter was a violation of the laws of honour, that no one ought to be judged or to be known by such testimonies, that no private correspondence could bear the eye of others" (204).

At this point in the scene, there is a new edginess in Anne, an increased scrupulosity. She stops Mrs. Smith, at the threshold of further disclosures, with a challenge to her authority:

> "My dear Mrs. Smith, your authority is deficient. This will not do. Mr. Elliot's having any views on me will not in the least account for the efforts he made towards a reconciliation with my father. That was all prior to my coming to Bath. I found them on the most friendly terms when I arrived."
>
> "I know you did; I know it all perfectly, but—"
>
> "Indeed, Mrs. Smith, we must not expect to get real information in such a line. Facts or opinions which are to pass through the hands of so many, to be misconceived by folly in one, and ignorance in another, can hardly have much truth left." (205)

Anne's challenge would seem rationally justified—by the facts in her possession, by Mrs. Smith's indirect manner of gathering her own—until it leads her, uncharacteristically, to cut Mrs. Smith off, in a violation of both fairness and courtesy. In her spirited attack on the legitimacy of certain modes of access to Mr. Elliot's character, it is hard not to see a displacement of her need to dismiss the evidence of his letter. Her animated reproach is also, however, an indirect request to be overwhelmed with proofs, so that the distance between her and Mr. Elliot might be safely increased, and she might once more be in a position to condemn him. Her response to the hearing that she grants Mrs. Smith tends to confirm this reading: "You tell me nothing which does not accord with what I have known, or could imagine" (207). Her initial reluctance to believe (grounded on very strict standards of verification) and this easy validation (based in part on what she "could imagine") make an odd sequence, unless we see the intensity of the need to repudiate in direct proportion to the threat of a recognized complicity. Once Mrs. Smith's revelations have been brought to the point where an identification with the character they disclose is no longer possible for Anne, then she easily admits that she has been able to imagine them all along.

The moral standards of the heroines, of course, *are* moral standards, and certainly can be discussed as such. They also, however, allow the heroines to savor the forbidden without having to acknowledge their affective and imaginative kinship to it. They are visibly the condition of a repression, which paradoxically permits repressed material to emerge by denying such material as *its own*. Freud calls this mental sleight of hand "negation" (*Verneinung*). "Negation is a way of taking cognizance of what is repressed; indeed, it is already a lifting of the repression, though not, of course, an acceptance of what is repressed."[23] Freud's suggestive concept allows us to formulate in a new way the equivocation operated by the novelist between the demands of construction and the pretensions of representational ideology. If the narratable in Jane Austen turns out consistently to coincide with a lapse from the novelist's moral vision, how can the narratable be entertained at all, without her text getting ideologically contaminated by it? By being entertained, precisely, I would argue, in a mode of negation. A moral negation exculpates the novelist from the sin of narrating, and hence permits the act of narration to go forward. Consider this very minor local instance:

> Such were Elizabeth Elliot's sentiments and sensations; such the cares to alloy, the agitations to vary, the same-

[23] Freud, "Negation," 19: 235.

ness and the elegance, the prosperity and the nothingness, of her scene of life—such the feelings to give interest to a long, uneventful residence in one country circle, to fill the vacancies which there were no habits of utility abroad, no talents or accomplishments for home, to occupy. (P 9)

And such the values that are inevitably deficient when measured against the novelist's insinuated standards. Yet the dead-pan sermonizing is a condition of our pleasure in the passage. Indemnified by the safeguard of a comic-satiric treatment, we can positively enjoy Elizabeth's moral infirmities, just as the narrator can delightedly put them on exhibition. The mode of moral disapproval shows the novelist—in the dimension that (officially, at least) means most to her—unable to "accept" a character like Elizabeth Elliot. It takes Elizabeth out of competition with Anne for the men who ought to matter, it trivializes the fascination that her haughtiness might exert, and it immunizes the text against any seeming affinity with the perversely aimless narrative governing her. However, it permits the novelist to *display* all the things she is also disarming and disowning. If this is regulated hatred, then we need to see hatred as an inverted form of love —the name for love when one doesn't want to feel any.

This strategy of negation protects the novelist from the morally deplorable structures of the narratable, and so allows them to generate her novels. Jane Austen's peremptory standards, her absolute moral vision, her definitive nominations never lend themselves to narrative—indeed, they are virtually unaffected by it. Of course, the novels often tease us with the possibility that this moral ideology will fail to be incarnated. It is just possible that Edward Ferrars will marry Lucy Steele, or that Captain Wentworth will go away again. If these possibilities were realized, however, they would have the status of sheer and utter mistakes. Our knowledge of what the proper settlement ought to have been would remain unshaken. Contingencies are allowed (if never ultimately) to threaten the incarnation of the right names and relationships in a social settlement, but never the rightness of these, which is intact no matter what happens in the novels. Revising the *mot* of Gide's immoralist, we might say, "What would be the narrative of transparent conduct and definitive language? Nothing but their disappearance or defalcation, nothing but a weak trace of them can be told." A morally insistent voice, installed in "the reality of reason and truth," always qualifies what *can* be told in Jane Austen, always reminding us that it doesn't quite make the mark, always denying it a certain ideological rightness or fullness. A reader becomes aware of this even on so elementary a level as that of screening eligible candidates for the heroine's hand. No, not Mr. Collins—too stupid; not Colonel Fitzwilliam—too impoverished; not Wickham—his manners are too easy; and not Darcy either (in the first half of the novel)—his manners are too rude. The proper solution cannot be these, but these define the proper solution in the only way a narrative text would seem able to define it before coming to an end—that is, by contrast, by what the proper solution is *not*.

"It was *not* my mother," says the patient, from which the analyst infers, "So it *was* his mother."[24] At one level, Jane Austen's narrator insinuates, "the narratable can relate to my ideology of closure only as a lapse. They have no necessary, or mutually dependent relationship with one another, for one is all insufficiency and void, and the other is all adequacy and plenitude." From which, at another level, we might infer that the transcendent or absolute status of this closural ideology is covertly dependent on its being voided in the moment of narratability. Much as in the child's game of *Fort!/Da!* described by Freud,[25] the reappearance of an ideally transparent world becomes meaningful only through its previous disappearance. Moreover, just as the child's game takes place in the context of an original loss of his mother,

[24] Ibid.
[25] Freud, *Beyond the Pleasure Principle*, 18: 14-16.

so Jane Austen's symbolic staging of the disappearance and retrieval of "the reality of reason and truth" would seem to take place within a certain anxiety about whether the full meanings of her ideology can ever be established once for all. Negation allows the patient at least to thematize his mother in the analytical discourse. Similarly, Jane Austen's moral negation permits her to bring into language what otherwise, according to a strict construction of her ideology, could never properly be mentioned. Her novels can bring forward a fascinated delight with unsettled states of deferral and ambiguity, provided that they also, gently or firmly, repudiate them as not belonging (so to speak) to their real selves. Reading Jane Austen, we engage a blinded dialectic, knowing itself in only the partial mode of denial.

Good Riddance

"The night was cold and stormy. The wind roared round the house, and the rain beat against the windows; but Elinor, all happiness within, regarded it not" (SS 316). For Marianne is now on the road to recovery from her fever, and implicitly, from her attachment to Willoughby as well. Suddenly, there is heard driving up to the house a carriage, which Elinor expects is bringing her mother.

> Never in her life had Elinor found it so difficult to be calm, as at that moment. The knowledge of what her mother must be feeling as the carriage stopt at the door,— of her doubt—her dread—perhaps her despair!—and of what *she* had to tell!—with such knowledge it was impossible to be calm. All that remained to be done, was to be speedy; and therefore staying only till she could leave Mrs. Jenning's maid with her sister, she hurried down stairs.
> The bustle in the vestibule, as she passed along an inner lobby, assured her that they were already in the house.

She rushed forwards towards the drawing-room,—she
entered it,—and saw only Willoughby. (316)

Willoughby's arrival is a surprise, of course, but it fits
into a series of surprising episodes in the novel, in which one
character is expected and another arrives. At Barton, for instance, Marianne thinks that "a man on horseback riding
towards them" is Willoughby returning to her; it turns out
to be Edward Ferrars, in disquietingly "low spirits" (86,
96). In London, a knock is heard at the door, and both sisters instantly assume that it is Willoughby coming to call
on his mistress; in walks Colonel Brandon instead (161). The
same mistake is repeated, less explicitly, later in the London
stay (203). Once more back at Barton, Elinor imagines that
"the figure of a man on horseback" is Colonel Brandon on a
visit, and her visitor proves to be Edward Ferrars, come to
propose (358). These recurring cases of mistaken identity
serve a number of functions in the novel. Most obviously,
they are comic blunders, meant to reveal the heroines' characters and the particular blindnesses attending each. Typically, Marianne assumes that events will fulfill her wishes,
Elinor that events will frustrate hers, and actuality adheres
to the program of neither. Yet if these mistaken identities
are clearly *mistakes*, the novelist may also be hinting that
they are, in some sense, identities too. It is as though events
were asserting an interchangeability that threatened to obtain among the three men and between the two sisters. Both
sisters are erotically involved with all three men, whatever
safeguards are imposed by the categories (love/esteem/dis-
gust/mistrust/quasi-sororal affection) that differentiate this
involvement. Do Elinor and Marianne cultivate their difference from one another in part to avoid the threat of a
sameness of situation and choice? An interesting gloss is suggested on the novel's governing antithesis—on the need for
such an antithesis, despite the novelist's apparent preference
for one of its terms. Elinor, we know, is not unfeeling, nor

is Marianne entirely senseless. When they play their different dominant traits off one another, this is (whatever else) their way of making a preliminary classification on the basis of which they can be distinguished, along with the eligible men who approach them.

For our purposes, however, these mistaken identities most importantly refer us to the workings out of novelistic closure. They frustrate the pseudoclosures that in different ways Elinor and Marianne are both eager to impose, and ultimately work toward the real closures of the novel. The London visitor is not Marianne's lover, but the man she will later learn to love, in a lasting way; the Barton visitor is not Colonel Brandon, come to give an accurate account of Elinor's definitive loss of Edward, but Edward himself, come to propose marriage. In this scene at Cleveland, Elinor expects her mother—a figure of comfort who will allow their situation to settle into a state of equilibrium. Willoughby comes instead, who has always been a figure of disturbance, but we have been taught to suspect that what frustrates one closure may be made to issue in another.

For insofar as Willoughby's confessional visit meets an obvious closural requirement, his appearance is no surprise at all. There must be no mysteries left over at the end of a Jane Austen novel, and although it is unlikely that Willoughby's actions can be justified, they still must be explained. Some problems of motivation have not yet been laid to rest. What was the meaning of his initial treatment of Marianne? of his sudden departure from Barton? Is his character libertine, mercenary, or just plain weak? Willoughby's explanations to Elinor cannot clear his conduct, but they do the next best thing by clearing it up. A better knowledge of his character comes to reinforce his removal from the novel's center stage.

Yet from another angle, Willoughby's justification of himself reintroduces into his motives and intentions the same suspense that has made him a puzzle all along. Only the ante has been raised. What once was an apparent affection for Marianne has now become an explicitly acknowledged one,

whose reality is no longer suspect; and what was a seeming
dismissal of Marianne at the London party now ought to
become an effective one, through his marriage to Miss Grey.
The ambiguity of his desire has been preserved at a more
dangerous level, and the ambivalence of a response to him
must be riven by attraction and repulsion more potently
than ever. Furthermore, Willoughby wants his dangerous
narrative—charged as it is with the suspense of which further narrative could be made—relayed to Marianne herself.
"Will you repeat to your sister . . . what I have been telling
you? . . . Tell her of my misery and my penitence. Tell her
that my heart was never inconstant to her, and if you will,
that at this moment she is dearer to me than ever" (330). Is
Willoughby putting an end to their affair, or hoping to re-
new it? One sees the possibilities that his ambiguous performance opens up. It is just possible, for instance, that Marianne might yet run off with Willoughby, if this declaration
met her with all its force. This at least seems the point of
including the stories of Eliza Williams and her daughter in
the novel, and their motifs of marital infidelity, of prostitu-
tion, of seduction and abandonment. By a kind of melodramatic projection, these stories double for the issues potentially at stake in Marianne's own. We may of course want to
trust Marianne more than this implies; at the very least, however, a direct confrontation with Willoughby's "still ardent
love" for her would impede the enforced oblivion that a decent settlement must entail. If Marianne is never capable of
the behavior of a Lydia Bennet or a Maria Rushworth, she
always courts something like the fate of a Mary Crawford:
the inability to put the man she has loved and lost "sufficiently out of her head" (MP 469).

Willoughby's narration can move in the direction of either
sense or suspense. The sense of his disclosures tranquilizes
the disturbing inconsistencies enigmatically propounded by
his conduct; it fixes him, or ought to, outside the pale of
whatever might constitute settlement for Marianne. To the
extent, however, that Willoughby's meaning betrays an

easily exploitable ambiguity, it is troubled by a suspense that undermines its closural fixity. Elinor recognizes the dangerously ambiguous status of Willoughby's narration, and her reply to his request that she repeat it to her sister marks the beginning of a strategy of redaction: "I will tell her all that is necessary to what may comparatively be called your justification" (SS 330). She has implicitly reserved the right to edit Willoughby's confession—to bowdlerize his text so that an impressionable young woman such as Marianne might read it without harm. Elinor is the character best fitted for this task, but even for her it is no easy labor (proof of an emotional sensitivity in her that goes unperceived under cover of the boisterous demonstrations of her sister and her mother). The most important fact about Elinor's revision of Willoughby's narration (part of which takes effect immediately, and part gradually) is that it is an *exertion*. This is a word that the novelist has frequently used to describe Elinor's mental processes, and it refers us not only to the work involved in them, but also (in its root sense of a "thrusting out") to the purpose of the work. The forces at play in the work of Elinor's censorship need to be followed in some detail.

Elinor responds to Willoughby's appeal more intensely and fully than she ever has done, only when a protective context of "sadness" has been invoked:

> Elinor, for some time after he left her, for some time even after the sound of his carriage had died away, remained too much oppressed by a croud of ideas, widely differing in themselves, but of which sadness was the general result, to think even of her sister.
>
> Willoughby, he, whom only half an hour ago she had abhorred as the most worthless of men, Willoughby, in spite of all his faults, excited a degree of commiseration for the sufferings produced by them, which made her think of him as now separated for ever from her family with a tenderness, a regret, rather in proportion, as she

soon acknowledged within herself—to his wishes than to his merits. She felt that his influence over her mind was heightened by circumstances which ought not to have weight; by that person of uncommon attraction, that open, affectionate, and lively manner which it was no merit to possess; and by that still ardent love for Marianne, which it was not even innocent to indulge. But she felt that it was so, long, long before she could feel his influence less. (333)

The sadness has been implicitly grounded in the pathos of irreversibility with which she has invested Willoughby's case. If she cannot quite say, in view of the facts, "O! what a noble soul is here o'erthrown," she thinks something a bit like it:

Her thoughts were silently fixed on the irreparable injury which too early an independence and its consequent habits of idleness, dissipation, and luxury, had made in the mind, the character, the happiness, of a man who, to every advantage of person and talents, united a disposition naturally open and honest, and a feeling, affectionate temper. (331)

Elinor's melancholy depends upon and preserves a preliminary judgment that the "injury" is "irreparable." In this sense, her sadness coincides with the relief of closure—to be sad over Willoughby implies that he is now essentially *hors jeu*, "now separated for ever from her family." This, however, is a proposition that Willoughby's ambiguous narration by no means entirely confirms, for as we have seen, Willoughby only half sees his actions from Elinor's perspective. The confessional nature of his explanations suggests that he may be seeking remission of his sins; and if he talks the language of irreparability and permanent loss, there is some question whether he really means it. The chief point of some of Elinor's interventions has been, precisely, to insist on an irreversibility that Willoughby, in the slight hope of fresh peripeties, never fully wants to accept.

"Marianne to be sure is lost to me for ever. Were I even by any blessed chance at liberty again—"

Elinor stopped him with a reproof.

"Well"—he replied—"once more good bye. I shall now go away and live in dread of one event."

"What do you mean?"

"Your sister's marriage."

"You are very wrong. She can never be more lost to you than she is now." (332)

Yet even Elinor's own insistence on the irreversibility of events can grow fainter under the intensity of that tender and regretful response that it permits and controls, and it needs to be continually reaffirmed. For a moment, she "wished Willoughby a widower. Then, remembering Colonel Brandon, reproved herself, felt that to *his* sufferings and *his* constancy far more than to his rival's, the reward of her sister was due, and wished any thing rather than Mrs. Willoughby's death" (335). Like a magic wand breaking a spell, the recollection of Colonel Brandon would seem to dissolve the force of Willoughby's "influence"—except that his influence later revives, and the wand will have to be applied repeatedly, like the unmagical rod of discipline. Soon after her arrival, Mrs. Dashwood begins projecting the very match that her prudent daughter has envisioned, but Elinor is no longer so certain of its validity. Mrs. Dashwood insists that "Marianne would yet never have been so happy with [Willoughby], as she will be with Colonel Brandon," but Elinor "could not agree with her," and she withdraws "to think it all over in private, to wish success for her friend, and yet in wishing it, to feel a pang for Willoughby" (338, 339).

Ultimately, however, Elinor's complex response to Willoughby's narration gets simplified, as she rethinks and retells it. She has been reluctant to keep her promise to Willoughby (qualified though that was) because she feared "she had that to communicate which might again unsettle the mind of Marianne" (343). But not only is a revived Marianne now prepared to respond to the sense (rather than the suspense) of his narration, she also understands that this sense can complete her cure ("If I could but know *his* heart, everything would become easy" [347]). Rather than risk a lingering response to the empirical Willoughby whom she remembers, with his apparent sincerity and apparent duplicity, she needs to know what his conduct *meant*. Reassured by Marianne's proper attitude (more proper than her own has been when she wished Willoughby a widower), Elinor hazards her narration:

> She managed the recital, as she hoped, with address; prepared her anxious listener with caution; related simply and honestly *the chief points* on which Willoughby grounded his apology; did justice to his repentance, and *softened only his protestations of present regard.* Marianne said not a word.—She trembled, her eyes were fixed on the ground, and her lips became whiter than even sickness had left them. A thousand inquiries sprang up from her heart, but she dared not urge one. She caught every syllable with panting eagerness; her hand, unknowingly to herself, closely pressed her sister, and tears covered her cheeks.
>
> Elinor, dreading her being tired, led her towards home; and till they reached the door of the cottage, easily conjecturing what her curiosity must be though no question was suffered to speak it, talked of nothing but Willoughby, and their conversation together; and was carefully minute in every particular of speech and look, *where minuteness could be safely indulged.* (347-48)

Elinor's repetition of Willoughby's narration involves censoring it as well, as those parts of the passage I have emphasized easily bear witness. Moreover, the way in which the novelist presents Elinor's recital (in summary rather than scene) strongly supports an impression that Elinor's mode of telling must differ radically from Willoughby's. In that coolly ordered parade of semicoloned clauses, we are tempted to recognize both Elinor's rational style of discourse (versus Willoughby's melodramatic theatrics) and its efficient dispatch (versus Willoughby's insidious diffuseness). When at Marianne's request ("Tell mama"), Elinor rehearses Willoughby's narration a second time to Mrs. Dashwood, the same principles of abridgment and reorganization are at work, not only in the way she packages the material for consumption by others, but in her own increasingly constricted response.

Had Mrs. Dashwood, like her daughter, heard Willoughby's story from himself—had she witnessed his distress, and been under the influence of his countenance and his manner, it is probable that her compassion would have been greater. But it was neither in Elinor's power, nor in her wish, to rouse such feelings in another, by her retailed explanation, as had at first been called forth in herself. Reflection had given calmness to her judgment, and sobered her own opinion of Willoughby's deserts;—she wished, therefore, to declare only the simple truth, and lay open such facts as were really due to his character, without any embellishment of tenderness to lead the fancy astray. (349)

("*Only* the simple truth"? There would be, then, more to tell.) By the time the two sisters are ready to discuss Willoughby's character, there is no remaining trace of his influence over Elinor, who makes her judgment with untroubled confidence: "Your marriage must have involved you in many certain troubles and disappointments. . . . The whole of his behaviour, from the beginning to the end of the affair, has been grounded on selfishness. . . . His own enjoyment, or his own ease, was, in every particular, his ruling principle" (350, 351). Now that Willoughby's story has been completely rewritten in the interest of the knowledge that passes debate (and bypasses all further narrative possibilities), even a moral can be drawn from the tale: proof, if any were needed, that his story has become a closed book to the Dashwood family. "One observation may, I think, be fairly drawn from the whole of the story—that all Willoughby's difficulties have arisen from the first offence against virtue, in his behaviour to Eliza Williams. That crime has been the origin of every lesser one, and of all his present discontents" (352). This may seem odd morality for Elinor to conclude with, in a group of women, since the crime whose punishment is supposed to edify them could only have been committed by a man. Of course, however, the real point of this "observation drawn from the whole of the story" is to establish that the story is a *whole*, without further ramifications worth considering. Confirming Willoughby's fallen state, Elinor's observation also confirms how thoroughly vacated is the place that he might have occupied in their lives, and in the mention of Eliza Williams, it points clearly enough to a new and permanent locum tenens in Colonel Brandon.

I have dwelt on this sequence in *Sense and Sensibility* because it offers us, in miniature and in plain, almost diagrammatic form, the mechanics of closure. Willoughby's narrative, dangerously open, gives way to Elinor's retailing, modifying it in order to close it up. Willoughby's account does not inherently resolve itself; only when reconstructed and reduced by Elinor's account does it acquire a meaning of closural force. His account has a quasi-empirical richness of detail (his "person of uncommon attraction," his "open, affectionate, and lively manner," the hints that more is being said and unsaid than he quite knows), troubling and complicating Elinor's cognitive and moral judgment. Her account voids what it must see as the excesses and irrelevancies of his, in order that a judgment can stand, unsubverted by any fermenting residue. The first account mainly takes place, as it were, on the level of the signifier—that is, it offers a wealth of pointers to future possible meanings, not yet fully available. There are more signifiers, ambiguous and pointing in conflicting directions, than can be comfortably integrated into a definitive meaning by either Willoughby or even Elinor. By contrast, the second account takes place on the level of the signified—unambiguous, fully present meaning. It resolves the ambiguities of the first account and removes from it whatever "ought not to have weight." The work of closure, then, would seem to consist in an ideologically inspired *passage* between two orders of discourse, two separable textual styles. One of them (polyvalent, flirtatious, quintessentially poetic) keeps meaning and desire in a state of suspense; the other (univocal, earnest, basically cognitive) fixes meaning and lodges desire in a safe haven; and the passage from one to the other involves a voiding, a strategic omission—so to speak, a good riddance.[26] The interest of Jane Austen, on this perspective, is that her novels, far from merely operating the passage, tellingly dramatize it, so that one has a more complicated and less comfortable awareness of what it involves.

Elinor's secondary revision of Willoughby's primary narration is not, of course, the most compelling instance of such passage. Willoughby is hardly so interesting a character as to make his reconstruction by a different order a serious loss. What is lost in the translation (that is, all that is comprehended by his "influence" on Elinor's mind) is not something a reader has much cared about. Throughout the novel, Willoughby's appeal has been rather designated than dramatized. Its terms have been provided with explicit fullness by the narrator and the characters, and no very wide margin has been left to solicit the reader's active fascination. If Eli-

[26] I am somewhat indebted here to Galvano della Volpe's attempt to distinguish (partly on the basis of Saussurian linguistics) between the "univocal" language of scientific discourse and the "polysemic" (*polisenso*) language of poetic discourse. He collapses the distinction —prematurely, I think—at the level of a "search for truth" supposedly common to both languages. Moreover, by insisting that the *polisenso* is always reducible to what he calls a "sociological quid," he takes away whatever force the concept might have had. See his *Critica del gusto*, especially the second chapter.

nor responds to his narration with unwonted intensity, few
readers find much to sway them in his alternately breathless
and periodic style. The good riddance seems, quite simply,
a good. Moreover, since Willoughby himself has imposed a
sort of moral grid on his narration (however doubtfully
tenable), the difference between the two orders of discourse
is less marked than it might be. We need to turn to the
closure that has troubled readers of Jane Austen most, where
both the incommensurability of the two orders is more
pointed, and the loss involved in passing from one to the
other more poignant.

"Let other pens dwell on guilt and misery. I quit such
odious subjects as soon as I can, impatient to restore every
body, not greatly at fault themselves, to tolerable comfort,
and to have done with all the rest" (MP 461). A moral decorum informs the narrator's pose. Just as perfect ladies
know to let certain subjects drop, the perfect lady who is also
a novelist (strictly: who is about to cease being a novelist)
needs to "have done" with certain subjects, on which, on
whom it is not proper to "dwell." Jane Austen defines her
conception of the operation of closure in a nutshell: a restoration of "comfort" proceeding by an exclusion of what
made things uncomfortable. Most obviously, what has to be
got rid of are certain characters—mainly the Crawfords, but
also Maria Bertram and Mrs. Norris. To get rid of certain
characters, however, is perhaps only a broad way of getting
rid of *what characterized the text* under their sponsorship,
an insufficiently purposeful or wrongly opaque language.

Inevitably, we single out Mary Crawford, whose language
has made up so much of the text. What has most interestingly characterized her in the novel, as we have seen, is the
uncertainty she promotes—in herself as well as in others—
about how to take her discourse, how to take the subjects it
treats and the subject who utters it. Unlike her brother, who
"loves to be doing" and hence creates "a public disturbance
at last" (57, 163), Mary never commits an act that polite
society can quasi-automatically take for a clarification of

her real character. A seamlessness and a reserve mark her speeches, despite their articulateness and their volubility. It is hard not to feel that something is being withheld in them, and easy not to know where, precisely, one motive or trait overlaps with another. For a time even the narrator respects the reticence of Mary's self-presentation. Our fascination with Mary Crawford springs from the absence of full terms to grasp her, much like Edmund's and even Fanny's fascination with her (208), or Mary's own fascination with herself. ("Ignorance," Barthes suggests, "is the main characteristic of fascination."[27]) To *know* Mary must be the work of an active interpretation, reconstruing the ignorance that she ironically propagates into a valid cognition. Derived from a set of terms that Mary does little to provide, this interpretation must always be forced, in the sense of being incommensurable with its object. As if to underline the gap between Mary as she is and Mary as she will come to be known, the novel develops the "knowledge of her real character" (459) along a different track from the one that she herself sponsors: in the conversations between Edmund and Fanny, reviewing her character and revising it on the basis of moral principles that she does not intrinsically share. Here is the first of them, suggesting the operation involved as well as what menaces its success:

> "Well Fanny, and how do you like Miss Crawford *now?*" said Edmund the next day, after thinking some time on the subject himself. "How did you like her yesterday?"
>
> "Very well—very much. I like to hear her talk. She entertains me; and she is so extremely pretty, that I have great pleasure in looking at her."
>
> "It is her countenance that is so attractive. She has a wonderful play of feature! But was there nothing in her conversation that struck you Fanny, as not quite right?"
>
> "Oh! yes, she ought not to have spoken of her uncle as

[27] *Roland Barthes par Roland Barthes* (Paris: Seuil, 1975), p. 5.

she did. I was quite astonished. An uncle with whom she has been living so many years, and who, whatever his faults may be, is so very fond of her brother, treating him, they say, quite like a son. I could not have believed it!"

"I thought you would be struck. It was very wrong—very indecorous."

"And very ungrateful, I think."

"Ungrateful is a strong word. I do not know that her uncle has any claim to her *gratitude*; his wife certainly had; and it is the warmth of her respect for her aunt's memory which misleads her here. She is awkwardly circumstanced. With such warm feelings and lively spirits it must be difficult to do justice to her affection for Mrs. Crawford, without throwing a shade on the admiral. I do not pretend to know which was most to blame in their disagreements, though the admiral's present conduct might incline one to the side of his wife: but it is natural and amiable that Miss Crawford should acquit her aunt entirely. I do not censure her *opinions*; but there certainly *is* impropriety in making them public."

"Do not you think," said Fanny, after a little consideration, "that this impropriety is a reflection itself upon Mrs. Crawford, as her niece has been entirely brought up by her? She cannot have given her right notions of what was due to the admiral."

"That is a fair remark. Yes, we must suppose the faults of the niece to have been those of the aunt; and it makes one more sensible of the disadvantages she has been under. But I think her present home must do her good. Mrs. Grant's manners are just what they ought to be. She speaks of her brother with a very pleasing affection."

"Yes, except as to his writing her such short letters. She made me almost laugh; but I cannot rate so very highly the love or good nature of a brother, who will not give himself the trouble of writing any thing worth reading, to his sisters, when they are separated. I am sure William would never have used *me* so, under any circumstances.

And what right had she to suppose, that *you* would not write long letters when you were absent?"

"The right of a lively mind, Fanny, seizing whatever may contribute to its own amusement or that of others; perfectly allowable, when untinctured by ill humour or roughness; and there is not a shadow of either in the countenance or manner of Miss Crawford, nothing sharp, or loud, or coarse. She is perfectly feminine, except in the instances we have been speaking of. *There* she cannot be justified. I am glad you saw it all as I did." (63-64)

This is Edmund's crucial first step—in knowing Miss Crawford and in failing to know her. That he chooses to hold this retrospective with Fanny suggests that he recognizes a need for it, and his division of Mary's conduct into improprieties and allowable amusements is a preliminary attempt to sort out their confusion in Mary herself. The very scrupulosity of his analysis can seem to pay tribute to a highly proper flexibility, a moralist's sensitivity to the nuances of his case. However, it also seems a symptom of an unexorcised fascination that, far from making his principles more flexible, threatens to bend them out of shape. Edmund's incipient moral knowledge of Mary tends repeatedly to collapse back into the sheer fascination of his empirical response to her ("She has a wonderful play of feature . . . such warm feelings and lively spirits . . . a very pleasing affection . . . not a shadow of [ill humor or roughness] in [her] countenance or manner"). Implicitly, Jane Austen insists on what Edmund does not realize—that a moral knowledge (if it is to have cognitive status) must reconstitute the empirical phenomena brought before it according to its own principles; and that a rigorously maintained distance from the empirical is therefore a condition of its possibility. A moral knowledge of Mary Crawford will never take her up as she appears, for her appearances are designed to undermine such knowledge. It can only take her up when she has been "converted" (in the sense that currency is converted from one unit to another): reconstituted as its own object. Behind Edmund's error of judgment stands the full unabandoned wealth of his actual response to her, and he turns her own categories of self-presentation (irony, ambiguity, fascination) into a pseudoknowledge camouflaging the desires that these arouse in him.

> "I heard enough of what she said to you last night, to understand her unwillingness to be acting with a stranger; and as she probably engaged in the part with different expectations—perhaps, without considering the subject enough to know what was likely to be, it would be ungenerous, it would be really wrong to expose her to it."
> (154-55)

Dismayed at "Edmund so inconsistent," Fanny correctly sees Miss Crawford's "influence in every speech" (156). Or again:

> "Miss Crawford . . . has great discernment. I know nobody who distinguishes characters better.—For so young a woman it is remarkable! She certainly understands *you* better than you are understood by the greater part of those who have known you for so long; and with regard to some others, I can perceive, from occasional lively hints, the unguarded expressions of the moment, that she could define *many* as accurately, did not delicacy forbid it. I wonder what she thinks of my father! She must admire him as a fine looking man, with most gentleman-like, dignified, consistent manners; but perhaps having seen him so seldom, his reserve may be a little repulsive. Could they be much together I feel sure of their liking each other. He would enjoy her liveliness—and she has talents to value his powers. I wish they met more frequently!"
> (198-99)

What we see, through the blinds of Edmund's narrative *inconscience*, is the suggestive ambiguity of Mary's performance: how unguarded are her unguarded expressions? and who are the people whom delicacy forbids her to define accurately? Stuart Tave thinks it likely that "Sir Thomas is the one character she is forbidding herself."[28] He is one character, certainly—that is the obvious joke—but hardly *the* one. Surely, the point of the passage comes in the contrast between what must have been Mary's ambiguously understated and not quite decidable meaning and Edmund's duped eagerness to confer on it the easy legibility of his desires. As usual, Mary has suggested a mystery of there being more to her than she cares to reveal, which Edmund—not even recognizing it as a mystery—resolves as he likes. The instance of Mary Crawford makes it a particularly urgent matter to maintain the gap between the empirical and the cognitive orders; and to collapse the two, as Edmund is always doing, subverts the autonomy of a genuine moral knowledge—brings it back under Mary's corrupting "influence."

This is probably dotting too many i's, but the point, however one wishes to put it, is an important one. Jane Austen's novels implicitly draw this distinction between the empirical and the known, defining it by a coterminous distinction between the polyvalent language of the novelistic (oriented toward the signifier) and the univocal language of the ideological (oriented toward the signified). The novelist wants to end with full and definitive knowledge, in part because such knowledge (whether we compare it to the conclusion of a Socratic dialogue or a detective story) traditionally marks the enclosure of discourse. By dramatizing the shift from one order to another, however, by making this shift the *agon* of her novels, Jane Austen lays her cards on the table, as perhaps only a novelist extremely confident in the validity of her ideology can do. There is no hiding the fact that the imposition of knowledge necessarily coincides with a depletion of empirical reality, or that the closural meaning depends on a purgation of excess signifiers.

[28] Tave, *Jane Austen*, p. 164.

In the last hundred or so pages of *Mansfield Park*, Mary Crawford disappears from direct view. She is represented only by her letters to Fanny and by Edmund's report of his last meeting with her. It is as though the novelist could work toward Mary's expulsion from the Mansfield scene only by giving her a preliminary vacation—as though Mary had to be distanced before being known and dismissed. In a sense, it ought to be a nice proof of our reading of Mary's character that she finally becomes—within the novel's representation itself—only a text: the text of her letters, the text of her conversation as Edmund reports it. Just as a letter bespeaks the absence of its writer, so Mary's thoughts and speeches have always seemed to juggle away the presence of a central self that could be fixed in knowledge and truth. One might be tempted to say that, when represented by her written texts alone, Mary becomes quintessentially herself—that is, a self whose whereabouts (in every but the geographical sense) are in question. Fanny's response to one of her early letters—written before Tom's illness or Henry's elopement—tends to confirm this view:

> This was a letter to be run through eagerly, to be read deliberately, to supply matter for much reflection, and to leave every thing in greater suspense than ever. The only certainty to be drawn from it was, that nothing decisive had yet taken place. Edmund had not yet spoken. How Miss Crawford really felt—how she meant to act, or might act without or against her meaning—whether his importance to her were quite what it had been before the last separation—whether if lessened it were likely to lessen more, or to recover itself, were subjects for endless conjecture, and to be thought of on that day and many days to come, without producing any conclusion. (417)

In fact, however, Mary's letters come to be much less equivocal and (like those of Lady Susan) more positively wicked than her speeches and reported thoughts had ever been. "The influence of the fashionable world" and " the influence of London," of course, provide a blanket motivation for this sudden self-simplification (421, 433), but it can also be accounted for in terms of a restructured interplay of textual styles. One might say that the context in which Mary's irony is viewed has changed. While the novel was itself in a state of suspension, Mary's ironical discourse seemed attractively (if also somewhat dangerously) to embody the narratable moment. In the closural context of crisis and decision (brought about by Edmund's ordination, Tom's illness, Henry's elopement), the relative weight of this discourse has altered, and Mary's typical response now seems almost a failure to respond at all to the importance and the urgency of what has happened. Dominated by the novel's newly reinforced earnestness, Mary's characteristic liveliness now seems a hardened sarcasm, a thoroughly corrupted cynicism. Alternatively, one might say that Mary's irony itself has defaulted under the pressure of crisis, which forces the basic desires that her irony has tamed into playfulness to reassert themselves sharply. The language of her later letters comes surprisingly close to direct assertiveness:

> I really am quite agitated on the subject [of Tom Bertram's illness]. Fanny, Fanny, I see you smile, and look cunning, but upon my honour, I never bribed a physician in my life. Poor young man!—If he is to die, there will be *two* poor young men less in the world; and with a fearless face and bold voice would I say to any one, that wealth and consequence could fall into no hands more deserving of them. (434)

When Mary was present at Mansfield, all the strategies of her discourse tended to throw dust in everyone's eyes—to make her inaccessible to a direct purchase, or to exceed such a purchase (like Fanny's) by more complexity than it was able to grasp. Now that she is absent from Mansfield, the margin of uncertainty that her irony had needed to introduce is all too fully provided for; and it is as if Mary were compensating for the inaccessibility built into her situation by an increasing directness of desire, which can now be revealed, decisively, as desire of the wrong kind.

All along, however, the suggestiveness and implied incompleteness of Mary's discourse have made it liable to being construed in less suggestive and more complete ways. To the extent that it has posed a scandal to oversimple notions of legibility (such as Edmund and Fanny tempt readers to entertain), it is—like most scandals—susceptible to being tamed. Edmund is ready to blame himself "for a too harsh construction of a playful manner" (421); and though he is right, I think, about his construction being "too harsh" (so is Fanny's [367]), this seems to be called for by the requirements of closure. Here is our last dramatic view of Mary Crawford in the novel, presented through Edmund's haunted recollection. He has expressed his disappointment at her response to the elopement.

"She turned extremely red. I imagined I saw a mixture of many feelings—a great, though short struggle—half a wish of yielding to truths, half a sense of shame—but habit, habit carried it. She would have laughed if she could. It was a sort of laugh, as she answered, 'A pretty good lecture upon my word. Was it part of your last sermon? At any rate, you will soon reform every body at Mansfield and Thornton Lacey; and when I hear of you next, it may be as a celebrated preacher in some great society of Methodists, or as a missionary in foreign parts.' She tried to speak carelessly; but she was not so careless as she wanted to appear. I only said in reply, that from my heart I wished her well, and earnestly hoped that she might soon learn to think more justly, and not owe the most valuable knowledge we could any of us acquire—the knowledge of ourselves and of our duty, to the lessons of affliction—and immediately left the room. I had gone a few steps, Fanny, when I heard the door open behind me. 'Mr. Bertram,' said she, with a smile—but it was a smile ill-suited to the conversation that had passed, a saucy playful smile, seem-

ing to invite, in order to subdue me; at least so it appeared
to me. I resisted; it was the impulse of the moment to resist, and still walked on." (458-59)

The entire scene is the last climax of the novel, but it is an
untypical last climax for a Jane Austen novel to have. In
the other novels, the last climactic scene is the one in which
Mr. Right—usually with a proposal—confirms his attachment to his lady. Sufficiently freed and illumined, the desires of each fix on the other. In *Mansfield Park*, that scene
is reduced to a paragraph or so of summary in the windup of
the last chapter (as in "Edmund did cease to care about Miss
Crawford, and became as anxious to marry Fanny, as Fanny
herself could desire" [470]). Instead, in its rightful place,
comes this scene in which an attachment is disconfirmed,
broken off. Mary is given the typical structural position of
a heroine, without a heroine's typical good luck. In the context of all the novels taken together, the *hapax* here under-
lines the importance of Mary Crawford's appeal (much
more than that of an ordinary rival like Lucy Steele or Harriet Smith) and the consequent strain of expelling her from
Edmund's life. It is telling, too, that Jane Austen gives us
the scene through a character's narration of it—that is, from
a point of view that she has never fully embraced. Edmund's
narration is charged with emotional revulsion and disgust,
bespeaking by negation his attraction and desire. Seen by his
anxious fears of her powers of performance, Mary turns into
a vulgar Delilah, openly gesturing sexual solicitation. One
must wonder whether such a perspective does not invite us—
on the evidence of its own self-betraying bias—to imagine
a different version of the scene, more ambiguous and less
obvious than Edmund's. (It is hard to envision Mary's smile
—or any smile this side of a leer—yielding so full a sense
as "seeming to invite, in order to subdue me.") But the necessity of Edmund's point of view becomes clear when Fanny
comes to its support: "Fanny, now at liberty to speak openly, felt more than justified in adding to his knowledge of

[Miss Crawford's] real character, by some hint of what share his brother's state of health might be supposed to have in her wish for a complete reconciliation" (459). Who wants Mary's "real character," or the strategies of irony, ambiguity, and fascination that have been part of its self-composition, when what is now needed is the *knowledge* of her real character? (Is Mary removed from the foreground of the novel so that this may be more easily secured—behind her back, as it were?) If the categories of moral knowledge are to be brought to bear on her effectively, then the linguistic polyvalency that has made up her empirical reality in the novel must be forcibly reduced. The closure that Mary is subjected to involves a necessary simplification of her discourse and the implications that it has sustained.

Yet after this closure has taken place, fixing Mary as essentially mercenary and meretricious, she is curiously allowed to recover (in the narrator's final wrap-up) some of her earlier complexity.

> Mary, though perfectly resolved against ever attaching herself to a younger brother again, was long in finding among the dashing representatives, or idle heir apparents, who were at the command of her beauty, and her 20,000 £. any one who could satisfy the better taste she had acquired at Mansfield, whose character and manners could authorise a hope of the domestic happiness she had there learnt to estimate, or put Edmund Bertram sufficiently out of her head. (469)

The tones of Mary's self-irony have once more been allowed to infiltrate the narrator's discourse about her. "Perfectly resolved . . ." seems a more exaggerated formulation than the state of her feelings probably warrants, and hyperbole has been a typical mode of Mary's self-camouflage ("the *never* of conversation" [92]). "Dashing representatives, or idle heir apparents" recalls the mock romancing of her diction ("the former belles of the house of Rushworth" [87]). And the deliberate understating of her inability to "put Edmund Bertram sufficiently out of her head" suggests her own style much more than it does the narrator's (compare her comment to Fanny, "[Edmund] gets into my head more than does me good" [416]). Even in this closing summation, Mary recovers her capacity to unsettle the judgment made on her. It is clear that there is a discrepancy between this Mary and the Mary that Edmund and Fanny have just expelled from their lives. What keeps this Mary "long in choosing" is precisely "the better taste" that they have condemned that Mary for wanting. (Mary has acquired her better taste, moreover, "at Mansfield"; it is not, therefore, the belated fruit of repentant exile.)

The discrepancy points up the subtractive nature of Edmund's and Fanny's proceedings. Mary can add up to the siren and adventuress that they see in her only if something has been taken away—namely, everything that does not so add up. Only reduction and rescaling will produce a decisive knowledge of Mary Crawford (that is, one with closural force); but once a closure has thus been guaranteed and Mary become an effectively closed book (a "bad" character), then the novelist can put back some of what had to be taken away for closure and expulsion to take place. Of course, the novelist is in deep sympathy with what Edmund and Fanny do; but her text gives full dramatic weight to the fact that it is *they* who do it. A narrator whose point of view cannot be identified with theirs simply watches on, as it were, not hostile to their activities, but neither wholly committed to them. The consequences of this construction are interestingly double. On the one hand, the interpretation that Edmund and Fanny impose on Mary secures the enclosure of the form; it provides the form with an alibi for its own rounded termination. On the other hand, this closure is made to issue from claims on our awareness (those represented by the crises of Edmund and Fanny) whose limited and partial scope has been repeatedly defined: by the status of Edmund and Fanny as characters, deprived of a fully authoritative overview; by the separate track on which they have conducted their discussions about Mary; by the narrator's point of view, different from theirs; and finally, by the complex modes of portraying Mary in the novel. Closure is thus effective, rounding off the novel, bringing this sequence and that development to an end; but its efficacy is shown to depend on a suppression, a simplification, a sort of blindness. This is what is theoretically recognized in the difference between the narrator's last view of Mary and that of Edmund and Fanny. Can the theoretical recognition be made because, in practice, it operates in benign interests? Jane Austen would seem to be saying: "Moral knowledge, of the kind Edmund and Fanny impose, *is* 'unfair'; it does involve a reduction of Mary's complexity. But this reduction is the necessary price of settlement. If one needs knowledge and settlement badly enough, as Edmund and Fanny do, the cost of obtaining them is rightly paid." At the moment it takes place, the closure practiced on Mary Crawford voids the text of a certain linguistic richness, but the riddance is felt to operate in the interest of the good. Nonetheless, to dramatize the movement of closure as it works to translate the polyvalent into the univocal is also (in however backhanded a way) to recognize the intrinsic incapacity of such a closural system ever to totalize the novel, or to absorb the full dimensions of its signifiers within an ostensible meaning. To this limited extent, the richness of, say, Mary Crawford is given back to us once we recognize the self-enclosed nature of the closural system, which closes only what *can* be closed (what has been remade into its own object) and has done with "all the rest."

"Seldom, very seldom, does complete truth belong to any human disclosure; seldom can it happen that something is not a little disguised, or a little mistaken" (E 431). In the context of our argument, the suggestiveness of this text is obvious. It describes the mechanism of closure *almost* as we have seen it operate: at the moment settlement takes place, something gets left out. *Almost*, for the text does not quite say that disclosure, proceeding by mask and mistake, must forgo its claims to a "complete truth"; even less does it say that a masking or mistaking of the complete truth is a necessary condition if disclosure is to take place at all. This is what it teasingly stops just short of saying, merely claiming that it "very seldom" happens that a masking or mistaking fails to accompany the truth of a disclosure. However, even if we take the text at face value (even before recognizing that its face value is two-faced), it is evident that this reflection about human disclosure in general is itself a disclosure; and that, as such, it puts into question its own status (as a "truth" being "disclosed"). To what extent is it subject to the liabilities of human disclosure revealed in it? Does it abide by the general rule that it articulates (and if it does, then what is being disguised or mistaken?), or is it one of those exceptions such as "very seldom" occur?

The placement of the text, coming as it does at a crucial juncture in *Emma*, seems perversely calculated to raise these questions. We hardly expect reticence, much less suppression, at the supreme moment of mutual recognition uniting heroine and hero. On the contrary, it is at this very moment that Jane Austen's lovers typically indulge "in those retrospections and acknowledgements, and especially in those explanations of what had directly preceded the present moment" (P 241). Far from telling only and no more than what needs to be told, these conversations are characterized by redundancy and repetitiousness. "Between [two lovers] no subject is finished, no communication is even made, till it has been made at least twenty times over" (SS 364). In this case, however, "what had directly preceded the present moment" is precisely what is consciously withheld. Emma's initial reluctance to hear what Knightley has to say and her speedy acceptance of his proposal have produced an "inconsistency" (E 431) of conduct. Although Emma could easily have accounted for it (by revealing Harriet's newly revealed attachment to him and her own newly excited fears of his returning it), she chooses to let it stand. In the place where her explanation ought to be, an aphorism announces the omission of explanation.

Thus, at a decisive moment of truth in the novel, there comes a text that curiously subverts the completeness of the moment. The subversion is curious, moreover, not only because it comes unexpectedly, but also because it paradoxically tends to neutralize its own force. By suggesting that such moments of truth are "very seldom" more complete than this one, might not the text be in effect reinforcing the practical adequacy of the scene (which is, at any rate, as complete as can usually be the case)? For it may be true that at the moment in which truth is being disclosed, something is seldom not a little disguised or mistaken; "but where, as in this case, though the conduct is mistaken, the feelings are not, it may not be very material" (431). A theoretical distinction is insisted upon, but is oddly denied practical consequence. The text equivocates, both granting and taking away the truth of the proposal scene, simultaneously undercutting it and claiming that this undercutting doesn't much matter. We need to explore the possibility of a sense in which this quasi-proverbial text repeats or perpetuates the very process that it recognizes: specifically, a sense in which this discordant relationship between the truth of disclosure and the completeness of truth ("very seldom" obviated) is not a matter of mere probabilities. Might not what is presented as merely likely to occur, happen according to a certain necessity? And if so, then what is gained—or guarded against—by presenting this necessity in the disguised or mistaken form of a generally recurring accident?

Emma's secret is this: not only has Harriet Smith once more remade her object choice, she has attached herself (at Emma's unwitting instigation) to a man who no longer has even the possibility of reciprocating. Why does Emma find it necessary to suppress this information, even in a context of intimacy and unreserve? Why does she decide to continue suppressing it until Harriet's marriage to Robert Martin, when "all necessity of concealment from Mr. Knightley would . . . be over" and "the disguise, equivocation, mystery, so hateful to her to practise, might . . . be over" as well (475)? It seems unlikely that she is prompted by feelings of either protectiveness or rivalry toward Harriet (who now is "nothing"); nor would she need to be, at a moment of guaranteed discretion, moved by loyalty toward her sex— what the novel calls "the duty of woman by woman" (231). Why does the case of Harriet Smith assume such an importance that Emma feels a need not to betray it? What is the nature of her embarrassment?

We might begin to understand the necessity behind Emma's suppression of the "complete truth" here by taking up another, less deliberate instance of it in the novel. This is the censorship that she retrospectively imposes on the interest once excited in her by Frank Churchill. Here are the important articulations of that interest *before* Emma discovers her more potent feelings for Mr. Knightley. First, at Frank's first departure from Highbury:

> To complete every other recommendation, he had *almost* told her that he loved her. What strength, or what constancy of affection he might be subject to, was another point; but at present she could not doubt his having a decidedly warm admiration, a conscious preference of herself; and this persuasion, joined to all the rest, made her think that she *must* be a little in love with him, in spite of every previous determination against it.
>
> "I certainly must," said she. "This sensation of listlessness, weariness, stupidity, this disinclination to sit down and employ myself, this feeling of every thing's being dull and insipid about the house!—I must be in love; I should be the oddest creature in the world if I were not—for a few weeks at least." (262)

Then, during his absence:

> Emma continued to entertain no doubt of her being in love. Her ideas only varied as to the how much. At first,

she thought it was a great deal; and afterwards, but little
. . . pleasing as he was, she could yet imagine him to have
faults; and farther, though thinking of him so much, and,
as she sat drawing or working, forming a thousand amusing schemes for the progress and close of their attachment,
fancying interesting dialogues, and inventing elegant letters; the conclusion of every imaginary declaration on his
side was that she *refused him*. Their affection was always
to subside into friendship. Every thing tender and charming was to mark their parting; but still they were to part.
When she became sensible of this, it struck her that she
could not be very much in love; for in spite of her previous and fixed determination never to quit her father, never
to marry, a strong attachment certainly must produce
more of a struggle than she could foresee in her own feelings.

". . . I do suspect that he is not really necessary to my
happiness. So much the better. I certainly will not persuade myself to feel more than I do. I am quite enough in
love. I should be sorry to be more." (264-65)

Finally, at the news of his secret engagement to Jane Fairfax:

"That you may have less difficulty in believing this
boast, of my present indifference," she continued, "I will
farther tell you, that there was a period in the early part
of our acquaintance, when I did like him, when I was very
much disposed to be attached to him—nay, was attached
—and how it came to cease, is perhaps the wonder. For-
tunately, however, it did cease. I have really for some time
past, for at least these three months, cared nothing about
him. You may believe me, Mrs. Weston. This is the simple
truth." (396)

One needn't artificially raise the temperature of a response
whose limitations Emma acknowledges almost from the
start; one need only note that, however low, it is not at zero
degree. If Emma always qualifies the strength or the duration

of her attachment in these passages, she never denies its existence. Once she becomes aware of her feelings for Mr. Knightley, however, even the seemingly trivial fact that "for a few weeks at least" Emma was "a little" in love with Frank begins to be denied.

> How long had Mr. Knightley been so dear to her, as every feeling declared him now to be? When had his influence, such influence begun?—When had he succeeded to that place in her affection, which Frank Churchill had once, for a short period, occupied?—She looked back; she compared the two—compared them, as they had always stood in her estimation, from the time of the latter's becoming known to her—and as they must at any time have been compared by her, had it—oh! had it, by any blessed felicity, occurred to her, to institute the comparison.—She saw that there never had been a time when she did not consider Mr. Knightley as infinitely the superior, or when his regard for her had not been infinitely the most dear. She saw, that in persuading herself, in fancying, in acting to the contrary, she had been entirely under a delusion, totally ignorant of her own heart—and, in short, that she had never really cared for Frank Churchill at all!
> (412)

Implicitly, Emma's retrospective here censors and revises the texts that we have cited preceding it. "She looked back"; but she doesn't see what she saw when she was back where she is now looking. One odd sequitur: Emma now compares Knightley and Frank as they must have been compared by her at any time in the past (had it occurred to her then to institute the comparison); and she finds that "there had never been a time when she did not consider Mr. Knightley as infinitely the superior." If it did not occur to her to make the comparison in the past, how can it be that "there had never been a time" when she did not find Mr. Knightley winning it? Another: Emma begins by admitting that Frank

Churchill had once, for a short period, occupied a place in her affection; and she concludes that "she had never really cared for Frank Churchill at all!" Did she fail to make the comparison, or has she always made it? Did she once care for Frank, or has she never cared for him? One might account for these discrepancies by an appeal to common-sensical psychology: now that Emma is "really" in love, she realizes that what she called by that name wasn't "really" love at all. Yet this view would merely paraphrase Emma's forgetful revision, without explaining what makes it work, that is, precisely, the invocation of those "reallys." What strategic role do they play? What do they enforce?

I prefer to see Emma confronting the fact of desire's displacement (Knightley has succeeded to the place occupied by Frank Churchill) and then juggling it away (no displacement has ever occurred). Far from succeeding to Frank's place, as Emma is forced to think at the start of the passage, Mr. Knightley ends up having always occupied it. The oppositions of appearance versus reality, ignorance versus knowledge, are invoked, then, to keep desire whole: in one place and on one track, never divided, never transferred or redirected. The phenomena of division, transference, redirection come to be seen as effects of a delusion. Emma has always loved Mr. Knightley, but simply never known it; she has never loved Frank Churchill, but only imagined she did. By the time that Mr. Knightley arrives to condole with her over Frank's apparent betrayal, the processes of Emma's self-revision have fully taken:

> "Mr. Knightley," said Emma, trying to be lively, but really confused—"I am in a very extraordinary situation. I cannot let you continue in your error; and yet, perhaps, since my manners gave such an impression, I have as much reason to be ashamed of confessing that *I never have been at all attached to the person we are speaking of*, as it might be natural for a woman to feel in confessing exactly the reverse.—But I never have." (426-27, my italics)

Her claim blatantly contradicts what she has told Mrs. Weston earlier ("there was a period . . . when I was very much disposed to be attached to him—nay, was attached"). It would seem as though the psychology of being "really" in love required such retraction to help sustain itself. "This time, it's the real thing"; but the reality of the real thing is in part produced by treating previous erotic interest as unreal: inauthentic, delusional, even (as here) nonexistent.

In the proposal scene, this closure of desire becomes institutionalized. Desire has recognized its "proper object" and made itself capable of fixing on it; this recognition can now be incarnated socially, in marriage. Two "one and onlys" have found each other out: such is the implicit ideology of a romantic proposal, and it is not confined to Emma or Jane Austen or even literary texts. Here, however, there is a double urgency behind affirming the ultimate directedness of desire toward its proper object, since the ideology of romantic love carries the rationale of ending the novel as well. The assumptions under which erotic desire is locked into place—in holy matrimony and wholly in matrimony—also permit a story whose subject this is to come to a complete close. Enshrining the directedness of Emma's desire and *Emma*'s design, the proposal scene is thus doubly a staging of the sacred.

It is also likely to be, as René Girard would tell us, a staging of implicit violence: be it only, in this case, the genteel violence of barring a topic from conversation.[29] In a sense, merely to mention the career of Harriet's desire (at this particular crisis in it) would be an affront to the *vraisemblance* of the proposal scene. Romantic love assumes the existence of a right object, and a desire that transcends whatever contingencies have brought it into being. Harriet's case would put forward the incompatible themes of transference (desire sliding onto yet a new object) and mediation (desire crossed up and attached to somebody else's object). If Emma has

[29]René Girard, *La Violence et le sacré*.

needed to deny even what has been a very minor attachment
to Frank Churchill, then she might well want to eschew
these themes, defining the transcendency of her present attachment by an omission of what it is implicitly defined
against. There are more specific reasons for her censorship,
however. It is insofar as Harriet is a reminder of something
in Emma herself that she must be "forgotten": banished
not merely as an inappropriate reference, but as an embar-
rassing and potentially unsettling one.

Soon forgetting and soon supplanting its object, Harriet's
desire has been a parody of Emma's own wandering fancy.
(Consider how Frank Churchill gets displaced: other cares,
occupations, feelings crowd him out.) We have already
seen, moreover, how the revelation of Harriet's feelings for
Mr. Knightley has awakened Emma's own. Hence Emma
needs to protect her desire for him from resembling that of
her protégée, now become her "monstrous double." If common sense suggests that the difference is obvious, Emma here
is unwilling to trust to common sense. It is as though the
mention of Harriet's kind of desire in front of Mr. Knightley
were felt to hold synecdochal implications for her own, un-
dermining its implied transcendency at the very moment
that it needs most to be claimed. Suppression is Emma's way
to differentiate what might become an insinuated identity,
and it will cease only when later developments have made
the differentiation secure. When Harriet's desire has found
its truth in Robert Martin; when Harriet therefore no longer poses the problem of erotic and imaginative instability;
when two husbands and two social standings symbolically
articulate the difference between the two women; then and
only then will Emma give Mr. Knightley "that full and perfect confidence which her disposition was most ready to
welcome as a duty" (475).

On the coextensive level of the novel's own closure, we
observe a familiar pattern: at the moment of closure, the
novel arranges to put in parentheses the inherent instability
or suspense of character and situation that has initiated the

narrative movement. The narratable is shown being put *hors de combat*: not merely laid to rest in a settled outcome, or drained of its force by an "etc principle," but actively suppressed. Now if the narratable belongs to the "complete truth" of a novel (as it would have to do), then we begin to see why the complete truth "very seldom" belongs to closural disclosures. Very seldom?

> All Suspense & Indecision were over.—They were reunited. They were restored to all that had been lost. (P 263)

This is the moment of closure from the original version of *Persuasion*. The closure seems to be a trade-off between two orders or dimensions of the text, each presented as a mutually exclusive totality. *Retrouvé*, "all that had been lost" comes to supplant "all Suspense & Indecision"; and inversely, it is only because "all that had been lost" did get lost that "all Suspense & Indecision" have been able to crop up in the first place. The closural settlement accommodates the narratable only by changing its status, that is, by putting it in a past perfect tense and declaring it "over." Closure can *never* include, then, the narratable in its essential dimension: all suspense and indecision. What made the trial of Job so trying was doubtless the fact that he didn't know that it *was* a trial; as Kierkegaard tells us, "every explanation was still possible."[30] Once Job knew, the experience was radically changed. Similarly, the narratable disappears when it is looked back on from the point of view of closure. Its meaning is now perfectly clear—that is to say, its defining character ("every explanation was still possible") is lost. Elinor's exertion, Edmund's simplification, and Emma's suppression are all stagings of this loss of a dimension in the text, just as they are some of its main motivations.[31]

[30] Søren Kierkegaard, *Repetition: An Essay in Experimental Psychology*, trans. Walter Lowrie (New York: Harper & Row, 1964), p. 115.

[31] In a sense, of course, the loss that I have located at the end of the novels, in these gestures of suppression, is foreshadowed from the

If complete truth never belongs to novelistic disclosure, then why does Jane Austen's text preserve the possibility that there just sometimes might be a pure disclosure, with nothing to void and no history to hide? This ideal of a transparent state of affairs implicitly refers us to a nonnarratable world, where closure is not exclusion because there is nothing to exclude. Even though she finds no motivation for narrative except error, Jane Austen admits no *necessity* for error. If Emma had behaved as she should, Harriet would have done so as well, and there would have been nothing for Mr. Knightley to mistake or Emma to disguise. Characters may "fall" into narrative, but it is also insisted that they are "sufficient to have stood." When Anne and Wentworth are reunited in *Persuasion*, they conduct their retrospective in the perfect conditional ("you should have . . . you should have," "perhaps I ought to have," "I should have thought that"). The tense typically carries Jane Austen's doctrine of sufficient grace, and its full implications become clear in this last exchange:

> "Tell me if, when I returned to England in the year eight, with a few thousand pounds, and was posted into

---

start. The experience of the narratable may be like the trial of Job for some of Jane Austen's characters, but her readers never have it so rough. Most obviously, this security is a function of her "comic form" and its predictability of outcome. Comedy in Jane Austen invokes an overall context of assumptions and expectations that make the ultimate issue of the novels available from the start: in a hiding place easy to find in advance of the characters. We are assured that no one who matters in this game will be finally hurt, and that the narratable will be kept within the limits of a flirtation. As the case of Henry Crawford leads us to ask, however, what are the limits of flirtation, when flirtation would seem inherently to put its exact boundaries into doubt? What does the novelist's comic assurance ensure against? From the perspective of the reader's foreknowledge, the dangers of the narratable easily seem, like Lady Bertram's correspondence, "a sort of playing at being frightened" (MP 427). Yet why play at being frightened? Would a sort of playing at being frightened also be a sort of being frightened at playing?

the Laconia, if I had then written to you, would you have
answered my letter? would you, in short, have renewed
the engagement then?"

"Would I!" was all her answer; but the accent was decisive enough.

"Good God!" he cried, "you would! It is not that I
did not think of it, or desire it, as what could alone crown
all my other success. But I was proud, too proud to ask
again. I did not understand you. I shut my eyes, and
would not understand you, or do you justice. This is a
recollection which ought to make me forgive every one
sooner than myself. Six years of separation and suffering
might have been spared." (247)

Always when it is too late, the perfect conditional comes to
insist on the conditions of perfection, under which the narrative need not have taken place. The analysis of the past
is developed wholly in the terms of traditional moral choice.
Had Wentworth chosen to obey the dictates of justice rather than follow the promptings of pride, "six years of separation and suffering might have been spared." What this view
denies, or at least fails sufficiently to acknowledge, has been
basic to *Persuasion*—namely, the force of "persuasion" itself.
"Persuasion" is Jane Austen's subtle concept of social mediation, through which desire is nearly always made to pass
and nearly always made in passing.[32] The language of the

---

[32] "Persuasion" does not merely refer to Lady Russell's advice
against the original engagement. The title of the novel has been generalized so that it picks up all of the many usages and contexts of the
verb "persuade" in the text. Lady Russell's act of persuasion, however, does furnish a primary model, much like that of "triangular
desire" furnished by René Girard (*Mensonge romantique*): someone
persuades someone else's desires. "Persuasion" generally tends to an-
nounce the presence of a *third party*, so that even reflexive usages
(such as "Anne was left to persuade herself," or "These were [Eliza-
beth's] internal persuasions") come to point to mediation on the
sacred grounds of apparent authenticity.
Anne's curious insistence, to the very end, that she was right to have
followed Lady Russell's advice perhaps carries a suggestion that, if

perfect conditional implicitly claims an exemption for the two lovers, who transcend persuasion precisely insofar as they "should have" transcended it sooner.

Persuasion subjects the status of its narrative to Jane Austen's most moving equivocation. We have just seen how it insinuates that its narrative "might have been spared." The insinuation receives support from the fact that the closural settlement of the novel merely reconstitutes an original settlement disjoined before the novel even opens. The "truth" of *Persuasion* comes when the two lovers are "returned again into the past"—returned to a time before narrative, before the failure or *fêlure* from which a narrative has untowardly bulged (240). The narrative is thus foreclosed in an important way. In the guise of a souvenir, its ultimate configuration is shown held in reserve from the very start; and Anne Elliot, the novel's center of consciousness, maintains the intrinsic rightness of this configuration no matter what the actual outcome. "Their union, she believed, could not divide her more from other men, than their final separation" (192). The play of narrative complication is allowed to threaten the possibility of *incarnating* the right settlement,

---

"persuasion" ought to be transcended, it cannot be bypassed. Wentworth affirms that they might have been spared most of their separation and suffering, but Anne insists that at least some was inevitable. Wentworth is not yet entirely convinced. The double insistence—on the inevitability as well as the dispensability of "persuasion"—would seem to be another version of Jane Austen's ambivalence toward the status of narrative.

In view of the importance the concept of persuasion thus acquires in the text, it is worth reaffirming that the title of the novel is the author's own. In his introduction to *Emma* (Penguin, 1966), Ronald Blythe has given fresh currency to the error that the title was made up by Henry Austen when he had the novel published after his sister's death. But Jane Austen mentions *Persuasion* by name in a memorandum, of which the manuscript is extant in the Morgan Library, and a facsimile available in Jane Austen, *Plan of a Novel and Other Documents* (Oxford: The Clarendon Press, 1929). See also R. W. Chapman, *Jane Austen: Facts and Problems* (Oxford: The Clarendon Press, 1948), p. 81.

but it can never affect what ought to be as such. The developmental powers of the narrative are mainly restricted to the minor characters, whose formation is highly responsive to the "persuasion" of incident and situation (Louisa Musgrove and Captain Benwick, for example). Anne Elliot comes to the novel with her character and her choice already made, inalterable whatever happens. Even Wentworth is "constant unconsciously"; and far from shaping him, the narrative merely awakens his sense of what he always has been (241). *Persuasion* continually suggests that its proper issue can only be a return, and that its narrative can merely arrange or fail to arrange this return. The sheer elaboration of narrative thus begins to seem a perverse and almost gratuitous postponement.

The retardatory effect is partly obtained by the insistence of such foreclosure throughout the novel; but it is also ensured by a more properly intrinsic feature of the narrative. The unfolding of *Persuasion* is nearly wholly motivated by social occasions: visits, outings, parties. If these bring Anne and Wentworth together, they also never leave them alone. We might say that a *terzo incomodo* intervenes in every encounter between the two: the very publicity of social intercourse itself. In this way the narrative functions to prevent Anne and Wentworth from direct speech about what matters most. Each tentative communication between them must pass through the medium of polite sociability, which renders it opaque. Might not the medium of sociability be all the message there is? This is the position to which, at different moments, both Anne and Wentworth retreat. When Wentworth puts her in Admiral Croft's carriage, this passes with Anne for "an impulse of pure, though unacknowledged friendship"; and Wentworth thinks that Anne's encouraging manner to him at the concert "might be only the ease which [her] engagement to another man would give" (91, 245).

Can the narrative be written only because its protagonists cannot speak? It is at least certain that the ending of *Persuasion* explicitly coincides with the recovery of the means of direct speech. "I must speak to you by such means as are within my reach" (237). Thus Wentworth prefaces his proposal, but the means of speech within his reach are ironically only pen and paper. The proposal speech is made in writing, in a letter. Significantly, the letter tries to obviate some of the effects of its status as writing. Its forceful style gives the illusion of impetuous speech ("I can listen no longer . . . I must speak"), and the secrecy in which it is drafted and delivered restricts the possibility of publication intrinsic to a written text. Yet in one important sense, Wentworth's letter remains a letter, removed from the circuit of speech: it bars Anne from an immediate reply. Written within range of her voice, the letter acknowledges the frustrations of a written text that would be spoken: "I can hardly write. I am every instant hearing something which overpowers me. You sink your voice, but I can distinguish the tones of that voice, when they would be lost on others" (237). *Persuasion* ushers in its conclusion with a written text pleading for the unwritten communication of speech and gesture ("a word, a look will be enough"). The moment of full release in the novel comes, not when Anne reads Wentworth's letter, but later when they have recovered "the power of conversation." "Are you going near Camden-place?" Charles Musgrove asks Wentworth on the streets of Bath; "because if you are, I shall have no scruple in asking you to take my place, and give Anne your arm to her father's door."

There could not be an objection. There could be only a most proper alacrity, a most obliging compliance for public view; and smiles reined in and spirits dancing in private rapture. In half a minute, Charles was at the bottom of Union-street again, and the other two proceeding together; *and soon words enough had passed between them to decide their direction towards the comparatively quiet and retired gravel-walk, where the power of conversation would make the present hour a blessing indeed;*

and prepare for it all the immortality which the happiest recollections of their own future lives could bestow. (240, my italics)

The novel never even gives us the dialogue of the "conversation" that has this "power." Jane Austen's novels systematically elide full dialogue at such crucial moments of speech, as though reticence were the only way for a narrative to render them. " 'At present, I ask only to hear—once to hear your voice.' . . . She spoke, then, on being so entreated.—What did she say?—Just what she ought, of course" (E 430, 431). A mere indication that the crucial speech has occurred must suffice to bring in the untold reign of what ought to be.

Whether characterizing itself as a muzzling of a primary power of speech, an intermeddling in a primal union, or a distraction from the primacy of return, the narrative of *Persuasion* is always implicitly affirming its own secondariness. Yet if this secondariness is saturated with pathos, it is because it is secondary in every sense but one: it occupies the primary *position.* The narrative stands in the way, as it were, of characters and readers, an engrossing obstruction. *Persuasion* might well be taken for Jane Austen's "purest" novel, for the narrative of pathos ("separation and suffering," "division and estrangement") radicalizes a pathos in narrative itself. "Six years of separation and suffering might have been spared." The truth of the story should have made most of it dispensable. As if by a logic of reaction formation, however, the close of the novel is also the site of Jane Austen's most explicit attempt to redeem the moment of narrative for her characters. We return to the gravel walk:

There they exchanged again those feelings and those promises which had once before seemed to secure every thing, but which had been followed by so many, many years of division and estrangement. There they returned again into the past, more exquisitely happy, perhaps, in their reunion, than when it had been first projected; more

tender, more tried, more fixed in a knowledge of each
other's character, truth, and attachment; more equal to
act, more justified in acting. (P 240-41)

For having passed through a narrative of division and estrangement, the closural settlement apparently profits by a
bonus. The same feelings and promises "which had once
before seemed to secure every thing" now secure, curiously,
everything and more. "Everything" comes from the recovery of the original engagement; but "more" comes from
its recovery after "many, many years of division and estrangement"—that is, synecdochically, after the narrative.
On one view, the narrative delay has added nothing ("six
years might have been spared"); on another, it has produced a superfluity, what the original version called an
"overplus of Bliss" (268). The equivocation is sustained by
the reservation—"perhaps"—that interrupts the affirmation
of the bonus, a reservation absent from the canceled draft,
which claimed simply that Anne and Wentworth "were
carried back to the past with only an increase of attachment
and confidence" (263). Why "perhaps"? Is there a bonus or
isn't there? Not only is this attempt to recuperate the moment of narrative limited, it is finally ambiguous.

The bonus has to be qualified by equivocation and uncertainty because, if it were not, it could potentially undermine the very ideology that permits closure to take place. In
the context of Jane Austen's typical use of the verb "fix," to
say that Anne and Wentworth are "more fixed in a knowledge of each other's character, truth, and attachment" is
virtually a solecism. Jane Austen's novels close with confidence because settlement, knowledge, love are absolutes,
never matters of more or less. If sufficiently stressed, the
division of these absolutes into degrees would undermine the
novels' closural codes. How fixed would fixed be? Could
Anne and Wentworth be "even more fixed" than they are
now? Would they need another narrative to make them so?
Once the categories of more and less were admitted in the

final settlement, the logic of the narratable (a logic of the "not quite") would be inscribed in closure itself. "Six years might have been spared" can at least be affirmed as an acquired truth. But suppose that the narrative never reached a point at which even this could be affirmed? The pathos of a dispensable narrative is nothing next to the pathos of an unending narratability, indispensable because there are no safe grounds on which to dispense with it. No longer kept within limits and roundly terminated at the end, narrative would implicitly become all there is. Thus *Persuasion* very cautiously says "perhaps."

Chapter 2

———◆———

George Eliot: "The Wisdom
of Balancing Claims"

———◆———

IT WAS CHARACTERISTIC of Henry James's acuteness to see that *Middlemarch* "sets a limit to the development of the old-fashioned English novel."[1] It was equally characteristic of his tact that he never went on to specify what sort of limit it set, or even on which side of the limit the novel ultimately came down: whether the limit was set by remaining—just barely—within the assumptions of traditional form, or by going beyond them to a point where their validity would seem challenged. James's remark suggests *Middlemarch* as an inevitable reference in our study of traditional form in the nineteenth-century novel. Even the ambiguity of his comment offers a useful preliminary formulation of the doubleness that shapes George Eliot's novel itself.

Middlemarch indeed oscillates in a curious and exemplary way: between a confident reenactment of traditional form, in the magisterial manner of a *summa*, and an uneasy subversion of its habitually assumed validity, as though under the less magisterial pressure of a doubt. If we insist on the extent to which the novel retreads the itinerary of, say, *Emma*, we find ourselves embarrassed by those aspects of the text that put a question mark before its own traditional form.[2] Yet if we turn about and stress the novel's "self-

[1] Henry James, unsigned review, *Galaxy* 15 (March 1873), rpt. in David Carroll, ed., *George Eliot: The Critical Heritage*, p. 359.
[2] A perfect instance would be Arnold Kettle, *An Introduction to*

deconstructive" dimension, we are hard put to explain why
its deconstructive insights—far from issuing in a novelistic
form more fully commensurate with them—impede neither
the rhetorical power with which traditional form is able to
impose itself nor the earnest moral apology that is made for
traditional-formal usages.[3] Moreover, if we allow its full ambiguity to the presence of both a traditional ground and a
deconstructive abyss beyond its limits, we seem carried into
further ambiguity over the possible meaning of their co-
functioning. Does the novel intend to subject this traditional ground to a covert erosion, slyly destining it for the
abyss below? or does the novel mean to use the abyss in a
cautionary way, offering its sublime, vertiginous prospect
only to frighten us back from it—back to safer, beaten
ground whose value is proportionately enhanced by the
danger of having strayed?

Like one of those optical drawings that won't resolve
once for all into five cubes or six, a vase or two human pro-
files, *Middlemarch* seems to be traditional and to be beyond
its limit, to subvert and to reconfirm the value of its traditional status. We shall explore the double valency of such
a text as what matters most about it: not necessarily in the
hope of giving its terms their proper balance (as though this
were possible), far less of being able to favor one of them
over the other, but with the suspicion that their full contradictory value may best define the novel's peculiar relationship to traditional form.

---

the English Novel: Defoe to the Present. Kettle begins his chapter on
Middlemarch by claiming that the novel "is the same *kind* of novel
as *Emma*. . . . George Eliot extends the method of Jane Austen, but
does not substantially alter it" (p. 160). This perspective governs and
simplifies his entire reading of the novel.

[3] This seems to me the failing of J. Hillis Miller's two articles,
"Narrative and History," and "Optic and Semiotic in *Middlemarch*."
Despite it, the articles remain our most sophisticated treatment of the
novel's own sophistication, and I shall later, by a long and qualifying
detour, want to rejoin some of their conclusions.

I have already charted what I think are the two basic requirements of traditional novelistic form: a moment of suspense and instability, and a moment of closure and resolved meaning. The first institutes the narratable disequilibrium, which the second converts back to a state of nonnarratable quiescence. We might ask again our fundamental question: with what representations of content and value does *Middlemarch* motivate its constructional categories (nonnarratability, narratability, closure)? In answer, however, the novel presents not merely a variety of different determinations, but what are actually different *systems* of determination. How the constructional categories are motivated depends on the level at which the story is being told. Three main levels of motivation easily stand out. The novelistic community (Hegel's world of "maintaining individuals") views the story according to one scheme of reference and value; the protagonists (that world's "historical individuals") perceive it according to another; and the narrator (would he be the providential *Geist*?) collaborates with his invented reader to tell it according to still another. The text pluralizes the perspective from which traditional form is commonly perceived and delimited, offering not a single, univocal movement from the narratable to closure, but in effect three such movements. One recalls the virtual unanimity that obtained among levels of telling the story at the end of a Jane Austen novel: Emma finally came to share the narrator's view of her errancy, and even Mary Crawford ended up recognizing "the better taste acquired at Mansfield." In *Middlemarch*, the different ways of perceiving and delimiting the story all conspire to identify what is, in terms of its main actions, *the same story*. Yet if they are narratologically identical, they remain to the end hermeneutically distinct. Each system of delimitation accounts for more or less the same events, but each system derives meaning from different sources and puts its stresses and values in different places.

This pluralism of perspectives that are coterminous but

not covalent opens up some interesting possibilities. If one
perspective (such as the narrator's) includes a consciousness
of others, it may need to subvert or parody them, in order
to maintain its difference by an effect of transcendence. Yet
if despite its difference it shares a common structure with
its rivals, it may be running the risk of self-subversion or
self-parody in the very attempt to undercut them. The need
to protect against this risk may even give rise to certain de-
flections or hesitations of aim. The main force of the pluralism in *Middlemarch*, however, is surely to make us aware of
perspective itself. What traditional form shows us is no longer
exhibited in a spirit of naive realism, as simply what is there
to be seen. Instead it must now be taken as a function of a
perceiving system with its own desire, disguises, deletions,
and disinterests, *which might have been organized otherwise*. One inroad, then, would be to follow the story of
Middlemarch according to its three different tellings, its
three uncannily synoptic gospels.

Narrative One: The Community

"Sane people did what their neighbours did, so that if any
lunatics were at large, one might know and avoid them."[4]
Here is the mechanism of social control that allows the community in *Middlemarch* to maintain itself. Here as well is
the mechanism of narrative control that allows this community to function, in precise ways, like a traditional novel.
The collective scenarios of society constitute the nonnarratable equilibrium, and the violations of them (lunacy being

[4] George Eliot, *Middlemarch*, ed. W. J. Harvey (Penguin, 1965),
p. 31. All quotations from *Middlemarch* will henceforth be designated
in the text by their page number in this edition. There is nothing sacred about the Cabinet Edition (Edinburgh and London: Blackwood,
n.d.), and modern editions of the novel are based not on it, but on
the one-volume edition published in 1874, the last to pass through
George Eliot's hands. It seemed perverse to send the reader after the
Cabinet Edition, which, without particular textual or editorial advantages, is also rather difficult to get hold of.

only the most extreme form of exorbitancy) represent the narratable difference. This community/novel is apparently constructed to meet the requirements of an important task: to know the narratable in order to avoid it. It would designate a state of story-worthiness only to quarantine it elsewhere: anywhere but in the functioning of what the text ironically calls "that beneficent harness of routine which enables silly men to live respectably and unhappy men to live calmly" (720). The narratable is a paradoxical, ambivalent phenomenon. Much as the lunatic both affronts and reassures our own sense of mental health, the transgressions of routine both scandalize and ultimately confirm its normativeness.

Yet as the "socially uniting" Mrs. Cadwallader admits, "We have all got to exert ourselves a little to keep sane, and call things by the same names as other people call them by" (581). Like a proper harness, the "harness of routine" includes both blinders and reins. Within a field of potentially all-inclusive narratability, only some differences are acknowledged to operate, while others are denied and elided into the nonnarratable. Take the instance of Mrs. Cadwallader herself. If she is socially uniting in an eminent degree, it is because her differences are simply disregarded as not counting. Mr. Brooke might have quarreled with her over their difference of opinion about Dorothea's marriage, but he does not. "Who could taste the fine flavour in the name of Brooke if it were delivered casually, like wine without a seal? Certainly a man can only be cosmopolitan up to a certain point" (78). At the other end of the social scale, Mrs. Cadwallader's differences (her free-spoken tongue, her pride of birth, her hectoring parsimony) are similarly overlooked, maintained only at the level of the picturesque. "Such a lady gave a neighbourliness to both rank and religion," a sameness to difference (76). In the social world of a Balzac or Zola, her miserliness and snobbery would have engendered fully developed stories (think of Mlle. Gamard in *Le Curé de Tours* or even La Grande in *La Terre*). This community actively sets such possibilities aside. It celebrates a social mean in Mrs. Cadwallader, but only by an attitude of negligence that guards this mean from becoming a narrative of the *mesquin*.

To disallow one set of differences, however, works typically in this community to insist on the force of another set. Weak differences get erased so that strong ones may be underscored, and vice versa. Saussure aptly reminds us that the 8:45 p.m. Geneva-Paris express train is in fact a different train each day, composed of different cars, engines, personnel. "What constitutes the express train is the hour of its departure, its itinerary, and in general all the circumstances that distinguish it from the other express trains."[5] If we are to use a railway system properly, the differences within the series of "8:45 p.m. Geneva-Paris express trains" must vanish in the face of the differences between this series and others. The identity of the series is not absolute, but the effect of a pragmatic relevancy: some differences give way under the force of more pertinent discriminations.

By such a logic, for example, Dorothea's strong difference consolidates the weak differences of opinion about her into a conventional unanimity. It may be true that "of course all the world around Tipton would be out of sympathy with [her] marriage," but individuals have very different motives for their irritation (73). Mrs. Cadwallader sees in it the rejection of the advantageous match that "she had preconceived" (84). Mr. Brooke takes it as another sign of the irreducible capriciousness of the female sex. Celia dislikes it because Casaubon is unpleasant to look at, and Sir James Chettam because he fears Dorothea may have deluded herself. The criticism of Dorothea's womanhood is similarly developed out of several different theories, by no means fully compatible. If she is all too feminine for Brooke, to other tastes she is plainly not feminine enough. Lydgate, whose "distinction of mind . . . did not penetrate his feeling or

5 Ferdinand de Saussure, *Cours de linguistique générale*, p. 151.

judgment about furniture, or women," thinks women (not unlike furniture) should be decorative and comfortable (179). Dorothea is thus "too earnest"; "she did not look at things from the proper feminine angle" (119, 122). Mr. Chichely's ideal, on the other hand, is the spitfire: "A man likes a sort of challenge" (115). Dorothea is thus "altogether a mistake, and calculated to shock his trust in final causes, including the adaptation of fine young women to purple-faced bachelors" (120). Yet all these conflicting opinions have the magical force of an agreement: they all designate Dorothea along with her marriage as the odd one out, the strong difference allowing their weak differences to hide under the effective identity of a social norm.

Like a harness in its now archaic sense of war gear, the harness of routine does the work of protection and defense. It is obvious that the characters who find Dorothea such an oddity are themselves rather odd. By any intrinsic standard of eccentricity, they might well find each other as odd as they all find her. Yet why doesn't this happen? Why does a family resemblance of differences effectively give way to a binary opposition between the presence and absence of difference *tout court*? It can only be that Dorothea's difference is uniquely threatening. What is threatened are not merely traditional female roles and functions, but all the social arrangements that these maintain. Thus Dorothea's difference has the power to initiate the community's storytelling as the differences of the Mrs. Cadwalladers and Mr. Chichelys do not. The distribution of the narratable is not a common-sensical recognition of what is inherently interesting. Nor does it proceed according to an arbitrary logic of hit-or-miss. Rather, it marks the sites where an ideology feels itself in danger and has already begun to counter-attack.

Characters who are felt to threaten the ideology of social routine enter immediately into the network of chatter and gossipy observation that promotes their eccentricities to a state of story-worthiness. The community always characterizes the narratable difference in the same, telling way. Celia, for example, has "the feeling that her sister was too religious for family comfort. Notions and scruples were like spilt needles, making one afraid of treading, or sitting down, or even eating" (43). The transition made by Celia's thought is almost seamless: what begins as a social problem (of "family comfort") is raised up into a threat to nature itself, at its most basic level of bodily movement and biological need. In a similar operation, when acquainted with some of Lydgate's "new ideas," Mr. Standish replies, "Hang it, do you think that is quite sound?—upsetting the old treatment, which has made Englishmen what they are?" (119). Having made Englishmen "what they are," the old treatment is already a second nature, so that Lydgate's innovations inevitably pose a question of their soundness, as though they might be a form of disease or mental defectiveness. On this way of seeing things, a social novelty invariably becomes a lapse of nature. Even when the narratable difference is not construed as an unnatural monster, it is taken for a supernatural prodigy. Sir James comes to revere his quirky sister-in-law as a sort of local totem; and people remark, as if his "new ways" were sorcery, that Lydgate has "the merit of bringing people back from the brink of death" (488). To label certain social differences "against nature" is of course to propose a backhanded definition of nature, as fully equivalent to social routine. The Middlemarch community implicitly takes up the "Study of Provincial Life" as though it were a branch of natural history—and that branch only teratology: the study of nature's malformations and monstrosities. One is tempted to see a virtual emblem of the community's self-perception in Mr. Farebrother's study, where the naturalist's unexceptionable collections modestly contrast with an "anencephalous monster" on display in a glass jar (202).

Woe to those who shed this harness of routine. Farebrother warns: "Either you slip out of service altogether, and become good for nothing, or you wear the harness and draw a good deal where your yoke-fellows pull you" (204). To choose a battleground, however, is only a preliminary matter; battle must be waged and the enemy routed. Once designated, that is, the narratable needs to be put outside the boundaries of the community, outside its middling "marches"—if only in a root sense, exterminated. It therefore has to be developed into finished, fully narrated stories, whose narrative closure can double for a social exclusion.

Story production and social control coincide perhaps most plainly in the case of Lydgate. One recalls that, well before his arrival in Middlemarch, the practice of medicine there is an elaborate system of differences. A lowering system "including reckless cupping" is opposed to a strengthening system "of incessant port wine and bark" (118). Two rival surgeons or practitioners correspond to the two systems: Mr. Toller with "lazy manners" and "the easiest way of taking things which might be supposed to annoy him," and the "irascible," "irritable" Mr. Wrench (486, 487). In addition, there are two physicians of apparently different methods.

> Dr Minchin was soft-handed, pale-complexioned, and of rounded outline, not to be distinguished from a mild clergyman in appearance: whereas Dr Sprague was superfluously tall; his trousers got creased at the knees, and showed an excess of boot at a time when straps seemed necessary to any dignity of bearing; you heard him go in and out, and up and down, as if he had come to see after the roofing. In short, he had weight, and might be expected to grapple with a disease and throw it; while Dr Minchin might be better able to detect it lurking and to circumvent it. (212)

Yet such longstanding divisions of method and rank are kept thoroughly below the threshold of potential conflict. Only Lydgate is the pertinent difference: the threat that easily collapses other, older distinctions into a nonnarratable unity.

The vote of the hospital board is a preliminary occasion for social consensus at the medical level. The doctors' partiality for Farebrother is not merely an implicit pact against Bulstrode, but more important, against his new protégé as well. Before the vote, "the long-established practitioners, Mr Wrench and Mr Toller, were . . . having a friendly colloquy, in which they agreed that Lydgate was a jackanapes, just made to serve Bulstrode's purpose" (212). Similarly, "regarding themselves as Middlemarch institutions," Minchin and Sprague "were ready to combine against all innovators, and against non-professionals given to interference" (212). When it is a matter of plotting Lydgate out of Middlemarch, their rivalries and differences cease to count: "The two physicians, for a wonder, turned out to be unanimous, or rather, though of different minds, they concurred in action" (211). Significantly, it is one of the medical men, the irascible Wrench, who taunts the still undecided Lydgate into voting against them:

> "There is a casting-vote still to be given. It is yours, Mr Lydgate: will you be good enough to write?"
> "The thing is settled now," said Mr Wrench, rising. "We all know how Mr Lydgate will vote."
> "You seem to speak with some peculiar meaning, sir," said Lydgate, rather defiantly, and keeping his pencil suspended.
> "I merely mean that you are expected to vote with Mr Bulstrode. Do you regard that meaning as offensive?"
> "It may be offensive to others. But I shall not desist from voting with him on that account."
> Lydgate immediately wrote down "Tyke." (217)

Once all the exorbitancy of the narratable has been projected onto Lydgate, the plot thickens—or as the text puts it, "There were particulars enough reported of him . . . to intensify differences into partisanship" (483). Through Lydgate, the medical men are able to define themselves as a unified group and their activities as a nonnarratable state of affairs; but the reverse of this phenomenon is that they are a group under attack. The narratable excites an irritation that must be tranquilized, like a foreign body that must be assimilated or expelled. Thus Lydgate's differences are manipulated according to the system of self-defense already set up. He doesn't dispense drugs: does he mean to set himself above Toller and Wrench? does he mean to put himself on a level with Sprague and Minchin? Even before the convenient innuendoes occasioned by Raffles's death, Lydgate's differences have been put into duly scandalous form:

> Mr Gambit was told that Lydgate went about saying physic was of no use.
> "Indeed!" said he, lifting his eyebrows with cautious surprise . . . "How will he cure his patients then?"
> "That is what *I* say," returned Mrs Mawmsey. . . . "Does *he* suppose that people will pay him only to come and sit with them and go away again?" (485)

The scandal may be enforced by cool irony (the tack of Toller and Gambit) or by feverish complaint (the tack of Wrench and Mrs. Mawmsey); in either case, its effect is to deprive Lydgate of a decent share of paying patients so that he is finally obliged to seek a practice elsewhere. To ride the outlaw out of town is virtually the only form of closure that so naive a community/narrative can imagine.

There are other dimensions of Lydgate's story, of course, besides this professional scapegoating. The medical men can certainly not be held responsible for his marriage to Rosamond or for the carelessness with which the ménage incurs its debts. These would be domestic matters, unrelated to the fate of his practice. The lack of connection, however, is more apparent than real. "Is it not rather what we expect in men, that they should have numerous strands of experience lying side by side and never compare them with each other?" (634). What makes Lydgate's destiny uncanny (in a full Freudian sense) is that these apparently unrelated strands of experience come to function as parts of *a single strategy of enmeshment.* To the extent that no one person or group in the community is either conscious or in control of such a strategy, its imperatives are imposed all the more efficaciously. Rosamond unwittingly serves the same interests as the medical men—*or rather, though of a different mind, she concurs in action.* Her aggressive gentility and her indifference to her husband's "professional and scientific ambition" wage the community's battle surreptitiously, on what is supposed to be neutral ground. If the medical men aggravate his financial difficulties, Rosamond aggravates the misery attending them. "The sufferings of his own pride from humiliations past and to come were keen enough, yet they were hardly distinguishable to himself from that more acute pain which dominated them—the pain of foreseeing that Rosamond would come to regard him chiefly as the cause of disappointment and unhappiness to her" (754). The assimilation that a marriage to Rosamond seemed to promise turns out to be the community's deepest ruse. She and the medical men have been unconsciously waiting and preparing for the affair of Raffles's death—if it didn't occur, we feel, they would need to invent an equivalent event to put the seal on Lydgate's departure.

Indeed his bitterest moment comes with an awareness of this collective and unconscious "conspiracy" against him.

> He was ready to curse the day on which he had come to Middlemarch. Everything that had happened to him there seemed a mere preparation for this hateful fatality, which had come as a blight on his honourable ambition. . . . Lydgate thought of himself as the sufferer, and of others as the agents who had injured his lot. He had meant everything to turn out differently; and others had thrust themselves into his life and thwarted his purposes. (793)

To be sure, the text qualifies the plausibility of so distilled a paranoia. Pure victimization is simply impossible on George Eliot's thoroughgoing conception of moral responsibility. It always remains theoretically true that "if we had been great-

er, circumstance would have been less strong against us"
(632). To collaborate with Bulstrode, to marry Rosamond
and to espouse her style of living: these are authentic
choices, assumed by Lydgate in a deeply personal, fully sub-
jective way. Yet even his own responsibility for what happens to him—the very operation of his "spots of common-
ness" (179)—gives a further turn of the screw to the community's devious control. For without being aware of it, he
has chosen to be exactly what the others have wanted to
make him. Perversely, inward choices have turned out to
coincide with externally imposed necessity. The double insistence on social determination and moral responsibility that
has always baffled readers of *Middlemarch* shows up typically as another phenomenon of the uncanny. "A choice is
made where in reality there is compulsion."[6] Freud had a
certain logic of wish fulfillment in mind here, but his insight
has its sociological equivalent too, in cases where the oppo-
sitional character of "man in society" seems eerily collapsed
by the "society in man."[7]

Bulstrode provides another instance of the same paradox
of social scapegoating—that the scapegoat "deserves" his
undeserved treatment. On the one hand, the community's
combination against him is blatantly cathartic. "The sudden
sense of exposure" is made to follow on "the re-established
sense of safety" with melodramatic abruptness (781). The
theater of unmasking is (where else?) the Town Hall, at a
public meeting punctuated by liturgical "murmurs" and
"hisses" and succeeded by a ritual shunning. This paroxysm
of moral indignation is qualified by the resentful eagerness
with which it is prosecuted—as though the secrets in Bulstrode's closet were rather a lucky find. Yet on the other
hand, the banker is manifestly guilty, and his guilt also wears
melodramatic dress: usury and murder. The community's desire to expel him is disingenuous and justified at once. "The

[6] Freud, "The Theme of the Three Caskets," 12: 299.
[7] The phrases come from Peter L. Berger's excellent *Invitation to
Sociology*.

pitiable lot is that of the man who could not call himself a
martyr even though he were to persuade himself that the
men who stoned him were but ugly passions incarnate—
who knows that he is stoned, not for professing the Right,
but for not being the man he professed to be" (881).

Ironically, Bulstrode's crime bespeaks a profound con-
formism, an extreme need of assimilation. "The man he professed to be" is in essence a man without a past, without a
story; and he professed to be such a man in order to enter
and dominate a community that constantly connives at its
own nonnarratability. To repress his past and its return in
Raffles has been an extreme form of obedience to the community's own imperative. Bulstrode tries so hard to efface
the narratable difference in himself that he is betrayed by
the vigor of his effort—or better, by the singleness of that
effort. Such an effacement is effective only if collective and
collaborative. When attempted by a single individual, it is
correspondingly isolated: forced to become conspicuous, excessive, story-worthy, criminal. Bulstrode's uncovered history is a neat case of the *negativity* typically assigned to
narrative by this community and by the traditional novel in
general. Story and crime coincide: the signs that tell tales
are also telltale signs of malfeasance. As the *Middlemarch*
community sees and shapes them, all narratives constitute
offenses against its established order.

"There are practices and there are acts which, owing to
circumstance, the law cannot visit" (780). Although it is
actually Bulstrode's practices and acts referred to here, we
should say that his crime is the only one that the community
can visit directly with its law. When the crime has no legal
name, a less direct, more mediated visitation is required. The
injunction against the marriage of Dorothea and Will Ladislaw, for instance, is more subtly delivered, its origin dispersed among a number of pressure points. Dorothea's eccentricities might have been tolerated if she had remained a
widow whose story was over (Sir James's hagiographic
ideal) or made a routine second marriage (Mrs. Cadwalla-

der's secular program). A marriage to Ladislaw, however, involves an automatic loss of social status, and the work of Casaubon's dead hand is abetted by the general suspicion and dislike directed toward his cousin. Ladislaw is the quintessentially repulsive outsider: "cursed alien blood, Jew, Corsican or Gypsy" (773). As though in response to this antipathy, he chooses—in Middlemarch itself—the one career impossible there: that of a reformer actively trying to shape a history that is always just as actively and much more effectively denied. Dorothea chooses the very man, and Will the very career that obliges each of them to withdraw from the community. The arrangement is almost elegant in its economy: they choose their punishment together with their crime.

It is no accident that the four protagonists in the community (Lydgate, Bulstrode, Dorothea, and Ladislaw) are made to leave town at the end of the novel: ritual sacrifices to the recovery of social routine. To be sure, the text gives to each case its own series of mediations, its own balance of choice and necessity, its own moral implications. *Middlemarch* is rightly praised for its ability to complicate the easy analogies that bind different characters together as a single dilemma. Yet even the manifold richness of the text in this respect passes comment on the social processes involved: for if the text's perception is subtle and discriminating, the community's conduct is generally blunt and insensitive. Virtually any kind of history is rejected from its bosom, whether the crimes of Bulstrode, the reforms of Lydgate and Ladislaw, or the imprudent marriages of Dorothea. The community levels their differences by subjecting them to the same fate of social exclusion. The town fathers "decline to cooperate" with Bulstrode (783); a "general blackballing" is begun against Lydgate (796); Sir James "cannot bear to see [Dorothea] again," since Ladislaw "is not a man we can take into the family" (875, 876). Murder, meliorism, and misalliance are made to look like equivalent threats to social well-being. The wholesale rejection of the narratable is excepted only in the case of Mary Garth and Fred Vincy, where the narratable has merely designated the all-but-routine logistical snags of an orthodox social settlement. No wonder that such low-degree, "Trollopian" narratability is ultimately accommodated within the community: why *not* accommodate it? Even the extreme possibilities of Mary becoming a governess and Fred a genteel clergyman or wastrel mount no substantial challenge to the systematic "way things are." If the community seems eager to thwart Lydgate or Dorothea, it shows a surprisingly decent face (in Farebrother, Caleb Garth, Harriet Bulstrode) when it comes to helping this couple get settled. The novel's last scene presents a happy picture of their assimilation, in a sly salute to the only story that ends properly—in Middlemarch proper.

Much has needed to be scanted in this account of the community's telling of *Middlemarch*, but not so much, I hope, that its general correspondences with a certain kind of traditional novel are unclear. Socially given reality has the function of a nonnarratable base from which narratable derogations—in the form of ideological threats—can be isolated. Its overriding imperative is self-recovery: to know the narratable in order not just to avoid it, but to void it entirely. Closure is made to seem like a straightforward exorcism rather than the culmination of a dialectical development— like Jane Austen's narrator, the community acknowledges no necessity behind the narratable moment. Unlike in Jane Austen, however, the bonus of such a moment once it is over is fully apparent: in an increased social cohesiveness ("There was hardly ever so much unanimity among them as in the opinion that Lydgate was an arrogant young fellow"); in a reconfirmed normativeness (Lydgate's "pride must have a fall," Rosamond "needed a lesson," "late events . . . were likely to humble those who needed humbling"); and finally, in a renovated pedagogy for reproducing the community thus fortified in a younger generation.

Sir James never ceased to regard Dorothea's second marriage as a mistake; and indeed this remained the tradition concerning it in Middlemarch, where she was spoken of to a younger generation as a fine girl who married a sickly clergyman, old enough to be her father, and in little more than a year after his death gave up her estate to marry his cousin—young enough to have been his son, with no property, and not well-born. Those who had not seen anything of Dorothea usually observed that she could not have been "a nice woman," else she would not have married either the one or the other. (896)

Yet the *Middlemarch* text provides a more complex account of the community telling than the latter is able (or willing) to give of itself. We are never allowed to give its claims the same validity, or take its proceedings with the same artlessness, as the community does. "*Of course* all the world round Tipton would be out of sympathy with this marriage." It would only be a slight exaggeration to say that the difference between the community's storytelling and the text's presentation of it turns wholly on the semantic status of that "of course." To the community, "of course" means "naturally," "of necessity": it points to a self-sustaining obviousness in social patterns. In the text, however, the dead metaphor is demonstrably revived into an actual if surreptitious cursiveness—routine, so to speak, would merely be a particularly well traversed route. As I have implicitly been arguing, moreover, to demonstrate that socially given reality is a *busy* quiescence, continually needing to reinvent itself, is already to betray its main assumptions. Once the nonnarratable base is shown to be *produced*, to have a *dynamic* of self-maintenance, then a potential affinity with its narratable opposite begins to emerge. Indeed, it starts to seem as though such a nonnarratable base existed only by virtue of suppressing and projecting its latent narratability.

Gossip offers a typically blinded form of this busy quiescence. What characterizes gossip, after all, is that it never "minds its own business." Gossip is always about someone else, always oriented toward a story that both precedes its discourse and stands outside its frame. The opposition be-

tween someone else's story and its own discourse works to
neutralize its activity, staged as mere observation. What
keeps gossip from becoming the subject of a narrative is, precisely, the narrative that is the subject of gossip. One way
not to *have* a story is to tell one about somebody who does:
narration is a solid protection against the narratable. It is easy
to see how the logic of gossip makes it the inevitable practice of a community that would remain unhistorical. Yet
subversively, the text will sometimes suggest that gossip is
part of the very story it is supposed to be merely telling. For
example, the early gossip about Rosamond and Lydgate—
relayed by Mrs. Pymdale through Mrs. Bulstrode to Rosamond and Lydgate themselves—actively helps to produce
their marriage; far from simply observing narrative events,
such gossip substantially shapes them. Despite the moral reserves that Mrs. Bulstrode is ultimately capable of drawing
on, she is never troubled by compunction about her interference here—has she even seen its decisiveness? To get the
story straight, as she tries to do here, may successfully mask
the act of straightening it out. Gossip easily thinks of itself
as a more-or-less transparent medium for the stories of others. More interestingly, the text suggests that these stories
may only be the most visible dimension of the community's
own history, a history it never admits to having.

Middlemarch thus broaches the only scandal that its
community shows no eagerness to bring to light: the story
of the nonnarratable. Most of the time, of course, such a
story is not fully or even very overtly told by the novel;
rather, its existence is argued for theoretically, in discreet
but telling signs of its suppression. It is suggestive, for instance, that some "strict constructionists" of community
norms were formerly normbreakers. Maintaining individuals
like the Cadwalladers and the Vincys may currently have
no story, but they had one once upon a time. Mrs. Cadwallader descended through her marriage, Mrs. Vincy rose a
little: both have become aggressively *bien-pensant* when it
comes to arranging matches for others. The text subtly ob-

serves the way in which, late in the novel, the memory of the Cadwalladers' marriage threatens the judgment about to be made on Dorothea's: almost instantly, the disturbing recollection is reduced to orthodoxy (877). It is instructive, too, to notice the potential narratability of social routine itself. The text presents a society of highly detailed differences (between sex roles, social classes, ranks in the medical hierarchy), and places it in a concretely realized historical frame (the Catholic Emancipation and the Reform Act at either end, the railroads coming in the middle). At moments even the community seems vaguely conscious of social contradiction and historical becoming: at Brooke's dinner party, in Dagley's tirade, in the peripheral struggles over national politics. Yet to see the rich narrative possibilities implied by social differentiation and historical time is also to see how reluctant the community is to exploit them. Social differences have been embalmed by everyday repetition, so that a field of potential contradictions capable of generating a history is effectively held at the level of patterns in a picture. An urban bourgeoisie is easily distinguished from a county aristocracy, but one inevitably thinks of a single Middlemarch community: the two social spheres are never shown to resist the general ideological coherence binding them— their actions may be different, but never contradictory. Similarly, the community makes every effort to avoid the history in which the text embeds it: Brooke is forcibly brought back to the fold, and the Reform (whose vicissitudes, in any case, have been carried mainly through the newspapers) is defeated. Like those archaic societies studied by Mircea Eliade, the community substitutes a myth of eternal return for a history of its development.[8]

In short, the text implies a potential narrative field always richer than the community's organization of it, which is thus made to seem naively self-deceptive. Yet this naiveté also seems intrinsically more powerful than the text's strategy

[8] Mircea Eliade, *Le Mythe de l'éternel retour: archétypes et répétition.*

for exposing it, mainly because such exposure rarely has practical consequences in novelistic action. Here, for example, is the text's theory of what we *ought* to be finding in this community:

> Old provincial society had its share of this subtle movement: had not only its striking downfalls, its brilliant young professional dandies who ended by living up an entry with a drab and six children for their establishment, but also those less marked vicissitudes which are constantly shifting the boundaries of social intercourse, and begetting new consciousness of interdependence. Some slipped a little downward, some got higher footing: people denied aspirates, gained wealth, and fastidious gentlemen stood for boroughs; some were caught in political currents, some in ecclesiastical, and perhaps found themselves surprisingly grouped in consequence; while a few personages or families that stood with rock firmness amid all this fluctuation, were slowly presenting new aspects in spite of solidity, and altering with the double change of self and beholder. Municipal town and rural parish gradually made fresh threads of connection—gradually, as the old stocking gave way to the savings-bank, and the worship of the solar guinea became extinct, while squires and baronets, and even lords who had once lived blamelessly afar from the civic mind, gathered the faultiness of closer acquaintanceship. Settlers, too, came from distant counties, some with an alarming novelty of skill, others with an offensive advantage in cunning. In fact, much the same sort of movement and mixture went on in old England as we find in older Herodotus. (122-23)

The theory is remarkably barren, however, when we look for actual narrative developments that might confirm it. Mrs. Cadwallader has slipped downward, Mrs. Vincy gained a higher footing, only in a distant past; and Mr. Brooke is "caught in political currents" and "surprisingly grouped in consequence" only for a time—up to a certain point.

Whether with "an alarming novelty of skill" (Lydgate) or "an offensive advantage in cunning" (Bulstrode), settlers are consistently never allowed to settle here. Those who dare to shift "the boundaries of social intercourse" invariably fail, and if they find a "new consciousness of interdependence," they must go enjoy it elsewhere—in London, like Dorothea and Will. Even the coming of the railroad produces no raised consciousness that we see. The story of the "movement and mixture" behind a facade of "rock firmness" exists mainly as a theoretical potential. It is understandable why the community needs to hide this story from itself, but why the text discreetly maintains it *only as a potential*—in discourse never really supported by narrative action—requires some accounting for.

It might be helpful to consider a less discreet, less merely theoretical demonstration of the bad faith of a nonnarratable community: Zola's *Le Ventre de Paris*. Here too a community wants to suppress its story-worthiness. Here too only the outsider Florent, a returned political exile, carries its telling of events. *Le Maigre* in a community of *les Gras*, he alone is made to assume the burden of narrative, history, difference—a burden of negativity that, typically, gets him redeported. The collective scapegoating, presided over by his "respectable" sister-in-law Lisa, would seem to celebrate a community routine as regular as a healthy digestion. "Les ventres crevèrent d'une joie mauvaise." Yet the "joy" is "wicked" not because Florent doesn't have a story, but because the others do as well. Even the militantly normative Lisa is involved in narrative actions that have nothing to do with Florent—like, most notably, her subterranean flirtation with Marjolin, which ends in his near rape of her and her near murder of him. Marjolin survives an idiot, and Lisa can bury the episode in complete silence. "Elle ne se reprochait rien. Elle avait agi en femme honnête."[9] Clearly, however,

---

[9] Emile Zola, *Le Ventre de Paris*, in *Les Rougon-Macquart*, ed. Armand Lanoux and Henri Mitterand, 5 vols. (Paris: Pléiade, 1963-67), 1: 888, 796.

Florent seems a scapegoat for more stories than his own. A mechanism of Freudian projection obviously governs the formation of a nonnarratable base and a narratable difference: the base is nothing more than the difference disguised, cast out as an opposite. Lisa's telling of *Le Ventre de Paris* may be efficacious (Florent *is* redeported), but it is also fully a sham, a way not to tell her own story.

In *Middlemarch*, equivalents of Lisa's "own story" are missing. The differences that the community nullifies into a storyless backdrop are practically voided by the novelist as well. Mrs. Cadwallader's "life was rurally simple, quite free from secrets either foul, dangerous, or otherwise important" (83). "The Vincys had their weaknesses, but then they lay on the surface: there was never anything bad to be 'found out' concerning them" (799). And if characters like Celia and Sir James have a story, it is casually dropped in subordinate clauses ("Celia, who had lately had a baby"), as though snuffed out by its own predictability (516). Conversely, the community identifies the very stories that the text, too, wishes to tell (of Dorothea, Lydgate, Ladislaw, Bulstrode). The text corrects, enriches, even subsumes the content of the community's narrative-formation, but it is never quite willing to break with its fundamental form. Certainly, we shall see, other perspectives are imposed on this narrative-formation; other, richer meanings are derived from it. Yet these other perspectives and meanings are complicitous with the community's perception, if only in this one crucial sense: "though of different minds, they concur in action." Far from opening up an anarchy in the perceptual field, the practice of perspectivism in *Middlemarch* more basically works to avoid it. Indeed, it might be thought of as the most sophisticated reality effect of all. We are familiar with how, in life, various perspectives of an object come to be "proof" of its reality; how, in novels generally, different views of a character may suggest the depth of a full existence; how, in this novel in particular, weak differences unite to confirm strong ones. Similarly, though other levels of telling significantly overdetermine the community's narrative-formation, they ultimately corroborate the "reality" to which it gives rise: these stories, these nonstories.

Critics such as Arnold Kettle and Quentin Anderson have identified this complicity as a simple failure of imagination.[10] It seems to me more accurately thought of as an ambivalence of imagination. For the text resists complying with the Middlemarch telling, if only through its subversive insights into the bad faith underlying it. The community's narrative-formation is reduced to its source in the need to protect a fantasized self-image, and on theoretical grounds, the authenticity of every aspect of this formation is put into question. The nonnarratable base is merely a "forgetting"; the narrative difference is only a conspicuously partial fraction of what it might have been; and closure is only the tautological extension of these initial sleights of hand: a pretended, effective rather than plausible, ending of difference and history. Yet insofar as these have been insights about novelistic form, the text is reluctant to imagine a novel commensurate with them. Or perhaps better, the text is willing *only* to imagine such a novel, not to realize it. A genuinely open history, a continuity of narratable differences, a full suspension of closure: these are only ghostly possibilities that, as it represents the community's telling, the text glimpses rather than grasps. Like good ghosts, however, they persist in haunting the novelist's house of fiction—as though they knew how spooky an old-fashioned English stately home could be.

Narrative Two: Individuals

"There was a general impression that Lydgate was something rather more uncommon than any general practitioner

---

[10] Kettle, *English Novel*, p. 171; and Quentin Anderson, "George Eliot in *Middlemarch*," in *The Pelican Guide to English Literature*, ed. Boris Ford, rev. ed., 7 vols. (Penguin, 1963-67), 6: 274-93, and rpt. in George R. Creeger, ed., *George Eliot: A Collection of Critical Essays*, pp. 141-60.

in Middlemarch. And this was true" (171). In a sense that far outstrips the community's perception of difference, Lydgate *is* a different breed of doctor, much as Dorothea *is* a different kind of woman. The difference that the community disingenuously imposes on them from without is also determined from within, by their own projects. "Je veux autre chose," a Zola heroine declares bluntly at the start of her story, and she might be speaking for the heroes of nineteenth-century fiction in general. All the protagonists of *Middlemarch* want "something else": something not yet possessed or even available in their community. In a full sense of the word, they *desire*, and it is partly this that makes them undesirables in a world that has dampened all ardor into the routine pursuit of routine satisfactions. Clearly, such desire threatens to engender stories of a significantly different quality from those that are engineered by the community. The community sees desire as the sign of a dangerous excess, and its narrative correspondingly moves to suppress it. The protagonists experience desire as a deficiency, and their "scripts" naively attempt to satisfy it. The community's narrative belongs to the genre of realism, and the protagonists' scripts to utopian fiction. Moreover, it is further evidence of the text's ultimate deference to its community that the narrative action, stopped short of directly rebutting the "realistic" telling, emphatically disconfirms all the assumptions behind the "utopian" one. Doubtless this fact helps to characterize it as utopian in the first place. Paradoxically, however, it is also obvious that the text values the feckless enterprises of its main characters far more highly than it does the cleanly enforced "achievement" of its community. In a double ambivalence fraught with psychological and ideological antagonisms (parent versus child, community versus romantic individualism), the text shows a respectful courtesy to what it clearly resents, while persecuting with clearheaded insight what it profoundly seems to cherish.

The implicit framework in which the protagonists form their narrative projects is most conveniently located in the Prelude. Nonnarratable plenitude would consist in "some illimitable satisfaction, some object which would never justify weariness, which would reconcile self-despair with the rapturous consciousness of life beyond self" (25). Significantly, no attempt is made to narrate St. Theresa's "epos" beyond indicating that she found it. It would be superfluous to tell of such satisfaction, even if it could be told. Theresa's life didn't of course end with her epos, but its further possibilities were fully encompassed by it. She found a guaranteed meaningfulness—a great good place to which all worldly signifiers, no matter how apparently problematic, ultimately pointed. Conventual claustration is merely the negative, secular emblem of this mystical and blessed closure. Narrative appropriately ceases where mysticism begins, for there is nothing more for a narrative to produce except anecdotally, again and again, the same "rapturous consciousness." Conversely, the narratable disequilibrium depends on a lapse from this blissful state into fallen nineteenth-century provincial England: with a gap between sign and meaning constituted by the lack of a "coherent social faith and order which could perform the function of knowledge" (25). In Theresa's case, of course, her Christian belief bridged the gap. Paradoxically, however, her faith never really needed to be "taken on faith"; as the text implies (with nostalgic simplification), it was supported by a whole social order. What the text laments in the nineteenth century is not a loss of faith, but a loss of its social "naturalization." In days when everyone, so to speak, took the leap of faith, it could perform "the function of knowledge." Yet one might also say that faith thus lost its defining character, as belief in what one *cannot* know. (The more natural, the less like a leap: "natura non facit saltum.") In a sense, faith only comes into its own when it is deprived of its social sanctions, and without knowing it, the nineteenth century would be a privileged moment. The problem of meaningfulness that it poses perversely *invites* acts and projects of faith, much as deficiencies invite desires to supply them.

As one of Dorothea's favorite authors, Bossuet, reminds us in his *Panégyrique de Sainte Thérèse*: "Il n'est rien de plus opposé que de vivre selon la nature et de vivre selon la grâce."[11] Yet for the main characters of *Middlemarch*, there is also nothing more tempting. They are all seduced by a dream of reconciliation that is formed by the very disparateness of the terms to be reconciled: on one hand, an unacceptable social routine that passes itself off as a state of nature, and on the other, a transcendent meaningfulness that is nothing less than a state of grace. Dorothea, for instance, wants to reconcile "thought" and "deed" (25); "some lofty conception of the world" and "the parish of Tipton and her own rule of conduct there" (30); "ignorance" and "the right conclusion" (53). She wants "everyday-things" to mean "the greatest things" (51), and she marries Casaubon because he seems to her to unite "the glories of doctor and saint" (47). Lydgate's ardor, too, is kindled by contradiction and inconsistency. "The medical profession as it might be was the finest in the world, presenting the most perfect interchange between science and art; offering the most direct alliance between intellectual conquest and the social good" (174). As it is, however, "it wanted reform." Lydgate would resist "the irrational severance between medical and surgical knowledge in the interest of his own scientific pursuits, as well as of the general advance" (174). Medical theory and practice would intimately collaborate: "The two purposes would illuminate each other: the careful observation and inference which was his daily work, the use of the lens to further his judgment in special cases, would further his thought as an instrument of larger inquiry" (176). Dorothea and Lydgate seem implicitly ruled by what Peter Brooks

[11] Jacques Bénigne Bossuet, *Oeuvres oratoires de Bossuet*, ed. J. Lebarq, rev. Ch. Urbain, and E. Levesque, 7 vols. (Bruges: Pairs, Desclée, de Brouwer et cie., 1926-27), 2: 387.

has called "the melodramatic sensibility," enacted as "the search to bring into the drama of man's quotidian existence the high drama of moral forces."[12] This uneasily but attractively double commitment—to the details of "everyday-things" and "daily work" and to a transcendent significance —aims at seeing both in deeply mutual implication. It is a mode of living the separation of the socially given and the metaphysically meaningful as an ethical insistence that they be joined.

Most characters in *Middlemarch* present versions of this commitment, each of which is developed in unique terms. Nevertheless, they can be classed under two distinguishable types, depending on which of the two claims bears the emphasis. On one side, there are those cases in which the mundane details of everyday life are elevated or overridden by a pretentious meaningfulness they cannot plausibly sustain. The artist Naumann is easily twitted with "his excess of meaning" (245), "the divinity passing into higher completeness and all but exhausted in the act of covering [his] bit of canvas" (221). Bulstrode bloats his shabby career into a providential design. In a travesty of the ethical quest, faith takes the parodic form of "bad faith": he can see himself as *acted through* and hence, however luxuriously tortured, never entirely responsible. With more of our sympathy,

[12] Peter Brooks, "The Melodramatic Imagination: The Example of Balzac and James," in *Romanticism: Vistas, Instances, Continuities*, ed. David Thorburn and Geoffrey Hartman (Ithaca: Cornell University Press, 1973), p. 218. See also Brooks's later full-length study, *The Melodramatic Imagination: Balzac, Henry James, Melodrama, and the Mode of Excess.*

Brooks's redefinition of the melodramatic in the nineteenth century could not be more suggestive to a reading of *Middlemarch*, and my own will need to come back to it later on. I should say now, however, that I shall be redirecting the implications of Brooks's case to more strictly formal uses. Without denying the extent to which melodrama is (as James would say) a "value intrinsic," I have been more struck with the way that it functions in *Middlemarch* as a "compositional resource"—in particular, as a key strategy of closure.

Dorothea and Lydgate indulge in a meaningfulness that is insufficiently concerned with its own incarnation. Both have a sense of large and nourishing metaphysical possibilities, but it tends to scant the resistances of the actual. At the other extreme, there are those cases in which attention to the mundane leads to a reduction of possibilities for meaning. Farebrother offers a fairly benign instance of this type—"he had not escaped that low estimate of possibilities which we rather hastily arrive at as an inference from our own failure" (218). Less benign, Rosamond's "easy conception of an unreal Better" also produces a low estimate of possibilities, with no awareness that its estimate is low (810). Her *bovarysme* is as petty as the world that dictates its terms. In their anxious desire for a meaningfulness that would transfigure the socially given, the characters in *Middlemarch* either minimize the quotidian, or succumb to it, shortchanging the rich range of meanings that might be made available.

Why do the characters never strike a proper balance? Rosamond's case is particularly instructive, because it virtually abolishes the difference between the immanence of "everyday-things" and the transcendence of "the greatest things." Transcendence here throws a glamorous but transparent veil over everyday possibilities that are extraordinary only in their banality. To the extent that Rosamond participates in the "melodramatic" enterprise, she unintentionally points to one of its unrecognized dangers—namely, that it has a parodic double in already established social routine. It is not hard to see certain affinities between "that beneficent harness of routine which enables silly men to live respectably and unhappy men to live calmly" and "some illimitable satisfaction, some object which would never justify weariness, which would reconcile self-despair with the rapturous consciousness of life beyond self." As we observed earlier, the social norm of the Middlemarch community posited itself as the end of narratable difference. By reference to local tradition, everyday signifiers took on spontaneous meaning, and the practice of everyday life could become nature itself.

In a crude but also fundamental sense, the protagonists of the novel are questing after what its maintaining individuals have already got: an unproblematic relationship between "thought" and "deed," between ideology and everyday social scenarios. Dorothea, Lydgate, Bulstrode all seek to find a similarly spontaneous meaning in everyday signs, though this meaning would no longer be a mere masked contingency, but one whose validity would be metaphysically or scientifically guaranteed. It shouldn't therefore be surprising that Dorothea and Lydgate willingly embrace domestic ties, or that Bulstrode's evangelism never interferes with his unexceptionable business instincts: St. Theresa was able to live according to nature as well as grace. Far from intending to do away with everyday routine, these characters seem only to want higher or more reflective versions of it, sanctioned by more exciting or spiritually worthy ideologies.

If they carry out a less balanced program than intended, however, the very homology between their enterprise and the community's bears a large responsibility. As René Girard has argued, when homologies lay claim to the same primacy, their rivalry easily risks becoming a play of mirrors. Although there are obvious ways to differentiate the operation of socially given routine from the project of its utopian subsumption, the symmetry seems fearful enough to deflect the characters' ambitions even as they are being formulated. With an otherwise inexplicable perversity, the project of reconciling "everyday-things" with "the greatest things" leads again and again to a willful *denial* of everyday things— as though only thus could it keep from becoming an all-but-identical duplication of community routine.

On her own view, for instance, Dorothea's initial decision to marry Casaubon would promise the much-desired interpenetration of both terms, social nature and metaphysical grace. The circumstantiality of her choice, however, suggests that she in fact chooses one term in precise and determining *opposition* to the other. Without her quite realizing it, Dorothea's interest in Casaubon is crucially promoted by being mediated through a corresponding lack of interest in Sir James. When Celia bluntly points out to her that she has encouraged the baronet's intentions, Dorothea is frankly revolted: "All her dear plans were embittered, and she thought with disgust of Sir James's conceiving that she recognized him as her lover" (59). Though the revulsion partly derives from an obvious sexual naiveté, it is more deeply inspired by a fear of misinterpretation. "What was life worth—what great faith was possible when the whole effect of one's actions could be withered up into such parched rubbish as that?" (60). What disgusts Dorothea is not so much the sense that Celia and Sir James have reductively misconstrued her, as the more disturbing sense that their misconstruction *looks correct*. What exceeds their interpretation of her consists of invisible longings, unacted dreams, and private nuances. It is thus dangerously easy to ignore the quality and intensity of her responses to life—to dismiss them as piquant eccentricities or mere fads. Dorothea is momentarily forced to envision the doubleness of her dealings, which in social terms bear a different meaning from their meaning (or problematic lack of it) in terms of her own "great faith." The same split that gave her faith something to negotiate also seems to make negotiation impossible, too much like recanting. Rather it is the social world that must be forsworn, if the faith in its higher harmonies is to be preserved with any distinctiveness. Dorothea's "disgust" is already a preliminary strategy of retreat from the everyday: in the role of an offended *belle âme*, she can see her actual plight as nightmarish unreality. With such an attitude, she returns home to find Casaubon's pamphlets waiting for her in the library. "It seemed as if an electric stream went through Dorothea, thrilling her from despair into expectation. . . . The oppression of Celia, Tantripp, and Sir James was shaken off. . . . She was getting away from Tipton and Freshitt, and her own sad liability to tread in the wrong places on her way to the New Jerusalem" (61). Plainly, the "despair" over Tipton and Freshitt, Celia and Sir James, and

the prospect of "getting away" from their "oppression" contribute decisively to the attractiveness of a New Jerusalem.
It is as though the only way Dorothea could salvage her own
interpretative scheme were a wholesale psychological denial
of the world from which rival interpretations issue. The
marriage of things great and small is made to show only for
their continuing divorce.

The deflection here depends on the ambiguous status of
the everyday: as a signifier, which characters like Dorothea
must raise into high meaningfulness, and as a signified, already meaningful in the community's competing system of
interpretation. The nature of the characters' quest presupposes a rejection of the everyday as a signified; otherwise
they could live quite happily within the orbit of social
norms. Yet to repudiate the everyday qua meaning makes
a difficult job of retaining it qua sign. In effect, the two rival
systems of uniting sign and meaning polarize one another,
according to what G. H. Lewes once neatly called "the bias
of opposition."[13] The community has so stigmatized the
everyday field that characters like Dorothea and Lydgate
haughtily tend to leave it alone. They let the community
monopolize it, while they insist on their monopoly of grander realms of meaning elsewhere.

As a result, their narrative scripts simply become attempts
to impose a necessary form on a content whose contingency
has been already put into parentheses.

> "I should learn everything then," she said to herself, still
> walking quickly along the bridle road through the wood.
> "It would be my duty to study that I might help him the
> better in his great works. There would be nothing trivial
> about our lives. Everyday-things with us would mean the
> greatest things. It would be like marrying Pascal. I should
> learn to see the truth by the same light as great men have

[13] George Henry Lewes, "Dickens in Relation to Criticism," *Fort-
nightly Review* 17 (1872), rpt. in *Literary Criticism of George Henry
Lewes*, p. 99.

seen it by. And then I should know what to do, when I got older: I should see how it was possible to live a grand life here—now—in England." (51)

What Dorothea wants is clear: a world in which daily experience would have a cognitive transparency, and conduct would immediately translate into the moral necessity of duty. She proposes to herself a kind of apocalypse. After a revelatory moment virtually abolishing all further history, her life could become the straightforward practice of revealed truths. Yet the way in which Dorothea imagines this resolution betrays a telling sleight of hand. "And *then* I should know what to do, *when I got older*. I should see how it was possible to lead a grand life *here—now*—in England." What is at first a desired future is subtly absorbed into the present. Time has collapsed under the urgency of desire like the folds of a fan. What has begun as the project of transfiguration gets fatally mixed up with its imagined achievement. Dorothea's daydream anxiously solicits a narrative that it also complacently dispenses with.

The scripts of desire in Middlemarch are generally entrapped within this fantasy of foreclosure. The sequence between lack and its liquidation is made minimally complicated, or at least, any complications are held to be ultimately irrelevant. "When Fred got into debt, it always seemed to him highly probable that something or other—he did not necessarily conceive what—would come to pass enabling him to pay in due time" (163). Rosamond is convinced that Will Ladislaw's coming to visit will be a potent cause of Lydgate's going from Middlemarch, "without at all seeing how."

This way of establishing sequences is too common to be fairly regarded as a peculiar folly in Rosamond. And it is precisely this sort of sequence which causes the greatest shock when it is sundered: for to see how an effect may be produced is often to see possible missings and checks;

but to see nothing except the desirable cause, and close upon it the desirable effect, rids us of doubt and makes our minds strongly intuitive. (827)

The force of transitions is underplayed or altogether ignored. It is an article of faith that closure will eventually incorporate whatever immediately resists it into its grand pattern. Lest "to see how an effect may be produced" be "to see possible missings and checks," mediations (time, circumstance, the other) are reduced to vacant mediums in which desire transacts without a hitch. Indeterminate middles, they are eclipsed in the glory of the end. And as Dorothea's own temporal confusion betrays, the glory of the end tends to be lived *in place of* the here and now. She enjoys her marital prospect as though it were already her future utopia, much as the conduct of Lydgate or Casaubon presupposes the eminence that neither has yet achieved. Will Ladislaw is made easy in advance by his "generous reliance on the intentions of the universe with regard to himself" (109), and Fred Vincy by "the superfluous securities of hope at his command" (262). Fred would be only the most literal instance of a series of characters who live their lives on credit, borrowing upon future expectations.

As narratives, the wishful sequences proposed by these characters are little more than tautologies, seeking to reproduce what is already there in anticipation. Dorothea "had looked deep into the ungauged reservoir of Mr Casaubon's mind, seeing reflected there in vague labyrinthine extension every quality she herself brought" (46), and Fred "fancied that he saw to the bottom of his uncle Featherstone's soul, though in reality half what he saw there was no more than the reflex of his own inclinations" (147). Lydgate "had prearranged his social action" well before coming to Middlemarch (211). When he and Rosamond exchange bashful glances of recognition, the result, called falling in love, "was just what Rosamond had contemplated beforehand"; "she had woven a little future, of which something like this scene was the necessary beginning" (145). Indeed, "Rosamond had registered every look and word, and estimated them as the opening incidents of a preconceived romance— incidents which gather value from the foreseen development and climax" (195). No wonder that transitional mediations seem parenthetical, when all that is wanted is merely to duplicate the correspondences already assumed between dilemma and resolution, merit and desert, agent and action. One might say that Dorothea, Lydgate, Rosamond, and Fred wish to live their lives as though they were traditional novels, in which little can happen except the suspenseful delay of an outcome foreseen from the very beginning.

As embodied in their fantasies, however, the tautology of narrative form involves more than "merely" formal matters. Invariably, for instance, it coincides with a psychology of the ego, "taking the world as an udder" to feed its supremacy (243). Defined as "the flattering illusion of a concentric arrangement" and as "an exclusive optical selection," egoism compulsively tidies up the field of vision according to a single desired perspective. Dorothea, Rosamond, and Fred easily find what they have shaped their perspective to see, and Lydgate complains of unsightly blotches in his prearranged prospect as "a ridiculous piece of bad logic" (210). Neither loose nor baggy, the scripts of egoism are nevertheless monsters, based on a moral indifference to the other. Dorothea hasn't yet learned that Casaubon "had an equivalent centre of self, whence the lights and shadows must always fall with a certain difference" (243), and "the difficult task of knowing another soul" is not for young gentlemen like Fred "whose consciousness is chiefly made up of their own wishes" (147). In Rosamond's romance, "it was not necessary to imagine much about the inward life of the hero, or of his serious business in the world"—both she and Lydgate "each lived in a world of which the other knew nothing" (195). Moreover, egoism seems equivalent to a more prestigious form of blindness:

The universal order of things would necessarily be agreeable to an agreeable young gentleman . . . he at least
(whatever might be maintained about mankind generally)
had a right to be free of anything disagreeable. That he
should ever fall into a thoroughly unpleasant position—
wear trousers shrunk from washing, eat cold mutton, have
to walk for want of a horse, or to "duck under" in any sort
of way—was an absurdity irreconcilable with those cheerful intuitions implanted in him by nature. (262-63)

Fred's fatuous confidence that "the universal order of
things" will conform to the particular order of his desires
is undoubtedly meant to parody the main assumptions of
"metaphysics" as the novelist understood them. Bernard J.
Paris has usefully shown how, on the views of the positivists
from whom George Eliot learned, metaphysics was always
characterized by an unacceptable epistemological redundancy. The world and the subject, the structure of reality
and the structure of thought, merely mirrored one another,
and any discrepancies were only apparent, to be ultimately
worked out in the course of a teleological unfolding. Not
only would experience be unproblematical under these assumptions, the positivists argued, it would virtually be dispensable.[14] A workaday version of these "cheerful intuitions" nevertheless rules the narrative program of the main
characters of *Middlemarch*, who are (in a highly significant
constellation of naiveté) idealist philosophers, blinded ego-
centrics, and traditional novelists all at once.

This narrative program, of course, is destined to general
failure: "reality," or the realist text, unmoors it. As I have
been arguing, the anchors of traditional narrative are basically a system of restraints imposed on the field of the
narratable. A story is centered through the establishment of
a well-policed periphery, where narratable potentialities are
either nullified, reined in, or denied importance. Order and

---

[14] Bernard J. Paris, "George Eliot's Religion of Humanity," *ELH*
29 (December 1962): 418-43, rpt. in Creeger, *Critical Essays*, pp. 11-36.

orientation are thus secured by clear distinctions of relevance: between round characters, full of intriguing possibilities, and flat ones, reduced to a prescribed function or gesture that they aren't allowed to overstep; between the primary notation that constitutes an important sequence and the subsidiary notation that is felt merely to fill it in; between motifs that are bound in a pattern of inescapable coherence and motifs that are free to be deleted or not without substantially altering the story. As the *Middlemarch* characters attempt to realize their narrative program, these distinctions simply become untenable. Every effort to simplify and to restrict the narratable is refuted by enormous complication and expansion. Every sequence is sundered by possibilities it had overlooked. Middles and mediations—what the text calls *mediums* ("unfriendly," "petty," "embroiled," "dim and clogging")—elude the time-killing or merely catalytic function assigned to them, and actually deflect from the ending that they were meant to reach. For instance, Dorothea, Casaubon, Rosamond, and Lydgate all initially cast their spouses in the limited role of a Proppian "donor" or a Jamesian "ficelle": helpmates who will do nothing but help. In every case, the "compositional resource" insists on becoming a "value intrinsic," with the surprising power to instigate unforeseen developments. Similarly, Fred Vincy goes to trade horses, assured that the episode will be merely a catalyst in his prearranged scheme for getting out of debt; but the catalyst precipitates an outcome of its own, and Fred has afterward less money than before. Lydgate imagines that his vote for the chaplaincy is irrelevant to the larger shape of his life (a "free motif"), all the while his life is given shape by precisely such repeated failures of attention. The wills of Featherstone and Casaubon are both ultimately overthrown by posthumous developments that they were written to ensure against: Fred eventually settles in Stone Court, as Dorothea eventually marries Will. In one form or another, each character's attempt to impose narrative order is frustrated by a counterfinality. Projected

ends are forever lost in the incessant "retarding friction" of
the means. Circumstances—what the text calls their "force,"
their "small solicitations"—overwhelm the definitive pattern meant to keep them under supervision. As Lydgate
thinks, with a more general application than he intends,
"The circumstances would always be stronger than his assertion" (794).

When his asserted order fails, or is threatened with failure,
a character is occasionally overcome by a vision of all possible orders collapsed into chaos. The world becomes a
jumble of narrative fragments that can never be unified in
any meaningful organization. Rosamond sees her little world
"in ruins," and "she felt herself tottering in the midst as a
lonely bewildered consciousness" (837). One recalls, too,
Dorothea's hallucinated view of the "stupendous fragmen-
tariness" of "unintelligible Rome," a "vast wreck of ambitious ideals" (224-25); her depressed reflections on Casaubon's manuscripts, as "fragments of a tradition which was
itself a mosaic wrought from crushed ruins" (519); and the
initial havoc of her feelings after she has surprised Rosamond together with Will. Yet order fails in *Middlemarch*
much more readily than it disappears, and such visions of
pure chaos are only momentary. Are they the mere exag-
gerations of egocentric heartbreak, rightly moderated and
passed beyond? or do they represent the ultimate "truth" of
the text, which no one—including the narrator—is *able* to
sustain? (The ambiguity will be important in shaping the
narrator's own performance, which oddly combines a confidence in his superior version of narrative order with a
hesitant, almost sotto voce confession of its ultimate inadequacy.) At any rate, the visions scare the characters with
enlargements of the same inconsistency that they originally
wanted their narratives to eliminate. Rosamond is so terrified
that she almost loses "the sense of her identity" (836). Inevitably, the characters turn to revised orders, which—however pessimistic, inadequate, or simply blind—have the considerable advantage of keeping identity and its life story

whole and in one piece. It is easier to rewrite the story when it is disconfirmed than to forgo the psychological and moral forms of integrity inherent in the fully narrated.[15]

The most pessimistic kind of rewriting is the sheer admission of failure. When an experiment goes wrong, there at least remains the orderly satisfaction of calling it a failed experiment. Some *Middlemarch* characters salvage the order of their life stories only in this meager way: through an explicit acknowledgment that, due to unforeseen circumstances, the story anticipated by them will not take place. "There is no sorrow I have thought more about than that— to love what is great, and try to reach it, and yet to fail" (821), Dorothea tells Lydgate, in a mutual recognition. Though Lydgate becomes "a successful man," "he always regarded himself as a failure: he had not done what he once meant to do"; and though Dorothea never repents of marrying Will, she still feels "that there was always something better which she might have done, if she had only been better and known better" (893). Bulstrode, too, has a "quick vision that his life was after all a failure" (781). Yet it seems crucial to distinguish the failure of these characters from actual disillusionment. None of them wakes up, like Swann in Proust, to the bitter knowledge that he has wasted years of his life pursuing a chimera. Just as Bulstrode holds on to his religion, Dorothea and Lydgate continue to regard the utopia in which everyday things mean the greatest things as the ideal orientation of their lives. They never question its value or even really its possibility. The original project (what Lydgate meant to do, what Dorothea might have done, if she had been better and known better) may be frustrated, but it still insistently governs the perception of disarray. Mistaken paths function as implicit reminders of

15 What I should call the psychological modalities of closure in literature have been brilliantly discussed by Leo Bersani in *A Future for Astyanax: Character and Desire in Literature*. I have particularly profited from the chapter entitled "Realism and the Fear of Desire," which contains a brief but useful treatment of *Middlemarch*.

the proper but untraveled direction, and ignorant blunders as inferences of perfect but inaccessible knowledge. If only as an opposite, counterfinality points to the initial *telos*. Defining itself as the negative image of a successful transcendence, failure is a bottom-line strategy of paying homage to it. As such, it has the same closural force as a happy ending might have had. It preserves the wholeness of a life story and the related wholeness of its agent. In a sense, too, it even preserves the "happy ending," as the only interpretative perspective able to make final sense of the actual, unhappy outcome.

Yet not all the characters in *Middlemarch* fail, or fail completely: another form of closural rewriting involves a more agreeable retreat to the stabilizing forms of order immanent in social convention. Despite their confidence in some grandly unspecified destiny, Fred Vincy and Will Ladislaw have aspired in practice to a narrative of playful aimlessness. We can think of Fred's gambling as an undeclared fondness for indeterminacy, for unpredictable, rapidly shifting orders; and of his motley bachelor pleasures in general as perpetual distractions from a unified design. His desire is willingly dismembered among various options, so long as it is not castrated by irrevocable choices. Fred wants what proves impossible in the realist text: a narrative that will not limit his possibilities. In a world that includes the presence of uncoercible others, however, limits will be imposed with or without his consent. Featherstone's will removes his hope of fortune; his father sends him back to college in preparation for holy orders; and if he takes them, Mary refuses to marry him. With much help and even more sheer luck, Fred is able to reduce his desire to the scale of what "reality" can actually satisfy. At least part of desire's full program is thus preserved, in the role of a gentleman-farmer married to his heart's love. In the end, Fred is perfectly adjusted to the conventionally limited order that he had wanted—naively and half-heartedly—to transcend.

In a more deliberate and viable tack, Will Ladislaw has

avoided conventional limits through an incessant self-trans-
formation. Even his face is protean: "Surely, his very features changed their form; his jaw looked sometimes large
and sometimes small; and the little ripple in his nose was a
preparation for metamorphosis" (241). Significantly, he
thrives on "the very miscellaneousness of Rome, which made
the mind flexible with constant comparison . . . the fragments stimulated his imagination and made him constructive" (244). Of course, Dorothea's or Lydgate's response to
"fragments" is also "constructive," but their constructions
are directed toward a final, all-embracing totality. What
Will constructs is typically more modest—a charming drawing, a witty verbal conceit: momentary or transient appre-
ciations well short of full self-engagements. In apparent protest against "too one-sided a life," he declines to choose a
profession, having no "special object, save the vague purpose
of what he calls culture, preparation for he knows not what"
(239, 106). As Casaubon fittingly recognizes, his dilettantism
refuses the classical order of beginning, middle, and end:

> "I have insisted to him on what Aristotle has stated with
> admirable brevity, that for the achievement of any work
> regarded as an end there must be a prior exercise of many
> energies or acquired facilities of a secondary order, de-
> manding patience. . . . To careful reasoning of this kind
> he replies by calling himself Pegasus, and every form of
> prescribed work 'harness'." (107)

Yet it is his uniquely pliable appreciativeness that makes Will
ultimately susceptible to the seductions of form. His response to Dorothea is an unforeseen but not wholly illogical
consequence of his aestheticism, the fatal attraction exerted
on sophistication by the primitive. Dorothea is "adorably
simple and full of feeling"; "it would be a unique delight to
wait and watch for the melodious fragments in which her
heart and soul came forth so directly and ingenuously"
(241). One thinks of Henry James's fondness for Balzac, or
the Pre-Raphaelites' for the Quattrocento. Dorothea is a

living allusion to the possible satisfactions of naive (but also aesthetically "simple") commitments. "But for the desire to be where Dorothea was," Will would never be fighting the political struggles of Reform; "he would probably have been rambling in Italy sketching plans for several dramas, trying prose and finding it too jejune, trying verse and finding it too artificial, beginning to copy 'bits' from old pictures, leaving off because they were 'no good,' and observing that, after all, self-culture was the principal point" (501). It is as though Will abandons the order of surprise and discontinuity that he has been experimenting with because it can't match the qualitative intensities of Dorothea's aspiring holism. The consistency of Dorothea's character offers so strong and simple a unity that it virtually commands imitation by one whose life has been programmatically dispersive. Moreover, it is impossible to divorce Dorothea's appeal (primarily, I'd say, the attractiveness of formal coherence) from its underlying morality. Much as Beatrice provided Dante with erotic, poetic, and religious incentives in a single form, both simple and overwhelmingly suggestive, the beauty of Dorothea's character captivates Will in order to initiate him into a new life based on a "sense of duty." She makes him feel that "the quality of [his] action is not a matter of indifference" (501), and the association of "quality" with both aesthetic appreciation and moral excellence points to the double advantages of settlement.

It may seem pointless to insist, in the case of either Will or Fred, on the renunciations required for closure. Not much is sacrificed when Fred forgoes his irresponsible bachelor freedom to settle down with Mary in Stone Court—at least nothing that the text has trained us to care about. There is of course more to be said in favor of Will's original ambition: if his "mode of taking all life as a holiday" shocks Dorothea, she also finds in it "a source of greater freedom" (239, 242). Nevertheless, it too is surely well lost on Dorothea's behalf and in the cause of political reform. In the case of Dorothea herself, however, the conventional marriage solution (with its typical novelistic attributes of youth, fertility, and happiness) entertains a more disturbingly discrepant relationship with the original problem. Henry James noted with disapproval that Dorothea's story gets ultimately restricted to the question, Will she or will she not marry Will Ladislaw? "The question seems relatively trivial and the implied struggle factitious."[16] Yet to feel the inconsequence of the ending is also implicitly to recognize the claims being made for its traditional problem-solving appropriateness. If her second marriage in no sense answered the questions that have oriented Dorothea's life, it would not raise the same issue of its "slender poetic justice." Closure would be read as an ironic or tragic abandonment of *all* terms of the problem. Only to the extent that the ending is presented as a proper resolution does it seem unsatisfactorily restricted. We need therefore to ask: how is Dorothea's story restricted? how does the course of narrative rewrite her desire so that her second marriage represents an apparently (but not really) fitting satisfaction?

What happens—in a process of symbolic transference reminiscent of Claude Lévi-Strauss's theory of myth—is that the original unsolvable opposition between "the meanness of opportunity" and an "epic life" is replaced by an equivalent but reduced opposition between Casaubon and Will. By marrying Casaubon, Dorothea commits herself to an imagined solution that in fact only produces a restatement of the problem. Yet the restatement of the problem has the advantage of localizing its terms. Casaubon comes to symbolize everything that frustrates Dorothea's aspirations, which are thus refocused on what he most specifically enjoins her against: his cousin Will. As Mrs. Cadwallader puts it, Casaubon "made himself disagreeable . . . and then dared her to contradict him" (875). For Casaubon *can* be contradicted. His codicil, unlike the general social-metaphysical interdiction that it reductively exemplifies, can be broken.

[16] James, *Galaxy* review, p. 355.

Dorothea may not be able to perform a "far-resonant action," but it is a much easier business to marry Will Ladislaw. Synecdoche here is a highly ambiguous figure, both allowing for a closural solution and reducing the full dimensions of the problem. As a result, Dorothea's story is at once fittingly concluded and irrelevantly sidetracked. She herself seems puzzled by the status of her satisfaction when she announces: "It is quite true that I might be a wiser person, Celia, and that I might have done something better, if I had been better. But this is what I am going to do. I have promised to marry Mr Ladislaw; and I am going to marry him" (879-80). It is as though, knowing that this settlement only *appears* to satisfy her original and still persisting desire, she gratefully makes do with the appearance.

In general, the forms of closure managed by the protagonists ratify either a surrender of desire or its reductive rescaling. They are not proper endings in the sense of a neat quid pro quo, a clean solution to the problem that set events moving. The problem out of which Dorothea and Lydgate shape their stories remains unsolved. In her case, it is deceptively brought to term by being converted into an easier, different problem; in his, it is simply dropped: *non liquet*. True, their narratives derive a high degree of consistency from the original contradiction that they were supposed to resolve. Yet as we have seen in Dorothea's story, this consistency masks a logic of reformulation and transference that easily issues in a felt *in*consistency of solution. As a *revised* order, closure always implies a background of renunciation, sacrifice, and loss. It can never therefore provide an organization wholly adequate to the narrative that has preceded it. In *Middlemarch*, however, the specific reason why traditional settlement (marriage, family, career) is not an adequate solution is that the problem has been to find a settlement transcending these conventional arrangements. (The alternative community in which Dorothea and Will are relocated requires only a very ordinary tolerance to secure them the full benefits of social integration.) Characters retreat to the satisfactions of routine and social nature that they began by ambitiously rejecting. Without denying the obvious if partial advantages of so doing, the text never lets us forget that this is not what they "meant to do" or "might have done."

Yet "the medium in which . . . ardent deeds took shape is for ever gone" (896). Under these circumstances, what a character like Dorothea might have done is a baffling question, which neither she nor the text knows how to answer. It is probably in the nature of her desire that it *couldn't* be specified by a logically consequent fulfillment. Better than any other (why always Dorothea indeed?), her case points to the incompatibility of a transcendent, totalizing desire with its actual medium. The medium is easily named "nineteenth-century society," or alternatively, "the limits of grown-up reality"; but the workings of this society and this reality coincide with a more fundamental pertinence of the text: the novelistic system of narrative itself. We have been suggesting that narrativity dooms the characters' dreams of transcendence in two major ways: by dispersing them and by replacing them. Transcendent desire must always seem degraded when it is carried by metonymical sequences and synecdochical transferences that inevitably make fractions of it. It comes to inhere in its mediations—to get stuck in them. At a telling moment in his autobiography, the young André Gide refuses to tell a schoolmate about his uniquely inspirational love for his cousin Emmanuèle: "C'était le bloc d'une fortune immense, un lingot qui ne se laissait pas monnayer."[17] His silence is intuitively shrewd: he knows that to commit the secret of his transcendence to the elaborate alienations of narrative—or even language— must be to convert his precious bullion into small change. Like language itself, narrative intrinsically tends to subvert the categories of the whole, the irreplaceable, the authentic:

[17] André Gide, *Si le grain ne meurt*, in *Oeuvres complètes*, ed. L. Martin-Chauffier, 15 vols. (Paris: Nouvelle Revue Française, 1932-39), 10: 195.

fragmentation is a consequence of its syntagmatic nature, substitution a part of its logic of expansion, and mediation its central figure.[18] Narrative is thus a domain in which the absoluteness of value is *risked*, where nothing can be got whole or all at once.

Jane Austen resisted the subversions of narrative by having her characters suddenly wake up from it as from a bad dream, and by suggesting that it shouldn't (and needn't) have developed in the first place. If she didn't bracket her narrative in such ways, a full closural meaning might no longer be convincingly above the fray—or *frayage*—of relativizing mediations and displaced desires. In *Middle-march*, however, no authorial confirmation blesses the notion that the system of narrative might have been avoided (say, if Dorothea "had only been better and known better").[19] Not to enter the sphere of narrative translations is out of the question, and what is lost in translation is the original version. It is as though narrative didn't possess an adequate vocabulary to reader projects of transcendence, and could only clumsily approximate them in paraphrastic constructions that finally missed the point. When Jane Austen's precautions are no longer taken, then the implications of narrative find expression in one of the nineteenth-

---

[18] See Roland Barthes, "Introduction à l'analyse structurale des recits"; and René Girard, *Mensonge romantique et vérité romanesque*.

[19] In the first edition of the novel, George Eliot did imply that, in a well-ordered society, Dorothea's narrative need never have taken place. The Finale included this passage: "Among the many remarks passed on her mistakes, it was never said in the neighbourhood of Middlemarch that such mistakes could not have happened if the society into which she was born had not smiled on propositions of marriage from a sickly man to a girl less than half his own age—on modes of education which make a woman's knowledge another name for motley ignorance—on rules of conduct which are in flat contradiction with its own loudly-asserted beliefs." The passage would certainly make the novel more comforting (at least to present-day sensibilities—the first readers were disturbed by its quasi-feminist tones). Yet, as George Eliot knew, the implications of the narrative that has preceded this passage are better served by deleting it.

century novel's favorite themes: the impossibility of transcendence.

It is naturally an unhappy theme, and on the whole, *Middlemarch* pursues the logic of narrative process in a mood of sad resignation. The resignation carries some less sad possibilities, however. Systematically denied by the derogations of narrative, transcendence survives as the perspective from which they make sense. Precisely because it is never fulfilled, moreover, transcendent desire reinforces the tendency of narrative to remain in suspense. One might even say that it is the most available source of energy for continuing the attempt to write out that suspense. "The effect of [Dorothea's] being on those around her was incalculably diffusive" (896). One would regret the diffusion more, if it didn't hold in reserve a narratable future and a prospect of change.

Narrative Three: God

Middlemarch, we have observed, betrays crucial ambivalences toward the narrative ambitions of both its community and its characters. The only site for squaring such ambivalences—if indeed they are to be squared—is the narrator's own improved version of narrative organization. His[20] su-

[20] My use of masculine pronouns to identify George Eliot's narrator is meant to call attention to the problem of *gender* in the relationship between the novelist and her persona. In her earliest work, *Scenes of Clerical Life*, the narrator is plainly a male: he even recalls for us his first appearance in coattails! In the later fiction, such unequivocal evidence of masculinity disappears, but the narrator is still far from assuming a feminine gender. George Eliot preserved her male pseudonym long after it had been exposed, and she sometimes playfully used masculine forms to refer to herself even in letters. The role of the masculine mask in the novelist's psychic economy would be well worth knowing.

Even if the problem of gender never existed, of course, there would be formal grounds for not identifying the novelist with her narrator. The doctrine of the latter may be indistinguishable from the novelist's own, but his dramatic weight (as a presence felt more in some places

perior retelling of the novel, according to demonstrably different valences, is meant to resolve the text's ambiguous loyalties, divided between an ideal of community (achieved but discredited) and romantic projects of transcendence (valorized but dismantled). Most of the notable formal features of *Middlemarch* are easily seen as part of a reaction formation intended to counter the defectiveness of other perspectives on its materials. The reparations are obvious when we pass from the community's tyrannical blindness and the characters' egocentrism to the narrator's tolerant intelligence and his multiple points of view; or from the logic of lapsed mediation to the concern announced in the title with intermediate, transitional zones. The narrator's activity presupposes that the liabilities of other tellings will be rectified, prevented, or reduced to a negligible minimum in his own.

Such confidence, of course, derives from the traditional privilege of the narrator in the nineteenth-century novel, the "monological" control described by Mikhail Bakhtin. The narrator's all-embracing field of vision inherently enjoys an overwhelming superiority of information over the competing orders of perception such as are furnished by characters, social formations, hypothetical readers, or the stereotypes of other fiction. In consequence, Bakhtin argues, "every struggle of two voices for possession of and dominance in the word in which they appear is decided in advance —it is a sham struggle; all fully significant authorial interpretations are sooner or later gathered together in a single verbal center and in a single consciousness, and all accents are gathered together in a single voice."[21] One might add that this dramatized revision of rival orders is what constitutes their typical inferiority and the equally typical superi-

---

than in others) is more clearly separable. One might say that while the narrator's discourse is merely *in* the novel, the novelist's discourse quite simply *is* the novel.

[21] Mikhail Bakhtin, *Problems of Dostoevsky's Poetics*, p. 168.

ority of the novel's own vision. If the monological novel can never lose its sham struggles, it nevertheless *requires* them, as a source of increased plausibility. Its claims to truth become more believable through a repeatedly demonstrated power to confute or subordinate other claims. An effect of relative improvement is thus built into the very structure of the novel's perceptions. Since the logic of this effect rather easily carries an ideological program, it is no surprise that the narrator of *Middlemarch* finds the conventions of monologism an appropriate vehicle for expressing an urgent moral vision. Indeed, as we shall see, the very privileges accorded to the narrator come to be recast as forms of moral practice, and the tenets of meliorism and the quasi-melioristic implications of monological structure are made to reinforce one another. The conventions of writing and reading the novel will prove to contain its most basic model for "the growing good of the world."

Yet to describe *Middlemarch* wholly from within the terms of monological convention—as though its adequacy as a form could be taken for granted—is to be more generous to the novel than it is to itself. The critique of traditional form developed out of the other, subordinated tellings is sometimes sweepingly general, potentially applicable to *any* narrative oriented toward full closure. Just as the community's project deflected the characters' different but homologous project, we might see both projects exerting a pressure on the narrator's own—forcing it into ambiguity and self-irony if only to preserve its superior awareness. While an overriding ethical imperative directs the text toward a finalizing configuration of meaning, a subtle epistemological doubt is calling this enterprise into question.

The narrator's perception of *Middlemarch* is governed by an ideal of *sympathy*—or as he says, "a sense of fellowship deep enough to make all efforts at isolation seem mean and petty" (454). The dynamics of immured but colliding egos provide the narratable complications and expansions of the story, while the dramatic manifestations of fellowship in a "cry from soul to soul" have the force of closure. The ideal of sympathy is typically evoked in the narrator's most authoritative tones: "There is no general doctrine which is not capable of eating out our morality if unchecked by the deep-seated habit of direct fellow-feeling with individual fellow-men" (668). The distinction drawn between general doctrines and direct fellow feeling plays a crucial part in legitimizing his narrative perspective: based on no mere dogma, but on a deep-seated and virtually instinctive morality. Sympathetic fellowship is offered as an all-but-natural touchstone by which ideologies are tested and—at least in part—found wanting. Like the equivalent touchstones of "connection" in E. M. Forster or "life" in D. H. Lawrence, sympathy has a strategic double valence: far below, and therefore far above, the threshold of ideology. By its "deep," quasi-primal character, it is exalted to a position of transcendence, held aloft from the distortions of "doctrines."

Yet the text also places this vertical transcendence in horizontal relationship to such doctrines. The *nature* of sympathy may be supra-ideological, but its actual *role* is not. This is to figure as a kind of doctrinal compromise, or middle position, between the ideologies of community and romantic individualism. Defined as an interpersonal process able to penetrate through superficial layers of being to psychological and moral depths, sympathy is clearly poised between the characters' solipsistic egoism and the community's coercive banality. It inspires the religion of humanity on which the hopes both for a better community and for a more workable transcendence are founded. The narrator's perspective thus functions to rewrite, in a soluble form, the dilemmas posed at other levels of the novel. We have already touched on the notorious ambiguity of such rewriting, solving problems but also co-opting them in an alien frame of discourse. Readers of *Middlemarch* frequently complain about the inadequacy of suggesting that a community might be based upon an ideal of interpersonal relationships; or of implying that Dorothea's ambitions might be ultimately

achieved along the lines of her final melodramatic encounters with Rosamond and Will. Yet the mystification here is
too visible really to mystify, and these complaints about it
are actually backhanded recognitions of the text's full inscription of its difficulties. As we shall see, the narrator's
formation carries everywhere within it the imprint of the
discrepancies that it would seem to sublate. In every resolution offered by this formation, therefore, we shall have to
attend to the persistence of contradiction, dissatisfaction, and
incommensurability.

A major site of such equivocal sublation is the text's highly
developed system of narratorial asides, constructed on an
important opposition between what Emile Benveniste has
called "story" and "discourse." Story encompasses the series
of events whose existence is assumed to be self-generating;
discourse refers narration to its source in a situation of communication, an intersubjective relationship between an "I"
and a "you."[22] Few things are more impressive in *Middlemarch* than the narrator's finely balanced commitment both
to the opaque and ordinary experience making up the story
and to the philosophical, scientific, and moral commentary
propelling the discourse. The narrator may pay humble
compliment to Fielding's regularly spaced digressions (170),
but he is implicitly proud of the fact that his own discourse
is far more interwoven with the fabric of the story. It needs
to be, as part of his attempt to anneal the fragile coherence
of "everyday-things" and "the greatest things." Yet the very
distinction we are invited to make between story and discourse dramatizes a gap between them. Materials and their
organization, signs and the meanings produced by their interpretation, are kept on formally separate tracks, as though
there were no natural or automatic transition between them.

Indeed, the narrator's discourse often turns on the comic
or pathetic ironies ensuing from such incommensurability:

[22] Benveniste makes this distinction in "Les relations de temps dans
le verbe français," *Problèmes de linguistique générale*, pp. 237-50.

An eminent philosopher among my friends, who can dig-
nify even your ugly furniture by lifting it into the serene
light of science, has shown me this pregnant little fact.
(297)

Does the wit of this sentence tell against the furniture,
whose ugly triviality is unworthy of being dignified? or
against the "eminent" philosopher, whose appropriation of
it already risks being the inflationary demonstration of a
Molièresque savant? In either case, the ironic, bemused
tones suggest that tenor and vehicle, irreducibly discrepant,
resist adequation. All of this would matter less if the passage
didn't then go on to bring forward the famous image of the
pier glass, whose random scratches are falsified by "a lighted
candle" into a "concentric arrangement." The "light" of
science becomes considerably less serene in the context of
an imagery that links it with this distorting "centre of il-
lumination." "The scratches are events, and the candle is the
egoism of any person now absent." "Any person now absent" is another instance of wit, seemingly exempting but of
course implicating those persons now present. Yet who is
more present at the moment than the narrator himself? And
what is he doing other than centering the novel? And what
else does he center it on but an insight that undermines the
validity of centers? The entire passage insists on being radically paradoxical: it unites everyday things with the greatest
things in ironical language that keeps them apart; and it
centers the novel's events and themes in the very metaphor
that casts most doubt on such centering.

In short, it is implied that the narration shares the problematic quality of the world that it narrates. Again and
again, the narrator betrays the doubtful reality of the connections that his generalizing language makes with the story
by way of grasping it. Indeed, the explicitly discursive dimension of the narration lays stress on the exclusively *verbal*
nature of these connections. Behind them, obliquely pointed
to by the self-awareness of narratorial commentary, is a

frustrated relationship between language and the reality that language is supposed to represent and study. The structure of irony developed in the narration does more than discredit the traditional forms of order deployed by the characters or the community; it undercuts its own presumptive validity. To this extent, George Eliot is less removed from her contemporary Flaubert than is commonly realized. And yet her worries about the status of novelistic form are a far cry from his flat epistemological despair. Her narrator, unlike his, is never half in love with easeful silence. If he knows that talk overreaches and at the same time falls short of its object, he also insists on the ways in which it is insightful and productive. Let every attempt to grasp reality in narrative form involve a distortion by desire, ideology, language itself. He at least will give full play to the attempt, recognized in all its self-contradicting but perhaps also self-correcting variousness. On sheer moral ground, he finds the courage to be naive.

It is difficult to overstate the narrator's moral urgency, since he moralizes even the conventions of his own form. The most basic gestures of the monologizing narrator, the most ordinary reflexes of the monologized reader, are consistently overdetermined as paradigms of moral action. The reader's relation to the narrator, for instance, becomes no less than a formal enactment of the fellow feeling and self-transcendence lacked by the characters. To be sure, the reader is generally depicted as a figure of moral complacency: often prissy, cynical, stupid, always seemingly reluctant to give the sympathy solicited from him. It is feared that his taste will be offended by the "ungenteel" representation of Featherstone's vulgar relations (375); or that his patience will be tried by the lovingly detailed quaintness of Caleb Garth (265); or that his intelligence will reduce the subtle mixture of motives in Bulstrode to a dose of sheer hypocrisy (667). He will be steeled against the tragic dimension of Dorothea's tearful honeymoon by a jaded spirit of familiarity (226), and he will feel that Lydgate's money troubles are "miserably sordid, and beneath [his] attention" (698). Indeed, one is tempted to bring against the narrator the same charge that Dorothea makes against Casaubon: "You speak to me as if I were something you had to contend with" (316). Surely the reader for whom this intimidatingly wise novel is written cannot be the benighted creature presupposed in the narrator's addresses. (Like Minta in *To the Lighthouse*, the narrator's reader would probably abandon the third volume on the train.) Yet this misses the moral demonstration intended by such a strategy. The caricature exists precisely so that the reader may disaffiliate himself from it. With an easy inevitability, he transcends the portrait of himself to underwrite the narrator's perspective and to collaborate in his "we." The monologism of the novel— the legislated superiority of the narrator's insights—leaves him no other alternative. He thus automatically bears witness to the "life beyond self," because the characterization of him is already surpassed by the mere act of reading the novel. His perfectly orthodox responses are implicitly read by the text as acts of going beyond the reader he is assumed to be, or might otherwise have been. More than the narrator's distant vision, self-transcendence is offered as the reader's actual experience.

The narrator's own operations are similarly given moral status. In Chapter 15, for example, he presents us with a full biography of Lydgate: his origins and childhood; his medical vocation and study; his scientific aspirations; his personal failings. No practice is more ordinary in nineteenth-century fiction. For all its assumption that characters preexist the stories told of them, the traditional novel is practically obliged to substantiate their existence with this kind of *curriculum vitae*. Balzac's introductions are exemplary in the naked markings of their function: to relay the information that the narrative will later transform into meaning. (As he might have written: "Who was this new doctor in town? A retrospective is necessary to grasp the events that follow in their full significance.") As the narrator of *Middlemarch* relays information, however, the procedure doubles for a species of good conduct.

> At present I have to make the new settler Lydgate better known to any one interested in him than he could possibly be even to those who had seen the most of him since his arrival in Middlemarch. For surely all must admit that a man may be puffed and belauded, envied, ridiculed, counted upon as a tool and fallen in love with, or at least selected as a future husband, and yet remain virtually unknown—known merely as a cluster of signs for his neighbours' false suppositions. (170-71)

In the context of a community too busy appropriating Lydgate to know him properly, the narrator's presentation comes defined as a moral corrective. It is insinuated that only a moral laziness has kept Lydgate unknown thus far: to know him now has less to do with omniscience than with sheer moral attentiveness. Even our own ignorant position as readers at the beginning of a story is recast in these terms:

> We are not afraid of telling over and over again how a man comes to fall in love with a woman and be wedded to her, or else be fatally parted from her. Is it due to excess of poetry or of stupidity that we are never weary of describing what King James called a woman's "makdom and her fairnesse," never weary of listening to the twanging of the old Troubadour strings, and are comparatively uninterested in that other kind of "makdom and fairnesse" which must be wooed with industrious thought and patient renunciation of small desires? In the story of this passion, too, the development varies: sometimes it is the glorious marriage, sometimes frustration and final parting. And not seldom the catastrophe is bound up with the other passion, sung by the Troubadours. For in the multitude of middle-aged men who go about their vocations in a daily course determined for them much in the same way as the tie of their cravats, there is always a good number who once

meant to shape their own deeds and alter the world a little.
The story of their coming to be shapen after the average
and fit to be packed by the gross, is hardly ever told even
in their consciousness; for perhaps their ardour in generous unpaid toil cooled as imperceptibly as the ardour of
other youthful loves, till one day their earlier self walked
like a ghost in its old home and made the new furniture
ghastly. Nothing in the world more subtle than the process of their gradual change! In the beginning they inhaled
it unknowingly; you and I may have sent some of our
breath towards infecting them, when we uttered our conforming falsities or drew our silly conclusions: or perhaps it came with the vibrations from a woman's glance.
(173-74)

The passage discloses Lydgate's intellectual passion with an
air of supplying what we have been merely too complacent
to find out. If each of the "great originators" had "his little
local personal history . . . which made the retarding friction
of his course," this is implicitly because "most of us, indeed,
know little of [them]" (175-76). And if we know little of
them, our heartless indifference ("you and I may have sent
some of our breath . . . infecting them") bears the blame.
From the start, then, the text anticipates Lydgate's story as
a function of the characters' unwillingness (including his
own) to do what the narrator has already done. Had the
Middlemarchers or Rosamond only made this effort of understanding, and had Lydgate only seen his "spots of com-
monness" with this accuracy (179ff.), his story might have
been largely avoided. Conversely, had we persisted in ignoring his intellectual passion, or stayed on the side of conforming falsities and silly conclusions, we should have given aid
and comfort to the story's "retarding friction." Once it is
recognized how the convention of narrative omniscience has
been restaged in this presentation, such contrary-to-fact
speculations may no longer seem radically untenable. For
the narrator's formal privilege has become no more than the

performance of everyone's moral duty, and the characters' formal debarment from this privilege no less than a positive refusal of it.

In a famous letter to Charles Bray in 1859, George Eliot wrote: "The only effect I ardently long to produce by my writings is that those who read them should be better able to *imagine* and *feel* the pains and the joys of those who differ from themselves in everything but the broad fact of being struggling, erring human creatures."[23] In this light, monological convention (complete knowledge of characters, completely shared by readers) would only be a heightened, promotional version of a capacity at anyone's disposal: to imagine and feel with an other. As though to confirm the proposition that "struggling, erring human creatures" can raise themselves to the heights of his moral vision, the narrator of *Middlemarch* will sometimes even lower himself to the level of their struggles and errors:

> One morning, some weeks after her arrival at Lowick, Dorothea—but why always Dorothea? Was her point of view the only possible one with regard to this marriage? I protest against all our interest, all our effort at understanding being given to the young skins that look blooming in spite of trouble; for these too will get faded, and will know the older and more eating griefs which we are helping to neglect. (312)

Yet the equivocation of such a passage ought to be evident. On one hand, the narrator's scruple dramatically breaks forth as a plausible model of sympathy through self-abnegation. The similarities are obvious between his self-questioning here ("Why always Dorothea? Was her point of view the only possible one?") and Dorothea's own later ("Was she alone in that scene? Was it her event only?"). On the other hand, by abandoning Dorothea in mid-sentence to take up Casaubon's viewpoint, the intervention points to its

---

[23] *The George Eliot Letters*, 3: 111.

own artifice, in the tradition of Sterne and Diderot. Not only does it remind us of the narrator's playful power to do as he likes, it derives that power from a self-consciously fictive discourse freed from the criteria of practical operability. While the realism of the story assumes that the actions of a Dorothea or Casaubon might be duplicated outside the limits of fiction, only within these limits is the narrator licensed to make his spectacular gesture. The passage thus manages two incompatible effects: it naturalizes its discourse and simultaneously makes it strange. Thematically suggesting the continuity between story and discourse, it formally registers the impasse between them. The discourse may metaphorically contain all the conditions for fully resolving the story, but the metaphor, so to speak, cannot be transferred. To the extent, then, that the discourse recognizes its own utopian impossibility, it may be read like every other utopia in the novel: a transcendence betrayed by the attempt to narrate itself.

In the case of the discourse, of course, this attempt is the story itself. Turning on the problem of personal isolation, the story would appear to originate in a fall from the ideal relationship between narrator and reader, or between both and the characters. Critics who evoke the Tolstoyan dimension of the novel might do better to stress its proto-Chekhovian dynamic. The community of analogously "struggling, erring human creatures," whose possibility we glimpse from the vantage point of the discourse, is presented in the story as a disparate society of egos who collide with one another on an absence of common ground. "There are characters which are continually creating collisions and nodes for themselves in dramas which nobody is prepared to act with them" (223). Interpersonal relationships in Middlemarch often look like a tennis game that is merely a succession of alternating serves. The game may sometimes be comic (say, in the dialogues between Sir James and Mr. Brooke, or between Dorothea and Celia), but it comes into its full pathos when a more meaningful collaboration is presupposed. Between the Lydgates, for example, "there was that total missing of each other's mental track, which is too evidently possible even between persons who are continually thinking of each other" (632). Casaubon "knew little of Dorothea's sensations, and had not reflected that . . . they were comparable in strength to his own sensibilities" (463); and his wife has been "as blind to his inward troubles as he to hers" (232).

Ironically, the selfishness here is a perverse mode of living for others. Rosamond's determination "to live as she pleased" (331) secretly depends on "having always an audience in her own consciousness" (196). "The town's talk is of very little consequence," she declares to her aunt, though "inwardly gratified" by it (330). Her fantasy of triumphing over the others finds its symmetrical counterpart in Lydgate's fantasy of being defeated by them (793). Aggressive desires for recognition are consistently doubled in the novel by paranoid fears of misrepresentation. The dread with which Casaubon's authorial consciousness anticipates the judgments of his readers, or Bulstrode's ultimately criminal terror of Middlemarch gossip, are prominent examples. Featherstone's approaching death inspires a collective version of a quasi-Sartrian duel of glances: "There was a general sense running in the Featherstone blood that everybody must watch everybody else, and that it would be well for everybody else to reflect that the Almighty was watching him" (338). Even so independent a mind as Will Ladislaw is susceptible to the power of others to misconstrue him: "Like most people who assert their freedom with regard to conventional distinction, he was prepared to be sudden and quick at quarrel with any one who might hint that he had personal reasons for that assertion" (651). Dorothea and Will are kept apart for so long precisely by their overwhelming consciousness of what people might say. The symptoms of a missing sympathy between self and other (indifference, fascination, fear, hostility) are part of a single, highly narratable syndrome. The community's comic and inconsequential bickering may be thought to represent the disease in the form of its own "homeopathic" cure; but more ambitious measures will be required to treat the "continually-alienating influences" (712) that threaten to divide Rosamond and Lydgate, Dorothea and Will, or Nicholas and Harriet Bulstrode.

For the community intrinsically flattens the personality of its members. Within its choral chatter, the oppositions of self and other are contracted into the idiosyncratic variations of a shared perception. To stand outside this community, in whatever degree, is already to have hidden psychological depths. The protagonists' greater inwardness implies a more demanding mode of expression: a sympathetic—even telepathic—dialogue from soul to soul. The inadequacy of their relationships, then, exactly corresponds to the inadequacy of their *speech*. It is suggestive how much of the plot of *Middlemarch* depends on information withheld from utterance: by deliberate suppression (Bulstrode's dissembled past, Casaubon's secret codicil, Rosamond's unmentioned letter to Sir Godwin), accidental distortion (Brooke's misleading report of his invitation to Will, Will's own ambiguous scene with Rosamond), or unavoidable muteness (Lydgate's tongue-tied innocence). The alienating influences that estrange the protagonists are all dramatized in terms of blocked, refused, or evaded dialogues. Persistently, a baffling *silence* usurps the place of full speech.

Lydgate, to take a major instance, has "no impulse to tell [Rosamond] the trouble which must soon be common to them both" (797): "his indisposition to tell her anything . . . was growing into an unreflecting habit" (812). He wonders, "Would she speak to him about it, or would she go on for ever in the silence which seemed to imply that she believed him guilty" (813). "The silence between them became intolerable to him: it was as if they were both adrift on one piece of wreck and looked away from each other" (814). Even when Lydgate and Rosamond do speak, the real subject of their conversation never gets said:

"What have you heard?"

"Everything, I suppose. Papa told me."

"That people think me disgraced?"

"Yes," said Rosamond, faintly, beginning to sew again automatically.

There was silence. Lydgate thought, "If she has any trust in me—any notion of what I am, she ought to speak now and say that she does not believe I have deserved disgrace."

But Rosamond on her side went on moving her fingers languidly. Whatever was to be said on the subject she expected to come from Tertius. What did she know? And if he were innocent of any wrong, why did he not do something to clear himself? (814)

Or again:

He had conquered himself so far, and was about to speak, with a sense of solemnity, as on an occasion which was not to be repeated. He had even opened his lips, when Rosamond, letting her hands fall, looked at him and said—

"Surely, Tertius—"

"Well?"

"Surely now at last you have given up the idea of staying in Middlemarch. I cannot go on living here. Let us go to London. Papa, and every one else, says you had better go. Whatever misery I have to put up with, it will be easier away from here.

Lydgate felt miserably jarred. Instead of that critical outpouring for which he had prepared himself with effort, here was the old round to be gone through again. He could not bear it. With a quick change of countenance he rose and went out of the room. (815)

Things are not much different between Dorothea and Casaubon, whose "imperfect coherence" is also accounted for by "the brokenness of their intercourse" (228). "Mr Casaubon was silent," "He did not speak," "Mr Casaubon remained proudly, bitterly silent": the motif is an almost formulate marker of alienation.

"We will, if you please, say no more on this subject [Will's letters], Dorothea. I have neither leisure nor energy for this kind of debate."

Here Mr Casaubon dipped his pen and made as if he would return to his writing, though his hand trembled so much that the words seemed to be written in an unknown character. . . .

Dorothea left Ladislaw's two letters unread on her husband's writing-table and went to her own place, the scorn and indignation within her rejecting the reading of these letters, just as we hurl away any trash towards which we seem to have been suspected of mean cupidity. (317)

Significantly, Casaubon avoids further speech by attempting to write, and Dorothea—as if rejecting the value of the substitution—protests by refusing to read. Our equation is extended: alienation equals the absence of speech equals the presence of writing.[24] To be sure, the opposition between speech and writing here is made a less literal matter elsewhere in the novel. Even in conversation, Casaubon is never "speechlike." Adorned with a "frigid rhetoric" and "an appropriate quotation," his discourse is "a public statement," comparable to M. Liret's "conferences on the history of the Waldenses" or to "the inscription on the door of a museum." Rosamond's far less erudite diction has a similar prepared quality to it, as though she were plagiarizing "the best novels, and even the second best" that make up her reading (196). Conversely, Dorothea's writing (as in her letter of acceptance to Casaubon) is as plain and direct as her speech ("if she had written a book, she must have done it as Saint Theresa did, under the command of an authority that constrained her conscience" [112]). And so with the handwrit-

[24] My formulations here and in what immediately follows are generally indebted to the discussion of speech and writing in Jacques Derrida, *De la grammatologie.*

ing of Caleb Garth, who asks, "What's the use of writing at all if nobody can understand it?" (611). Theresa's "scripture" and Garth's "script" may not be fully adequate models of the narrator's own subtly designed enterprise, but it too seems directed toward the values of full speech.

What is formally speech, therefore, may sometimes be a modality of writing, and what is formally writing a modality of speech. Casaubon specifies the conditions of equivalence in the following exchange:

> The speckled fowls were so numerous that Mr Brooke observed, "Your farmers leave some barley for the women to glean, I see. The poor folks here might have a fowl in their pot, as the good French king used to wish for all his people. The French eat a good many fowls—skinny fowls, you know."
>
> "I think it was a very cheap wish of his," said Dorothea, indignantly. "Are kings such monsters that a wish like that must be reckoned a royal virtue?"
>
> "And if he wished them a skinny fowl," said Celia, "that would not be nice. But perhaps he wished them to have fat fowls."
>
> "Yes, but the word has dropped out of the text, or perhaps was *subauditum*; that is present in the King's mind, but not uttered," said Mr Casaubon. (102-103)

Perhaps the word was never written, perhaps it was never spoken. It is not the modality of suppression that matters, but the resulting inaccessibility of a meaning fully "present in the mind." The point is carried by the image of a *text*, pointing us toward secrets that its nature is to screen, teasing us into interpretations that it refuses to guarantee. Whether by the text of his speech or by the text of its transcription, what the king really meant is kept hidden. The debate made possible by the ambiguity of his wish is frivolous enough, but the terms of this ambiguity are closely related to those that formulate the characters' most serious difficulties. "Signs are small measurable things, but interpretations are illimitable" (47); and the necessity as well as the incommensurability of interpretation stands behind Dorothea's deluded representation of Casaubon. "Dorothea's faith supplied all that Mr Casaubon's words seemed to leave unsaid: what believer sees a disturbing omission or infelicity? The text, whether of prophet or poet, expands for whatever we can put into it, and even his bad grammar is sublime" (73-74); "she filled up all blanks with unmanifested perfections, interpreting him as she interpreted the works of Providence, and accounting for seeming discords by her own deafness to the higher harmonies" (100). In a similar way, Fred reads too much into Mr. Horrock's inscrutable profile ("accompanied by adequate silence"), while Lydgate doesn't read enough in Rosamond's blue eyes ("deep enough to hold the most exquisite meanings an ingenious beholder could put into them, and deep enough to hide the meanings of the owner if these should happen to be less exquisite"). Multiplying the examples, one could easily argue that the entire novelistic world functions like a text, a system of signs whose inherent equivocation leads to constant misreadings.

J. Hillis Miller suggests that such equivocation might be extended to include the novel's own signs. "The novel, like Dorothea, is 'incalculably diffusive.' It has such effect on its readers as it does have, making such interpretations of it as they can, none absolute, each a misreading in the sense that the text is expanded for what the reader can put into it."[25] Why put the novel's own status into privileged brackets? Miller would seem to ask. If the novel too is a text—often insistently so—then it too is deprived of a final or fully present meaning, and our provisional, erroneous interpretations can never make good the lack. Yet one shouldn't un-

---

[25] Miller, "Narrative and History," p. 470. Miller goes on to quote Nietzsche: "To be able to read off a text as a text without interposing an interpretation is the last-developed form of 'inner experience'— perhaps one that is hardly possible." If Nietzsche is "unwittingly echoing George Eliot herself" in this passage, as Miller believes, I should argue that it is precisely in his qualifying "perhaps."

derestimate the novel's need to get out from under the sway of textuality. What *Middlemarch* explicitly wants to diffuse is not its own narrative or textual dynamic, but the urgent moral ideology menaced by that dynamic. Only by collapsing the polarities responsible for its own existence (self versus other, sign versus meaning), can the novel convincingly argue for the practical validity of its religion of humanity. A closure, then, must take place, and it must take the form of a transcendent experience of fellowship whose transparent signs no longer require interpretation.

This is the dominant function of the four "great scenes" at the end of the novel ("Look up, Nicholas," Dorothea at the window, Dorothea and Rosamond, Dorothea and Will). Each of them stages an abreaction in which the "broken intercourse" of egos and texts is overcome in fellow feeling and a wholly present word. They are examples of what Brooks has placed at the heart of melodrama: scenes where the moral imagination finds its voice, naming and enacting its imperatives in a full recognition of "the sign of virtue."[26] Not by accident do they come at the end of a narrative whose ongoing production depends on withholding full expression and deferring final meaning. Perhaps the most fundamental moral value of these scenes (far more basic than the values they are "about") consists in the sheer pressure they put on narrative language to *mean something*, to end its teasing, frustrating suspensiveness. In this sense, their real sign of virtue would be their virtue of no longer merely being a sign.

Yet even with its primary evidence of transcendence, the *Middlemarch* text equivocates. One recalls the radically antimelodramatic stance of Valéry's M. Teste: "Je ne suis pas fait pour les romans ni pour les drames. Leurs grandes scènes, colères, passions, moments tragiques, loin de m'exalter me parviennent comme de misérables éclats, des états rudimentaires où toutes les bêtises se lâchent, où l'être se

---

[26] Brooks, *Melodramatic Imagination*, especially in the chapter "An Aesthetic of Astonishment."

simplifie jusqu'à la sottise."[27] "Being simplifies itself to the
point of foolishness." George Eliot assuredly *is* made for
novels and plays, and she would hardly share Teste's cere-
bral haughtiness. However, if "foolishness" is the wrong
term for the powerful scenes that carry the novelist's most
precious values, "simplification" may not be. The frustrations of the novelistic world—in the last analysis, the fric-
tions of the narrative text itself—are not made to vanish in
these scenes, but only vanish from view. Without exception,
the transcendence of such moments is shown to depend on
not seeing all that is taking place in them. In the full ambiguity of the phrase, the closures of *Middlemarch* "make-
believe." Apparently meant to demonstrate once and for all
the reality of transcendence, they undermine the reality of
their demonstration by basing it on an act of faith. Of
course, the transcendence can seem enhanced by the irony:
"Blessed are they that have not seen, and yet have believed."
But it can also seem impeached by it: for what is the nature
of the blessing that falls on those who do not see *so that* they
may believe? Once again the text will insist on its double
legibility.

"LOOK UP, NICHOLAS"

Harriet Bulstrode is a character whose stability has meant
ignoring the tissue of contradiction and division out of
which it is woven. "Knowing very little of [her] own motives" (328), she has never perceived the oxymoronic implications of her "imitative piety" or her "native worldliness"
(662). Her differences never seem discontinuities ("various
little points of superiority" over Mrs. Pymdale "served to
give colour to their conversation without dividing them"
[328]); and her limited curiosity is never faced as an active
system of suppression. Although she enjoys a "habitual consciousness that her husband's earlier connections were not
quite on a level with her own," it is "not that she knew

[27] Paul Valéry, *Monsieur Teste* (Paris: Gallimard, 1927), pp. 112-13.

much about them," or even tried much to find out. A bare, blanked outline of his past is "almost as much as she had cared to learn" (661). "She so much wished to ignore towards others that her husband had ever been a London Dissenter, that she liked to keep it out of sight even in talking to him" (662). In short, the presumptive unity of her character has been "an odd patchwork," stitching discrepancies together into a mere semblance of consistency (807).

With the news of the Raffles scandal, that patchwork starts to come undone.

> "God help you, Harriet! you know all!"
> That moment was perhaps worse than any which came after. It contained that concentrated experience which in great crises of emotion reveals the bias of a nature, and is prophetic of the ultimate act which ends an intermediate struggle. (805)

In a sense, the "intermediate struggle" is a struggle against the fact of intermediacy itself. Something has *come between* her and her husband: a secret—learned only "from others" (807)—and a silence. ("Leave me in quiet," she begs as she goes to her room; and Bulstrode, alone in his room, finds that "if he turned to God there seemed to be no answer but the pressure of retribution" [806, 807].) Simultaneously, something has also come between her and the entire world. All the social mediations that once seemed to assure her identity now throw it into crisis: into a search for a "piety" that would no longer be "imitative," and for a "native" mode of relating to the world that would no longer depend on "worldliness."

Much as trauma calls out for abreaction, or tension for catharsis, the sheer concentration of the struggle demands an ultimate act to end it. The silence, the secrecy, the "intermediate" barriers between husband and wife—these must be overcome. It thus becomes crucial to appreciate the cognitive ambition underlying Harriet's pledge of loyalty. To an important extent, she offers her sympathy in order to *know what she is offering it for.* Whatever else it might be, her gesture of support is an attempt to elicit her husband's admission of guilt. For her forgiveness will not bear the weight of meaning undertaken by it until she knows (and he knows that she knows) what there is to be forgiven. If their confrontation is to disarm the force of intermediacy, then, it must issue in far more than a mere emotional release: it must produce nothing less than a moment of truth, compassionated and confessed.

"Look up, Nicholas."
He raised his eyes with a little start and looked at her half amazed for a moment: her pale face, her changed, mourning dress, the trembling about her mouth, all said, "I know"; and her hands and eyes rested gently on him. He burst out crying and they cried together, she sitting at his side. They could not yet speak to each other of the shame which she was bearing with him, or of the acts which had brought it down on them. His confession was silent, and her promise of faithfulness was silent. Open-minded as she was, she nevertheless shrank from the words which would have expressed their mutual consciousness as she would have shrunk from flakes of fire. She could not say, "How much is only slander and false suspicion?" and he did not say, "I am innocent." (808)

Has a full reconciliation taken place or not? One might first notice the ambiguous status of nonverbal discourse in the scene. On one hand, the gestures are telling and the weeping fully expressive. "His confession was silent, and her promise of faithfulness was silent." It is as though their communication passed over the clumsy paraphrases of language, and its meaning were all the more unimpeachable for transcending them. On the other hand, there is evidence to locate this mute discourse not somewhere beyond speech, but well on this side of it: "They could not yet speak to each other . . . she shrank from the words . . . she could not say . . . he did not say." Does the speechlessness depend on an intuition that mere words could never be adequate to express the fullness of the present moment? Perhaps, but there is some question whether the moment is really full without them. "They could not *yet* speak" implies that at least part of the moment has already been postponed to a later date. All Harriet's gestures may say "I know," but it is clear at the end of the passage that she does not know and still wants to. "She could not say, 'How much is only slander and false suspicion?' and he did not say, 'I am innocent.'" That she should desire to put such a question, and hope for such an answer, suggests that she has entertained an incomplete conception of her husband's misdeeds. Implicitly, the validity of her pardon is based on an error about what it actually encompasses.

It is never known how she might face the truth, because she is never enlightened. The revelations here waived until later are later deferred indefinitely:

> The acts which he had washed and diluted with inward argument and motive, and for which it seemed comparatively easy to win invisible pardon—what name would she call them by? That she should ever silently call his acts Murder was what he could not bear. He felt shrouded by her doubt: he got strength to face her from the sense that she could not yet feel warranted in pronouncing that worst condemnation on him. Some time, perhaps—when he was dying—he would tell her all: in the deep shadow of that time, when she held his hand in the gathering darkness, she might listen without recoiling from his touch. Perhaps: but concealment had been the habit of his life, and the impulse to confession had no power against the dread of a deeper humiliation. (882)

The vicious circle is obvious: because he fears that Harriet will withdraw her forgiveness, Bulstrode never confesses; because he never confesses, the benefits of that forgiveness are already withdrawn. By this point, the closural reconciliation has been largely retracted: dissolved back into the nar-

ratable polarities and protractions that it wanted to overcome. The Bulstrodes' story is brought to term, but the term
seems only a permanent state of suspensiveness. The actual
meaning of their scene together remains in the air: blindness
matching up with concealment? or both transcending themselves? It is not, of course, that the novel underrates Harriet's
impressive gesture, however unseeing and incomplete it is
ultimately shown to be. Her character reveals its bias, and
she enters into the camp of those whose integrity is made
secure through "direct fellow-feeling." Yet such purely individual salvation is precisely what the doctrine of sympathy
had aspired to go beyond. In this case, at any rate, the "sign
of virtue" is still detached from its meaning.

DOROTHEA AT THE WINDOW

Not unlike Harriet Bulstrode's, Dorothea's spiritual crisis
contains the concentrated experience of what being in a narrative means in *Middlemarch*. "The limit of resistance was
reached, and she had sunk back helpless within the clutch
of inescapable anguish" (844). Will's presumed defection to
Rosamond has been a betrayal of "the vibrating bond of mutual speech" (844), and Dorothea's own utterances can
barely get further than "loud-whispered cries and moans"
and "helpless sobs" (845). The "detected illusion" of Will's
"lip-born words" closes every prospect but that of an endless, pointless narrative (845). In a sense, Will's loyalty to
her stood as a bulwark against the dispersive influences of
time and change: it offered a "sweet dim perspective of
hope, that along some pathway they should meet with unchanged recognition and take up the backward years as a
yesterday" (844). With that hope gone, Dorothea's life
threatens to be kept forever in a state of unresolved, unre-
solvable transition.

Her response to this threat—the narrative threat par excellence—comes with violent, all but masochistic intensity.
She locks herself in her "vacant room," as though to under-
score the void of her solitude; she presses "her hands hard

on top of her head," as though delivering again the psychic wound inflicted by Will; she lies "on the bare floor and let[s] the night grow cold around her," as though this were the only appropriate metaphor for her state of mind (844). One might argue that her dramatic gestures are already part of an effort to master the anxiety they repeat. For they stress her despair in a double sense: they emphasize it, *and* they put pressure on it to give way. Dorothea's acting out—what the narrator calls her "paroxysm" (845)—seems unconsciously organized by the expectation that, if she can only intensify her concentrated experience even further, she may finally provoke "the ultimate act which ends an intermediate struggle." To raise the fever might be to break it in the end; to cultivate nightmares might be at last to wake up from them. Compared by the narrator to "a despairing child," Dorothea unwittingly pursues the logic of tantrum, inflating itself in order to subside.

Her impatience, so to speak, is rewarded: "She had waked to a new condition: she felt as if her soul had been liberated from its terrible conflict; she was no longer wrestling with her grief, but could sit down with it as a lasting companion and make it a sharer in her thoughts" (845). Once more Dorothea struggles to assert a vision in which "everyday-things mean the greatest things," though this time with a crucial difference. In the past, we noticed, Dorothea's commitment to the signified took place at the expense of an attention to the signifier. Vehicles were overlooked or dismissed altogether by a peremptory tenor, which then found nothing to carry it. Suggestively, Dorothea's grief can now yield to a less disabling vision precisely through a new interest in detail *together with* a speculation about meanings. "She began now to live through that yesterday morning again, forcing herself to dwell on every detail and its possible meaning." What is generally identified as Dorothea's emancipation from ego involves, specifically, a dual challenge: to inspect the details overlooked by a repressively selective selfhood, and to consider the meanings these might have for *others*. In the light of the polycentric perspective Dorothea tries to achieve ("Was she alone in that scene? Was it her event only?"), the range of the world's details and the range of meanings that can be made available to them need no longer restrict one another. If one meaning only reductively grasps a scene, then another meaning—or a whole range of other meanings—may be more adequate to the task. And yet, if meaning may be finally adequate to scene, is scene adequate to meaning? Can scenes fully incarnate the meanings that grasp them? The view from the window would seem decisive in its affirmation:

> She opened her curtains, and looked out towards the bit of road that lay in view, with fields beyond, outside the entrance-gates. On the road there was a man with a bundle on his back and a woman carrying her baby; in the field she could see figures moving—perhaps the shepherd with his dog. Far off in the bending sky was the pearly light; and she felt the largeness of the world and the manifold wakings of men to labour and endurance. She was a part of that involuntary, palpitating life, and could neither look out on it from her luxurious shelter as a mere spectator, nor hide her eyes in selfish complaining. (846)

Meaningfulness and life are in this moment reconciled, immanently charged with one another. As Martin Price has seen, "the sublimity [Dorothea] has sought in heroic exertions of the ego gives way to a sublimity she finds at a new level of her own being as well as of the world's."[28] Under the pressure of Dorothea's insight, this tiny diorama of the everyday emblematically extends and insinuates itself beyond its borders so that it comes to implicate, virtually, the entire world. And the world, which before had been seen as irrelevantly petty, now encompasses all that there is to live for. Together with the vision that sees it so, it can

[28] Martin Price, "The Sublime Poet: Pictures and Powers," *Yale Review* 58 (Winter 1969): 213.

sustain the largest and most ambitious meanings available to it.

Yet—one says it almost with regret—even this scene invites us to question its adequacy to the meanings it is supposed to be at last fully representing. What Dorothea sees from the window is inevitably qualified by the text's showing of what she doesn't see. I don't simply mean the fact that the tentativeness of certain details (*"perhaps* the shepherd with his dog") implicitly refers us to her notorious shortsightedness (53), although this does suggest that her capacity to *feel* "the largeness of the world" depends partly on a physiological inability to *see* it. Her more telling lapse of vision involves passing over the social dimension of the landscape, along with the social conditions of her own observation. Dorothea is the owner of an estate: her view opens out from a window on it and passes directly through its "entrance-gates." The fields beyond may well be part of the property. Significantly, Dorothea never sees anyone she knows in this landscape; she never even sees anyone she could know. No male protagonist of *Middlemarch* would ever be seen laboring in the fields, nor would Celia or Rosamond ever appear on the road carrying her baby. The horizontal view across the landscape masks the vertical view downward to a different class. At the moment of Dorothea's greatest participation in "that involuntary, palpitating life," she is removed from it by obvious social divisions. During her most democratic vision, she is *looking down*, both literally and in terms of social hierarchy. In a sense, the same oversight that permits her to identify with those she sees ironically brings the validity of identification into question.

Moreover, if Dorothea unwittingly censors the scene by not reading its social codes, the resulting picture of the human condition in turn censors her problems by not admitting them into its space. For life seen from the window is stripped to its most essential imperatives: survival (hence work) and procreation (hence "child-bearing"). The synecdoche whereby Dorothea makes these imperatives stand for her own less elementary dilemmas has its obvious therapeutic uses, but it also leaves out a lot. To the figures in the landscape, of course, physical labor and child-bearing have an immediate and unquestioned relevance. Dorothea's situation, however, is precisely one in which work and womanhood have become *problems*. Both her income and her good faith have made it possible to embark on a quest determined neither by economic necessity nor by traditional social arrangements. In this light, the symbolic equations of the vision ("burden" equals production equals "man"; "baby" equals reproduction equals "woman") either make that quest irrelevant or are made irrelevant by it. Once again, the solution seems below the level of the problem, and the answer comes to a question we thought was very different.

Furthermore, the answer isn't all there. Much as in the Bulstrodes' reconciliation, its plenitude is both promised and postponed. The scene has only given voice to "an approaching murmur that would soon gather distinctness" (847): its full truth will come later. The deferment inevitably detotalizes the scene's glimpse of transcendence, as though it were always a receding vision needing to be filled in, even when it was taking place. Paradoxically, the seemingly all-inclusive moment *lacks something*: its meaning can have the status of an ultimate truth only if it is carried through, supplemented, translated. In other words, the scene commits its closural status to the very processes that define the narratable. The vision thus risks being lost in the effort to find itself. Even before considering the first consequence of that effort (Dorothea's "second attempt to see and save Rosamond"), one should recognize the insistent disjunction between this scene and that. How is Dorothea to transfer the basic and grand values announced in the view from the window to the sophisticated and petty issue of Rosamond's adulterous temptation? The largeness of Dorothea's vision seems already impugned by the smallness—or simply the otherness—of the first opportunity to carry it through. Since the vision has deferred its meaning until more explicit and specific revelations to follow, much might ride on the visit to Rosamond: no less than the possibility of answering the question, Has Dorothea's vision taken place?

DOROTHEA AND ROSAMOND

"Why had Mrs Casaubon come again? The answer was a blank which Rosamond could only fill up with dread" (850). By now, "dread" and "blanks" have become almost a shorthand code for the dynamic of the narratable itself: motivated by varieties of interpersonal estrangement and formulated according to the logic of a text (a "blank" to "fill up"). Not only is Rosamond's relationship to her rival situated well within this dynamic, she intends to keep it there, matching Dorothea's blank intentions with blank responses of her own. "Inwardly wrapping her soul in cold reserve, . . . she prepared herself to meet every word with polite impassibility" (850). Once again, the closural attempt to transcend egoism in direct fellow feeling—and thus to overcome textuality in an experience whose meaning is self-evident—takes place in a context of intensified opposition.

As it happens, the encounter between the two women *is* filled with blanks, but Dorothea's overmastering urgency at once seems to change their status: from blanks that turn aside sympathetic dialogue to blanks that gesture toward it:

> In looking at Rosamond, she suddenly found her heart swelling, and was unable to speak—all her effort was required to keep back tears. She succeeded in that, and the emotion only passed over her face like the spirit of a sob; but it added to Rosamond's impression that Mrs Casaubon's state of mind must be something quite different from what she had imagined. (851)

What follows is the most impressive instance of "mutual speech" we have considered so far. The Bulstrodes' reconciliation, one remembers, was conducted entirely in silence—a silence that ultimately reconstituted a textual blankness whose interpretation would never be sure. Yet if silence is likely to backfire, so is language, and it is interesting to note what sort of precautions must be taken here to ensure its text-transcending status. For one thing, the "cry from soul to soul" must first be literally a matter of crying (as in Dorothea's "rising sobs" and Rosamond's "hysterical crying"). Moreover, just as tears authenticate themselves by being involuntary, the speech facilitated by tears must refer its truth to a primal and as it were preverbal compulsion. The narrator has already invoked a mother-child relationship as one such authenticating context for dialogue, but it is not the only one. Animality is another (Dorothea's "utterance" is "like a low cry from some suffering creature in the darkness" [853]), and primitive instinct still another (Rosamond's "confession" is "urged by a myterious necessity to free herself from something that oppressed her as if it were blood-guiltiness" [856]).

Yet how can speech be adequate to its sources of inspiration, when these seem radically to *supersede* the verbal? "Poor Dorothea, in her palpitating anxiety, could only seize her language brokenly" (855), and Rosamond's discourse too is all in dashes. It is as though these dashes were precisely the means by which a faltering utterance could refer to all that it must leave unsaid. Speech here aims less to fill up blanks than to be filled up by them. It hollows itself out, leaving room for and thus containing its own ineffability. This ineffability, however, must not relapse into mere verbal ambiguity. An already broken speech must be further interrupted by unequivocal physical gestures that pin down its unspeakable implications:

> The waves of her own sorrow, from out of which she was struggling to save another, rushed over Dorothea with conquering force. She stopped in speechless agitation, not crying, but feeling as if she were being inwardly grappled. Her face had become of a deathlier paleness, her lips trembled, and she pressed her hands helplessly on the hands that lay under them.

Rosamond, taken hold of by an emotion stronger than
her own—hurried along in a new movement which gave
all things some new, awful, undefined aspect—could find
no words, but involuntarily she put her lips to Dorothea's
forehead which was very near her, and then for a minute
the two women clasped each other as if they had been in
a shipwreck. (856)

At such a moment, literal communication may seem no more
than the overspill of a sublime and almost erotic communion.
The actual disclosures that Dorothea and Rosamond make
to one another—that Lydgate is innocent and loves Rosamond, that Will is innocent and loves Dorothea—look like
the merely logistical working out of a more profound
revelation: their experience of fellow feeling "without other consciousness than their moving with kindred natures in
the same embroiled medium" (324). The power of the scene
surely depends on our sense that not just "pride," but every
obstacle "was broken down between these two" (854), in
a mutual sharing of one another's being. And the breakdown
would confirm the truth of Dorothea's vision as well as of
the narrator's ideology.

If, that is, we could be sure it had occurred. In fact, the
experience—almost like the governess's in *The Turn of the
Screw*—remains hypothetical, requiring further proof that
is never furnished. Rosamond's understanding of it, for instance, gives little support to most of the implications we
have just brought forward. She appears to draw sustenance
less from what may have happened between her and Dorothea than from what clearly did not happen. Her original
relief that Dorothea hasn't come to scold her continues to
be the note of her final acknowledgment: "I did not think
you would be so good" (857). What seemed to be accom-
plished in their meeting is virtually elided in her summing
up: "I was very unhappy. I am not happy now. Everything
is so sad" (857). It is easy to read all Rosamond's speeches
in terms well this side of transcendence. Her very confes-

sion has a petty dimension of self-acquittal: "Now I have told you, and [Will] cannot reproach me any more" (856). One could even argue that her confession, as a way to re-orient the scene around what *she* knows and can tell, begins a process of recovering her psychic territory. Certainly, "a faint taste of jealousy" soon comes to mark her questions to Dorothea (857), and afterward she gives Lydgate notice: "If you go to talk to her so often, you will be more discontented with me than ever!" (858). If it isn't obvious that this "tribute" to Dorothea is also an attempt to exempt the one who pays it from imitating her standard, it soon becomes so:

> [Lydgate] once called her his basil plant; and when she asked for an explanation, said that basil was a plant which had flourished wonderfully on a murdered man's brains. Rosamond had a placid but strong answer to such speeches. Why then had he chosen her? It was a pity he had not had Mrs Ladislaw, whom he was always praising and placing above her. And thus the conversation ended with the advantage on Rosamond's side. (893)

True, the passage goes on to retract some of the cattiness it has just dramatized: "But it would be unjust not to tell, that she never uttered a word in depreciation of Dorothea, keeping in religious remembrance the generosity which had come to her aid in the sharpest crisis of her life." By this time, however, the "aid" has been reduced to an irony. The murder metaphor with which Dorothea had cautioned Rosamond against the future ("the marriage stays with us like a murder") here serves Lydgate to describe an actual state of affairs, and its validity is borne out by his "premature" death. It looks as though even infidelity has only become a less technical matter, when Rosamond speaks of her happy second marriage as her "reward" for putting up with the first. What seemed a privileged moment of self-transcendence, then, has ultimately turned out to be an occasion for self-recovery. Dorothea's overwhelming force of personal-

ity (like that of a too-dominating parent) has only made it
possible and necessary for Rosamond to reconstitute her
own.

Dorothea's attempt to "save" Rosamond has really only
saved herself, salvation by sympathy coming once again at
a purely individual level. At the end of their encounter, the
spectacle of sympathy is regrounded in the pathos of specu-
larity. "With her usual tendency to over-estimate the good
in others, [Dorothea] felt a great outgoing of her heart towards Rosamond for the generous effort which had re-
deemed her from suffering, not counting that the effort was
a reflex of her own energy" (857). A reflex of her own
energy? The phrase repeats the novel's very formula of
blindness ("seeing reflected there every quality she herself
brought," "what he saw there was no more than the reflex
of his own inclinations"). Dorothea's most generous moment thus seems also the one in which her ego is most tyrannical: most able to coerce the other into a semblance of mir-
roring its aspirations. Rosamond has not exactly shared the
terms that Dorothea thought were being developed between
them, and Dorothea never recognizes the extent to which
she has merely imposed these terms. Once again, a possible
instance of recognition and truth is shown for an effect of
misunderstanding and error; and transparency is—what it is
never supposed to be—a matter of interpretation.

DOROTHEA AND WILL

At this juncture, our interest focuses on Dorothea less as a
character than as the carrier of a revelation, which continues
to be brought into question as long as it goes unrecognized.
If Dorothea (along with the novel) has found the unshak-
able basis of human relationships, it must be possible to
build something on such a foundation besides a house on
sand. As the last of the novel's great scenes of melodramatic
elaboration, her meeting with Will is under obligation to adduce "proof": to incarnate meaning in a sign that will no
longer slip away from it.

This is not to say that some familiar themes and patterns
do not recur in the scene, for what is else not to be overcome? The conversation between Dorothea and Will is
typically punctuated by silences and half-utterances and
subtended by the fear of "a new distance" and "the vision
of a fatality that kept them apart" (865, 868). Typically,
too, their incomplete discourse has a double valence. On
one hand, it implies a revival of the old duel between self
and other (Will fears humiliation, and he speaks "bitterly,"
"angrily"); and it registers the unwelcome presence of a
third in their dialogue (money, station, what people will
say). On the other hand, it marks an "unutterable affection"
(867): a state in which, as the narrator has put it earlier,
"consciousness overflow[s] to suppress utterance" (679).
Here, however, each set of implications is carried on a
separate track. Two easily distinguished kinds of nonverbal
display interrupt speech in the scene: the storm outside and
the hand holding and kissing inside—respectively, the "bad"
silence and the "good." Both occur in what is virtually a
single moment:

> While he was speaking there came a vivid flash of
> lightning which lit each of them up for the other—and
> the light seemed to be the terror of a hopeless love.
> Dorothea darted instantaneously from the window; Will
> followed her, seizing her hand with a spasmodic move-
> ment; and so they stood, with their hands clasped, like
> two children, looking out on the storm, while the thun-
> der gave a tremendous crack and roll above them, and the
> rain began to pour down. (868)

Similarly, when Dorothea and Will exchange their first
"trembling" kiss, "the rain was dashing against the window-
panes as if an angry spirit were within it" (869).
The polarity within silence is repeated in an equivalent
opposition between silence and speech. Brought together by
the storm and their less-than-stormy caresses, Dorothea and
Will are redivided once they try to talk. After their hand

holding, the conversation again takes up "the trouble of
[their] parting"; and after their kiss, Will exclaims, "it is
impossible!" and "We shall never be married." What the
narrator compares to a "spell" (865) seems able to be broken
only by repeating itself to the point of desperation.

There was silence. Dorothea's heart was full of something that she wanted to say, and yet the words were too
difficult. She was wholly possessed by them: at that moment debate was mute within her. And it was very hard
that she could not say what she wanted to say. (870)

Much as the storm shocked Will and Dorothea into embracing, so Dorothea's silence must be made to shock her into
speaking. Only when Will's abrupt "Good-bye" dramatically seals the silence, can a full speech—filled by its elo-
quent dashes—erupt:

"Oh, I cannot bear it—my heart will break," said Dorothea, starting from her seat, the flood of her young passion bearing down all the obstructions which had kept her
silent—the great tears rising and falling in an instant: "I
don't mind about poverty—I hate my wealth."
In an instant Will was close to her and had his arms
round her, but she drew her head back and held his away
gently that she might go on speaking, her large tear-
filled eyes looking at his very simply, while she said in a
sobbing childlike way, "We could live quite well on my
own fortune—it is too much—seven hundred-a-year—I
want so little—no new clothes—and I will learn what
everything costs."

Unlike the other scenes we have been considering, this
one seems uniquely privileged in that its achievement is
neither taken back nor put off to a later occasion. It thus
arrests, in a final configuration of meaning, the series of
postponements and retractions that began with the view
from the window. In fact, that series might now be thought
of as a sequence of symbolical relays in which meaning was

being worked through to its conclusive incarnation here. The irreversible order of the sequence (the view from the window sending Dorothea to Rosamond, who in turn makes it possible for her to see Will again) is also a quasi-logical ranking. Sympathy moves from a possibility (at the window) to an actual, if unstable moment (with Rosamond) to a permanent state of affairs (with Will); and its erotic content goes from the generalized (at the window) to the tentative (with Rosamond) to the explicit (with Will). Such fairy-tale logic (too big, too small, just right) suggests that the ideal of fellow feeling has been brought to its full and final expression, Dorothea literally abandoning her luxurious shelter for the total and lasting union represented by her marriage to Will.

Yet—as my reference to Goldilocks was meant to imply—the fabular logic of problem solving is not working according to custom.[29] We have already shown that Dorothea's desire for Will is a reduction of her original desire and, in the end, perhaps even a destruction of what its original value had been. Here we may similarly argue that their last scene together symbolically reduces and destroys the original import of Dorothea's vision from the window. In both scenes, Dorothea looks out the window, but what she sees and the implications of what she sees have been radically altered. In the first scene, the view encompasses no less than all of life, which Dorothea could no longer look out on "as a mere spectator." The outside offered the possibility of fully absorbing the inside and of abolishing the polarity between them. In the second scene, however, the window oracle to which Dorothea has instinctive recourse shows only "the

---

[29] At the end of her triple experiment, one will remember, Goldilocks *runs away*. As Bruno Bettelheim notes disapprovingly, in *The Uses of Enchantment*, "At the end of 'Goldilocks,' no resolution of the identity problem is projected" (p. 222). Interestingly, he blames this failing on the recent (that is, nineteenth-century) origin of the fairy tale. The trouble with "Goldilocks," we might say, is that it is too much like a nineteenth-century novel.

drear outer world" (869): forbidding, mute, exclusive. "See how dark the clouds have become, and how the trees are tossed" (867). The thoroughly humanized and benign landscape has turned savage and threatening, and the earlier invitation to go outside has been replaced by a firm suggestion that it is better to remain indoors. Once a transparency, the window has become a protective shield.

It is as though Will himself were a synecdochic equivalent of all that the outside had previously offered. Now that he has moved from the outside to the inside, the former is voided of all value except that of negation. Both Dorothea and Will are spoken of as "defiant" in the scene (865, 866), and the storm outside is an obvious symbol for the world that they must defy. Thus, one begins with a proposed union between Dorothea and the world; one substitutes Will for the world; and one gets a union between Dorothea and the world represented by a union between Dorothea and Will— *against the world*. At the same moment in which Dorothea's revelation is recognized, it is also betrayed into inconsistency. Suggestively, the storm both provokes recognition and symbolically dismisses most of what recognition might have meant. As such, it refers us to the ambiguous process of narrative transference itself, working meaning through and simultaneously working it *out*. Dorothea's vision of totality has shrunk to the dimensions of mere monogamy: a middle-class couple ("seven hundred-a-year") uniting in opposition to the "angry spirit" of the world. In the last analysis, perhaps "what everything costs" is simply the price always paid when "everything" commits itself to a narrative unfolding.

In every case, then, what the great scenes of *Middlemarch* aspire to signify is exceeded by their signifiers, which just as easily point to blindness, misunderstanding, egocentric tautology, and textuality, as they do to insight, recognition, fellowship, and transparency. It is as if the novelist could not help seeing the persistence of the narratable even in its closure. As a consequence, closure appears to take place only

through a strategic misreading of the data—a misreading
that is at once shown to be expedient (expressing a moral
command), efficacious (settling the final living arrangements of characters), and erroneous (deconstructed as a
repetition of what it is supposed to overcome). The resulting ambiguity, of course, is bound to make conclusion less
conclusive. George Eliot herself recognized that "conclusions are the weak point of most authors, but some of the
fault lies in the very nature of a conclusion, which is at best
a negation."[30] Or as we might say: the suspensive and dispersive logic of narrative is such that an effective closure—
no matter how naturally or organically it emerges from the
story—always stands in a discontinuous (or negative) relation to it. In different ways, the fiction of Jane Austen and
Stendhal thrives on this discontinuity. In Austen, it is used to
quarantine the final manifestation of truth from the suspect
processes of story production, and in Stendhal, more perversely, as we shall see, it carries an insistence on the asymp-
totic nature of desire, which satisfaction radically falsifies.
Sharing Jane Austen's belief in the morality of closural negation, the narrator of *Middlemarch* also shares Stendhal's
sense of the inauthenticity of this negation, although the
inauthenticity is based less on erotic than on epistemological
grounds. He is therefore condemned, as neither Jane Austen
or Stendhal ever is, to *worry* about closure, which, under
the sway of both a moral imperative and an intellectual

[30] *George Eliot Letters*, 2: 324. My attention was brought to the
letter in question by Darrel Mansell, Jr., "George Eliot's Conception
of 'Form,'" *Studies in English Literature* 5 (Autumn 1965): 651-62,
rpt. in Creeger, *Critical Essays*, pp. 66-78. In an excellent study, Mansell argues that "the more relations the novel establishes, the more
must be severed where they do not end . . . at best the conclusion
can only cut off this network at some arbitrary point" (p. 77). My
only quarrel with Mansell's theory of form in George Eliot (which
he bases on the novelist's own essay, "Notes on Form in Art") is that
his interest in the "relations which the novel itself sends outwards"
leads him to scant the extent to which a novel like *Middlemarch* tries
to master its internal dynamic in quasi-conventional resolutions.

doubt, must be at once definitive and inconclusive, simple and problematic, supremely real and perhaps impossible. It oscillates undecidably between negating the narratable and being negated by it.

The double bind continues to mark the novel to the very end. The narrator writes in the opening paragraph of the Finale:

> Every limit is a beginning as well as an ending. Who can quit young lives after being long in company with them, and not desire to know what befell them in their after-years? For the fragment of a life, however typical, is not the sample of an even web: promises may not be kept, and an ardent outset may be followed by declension; latent powers may find their long-waited opportunity; a past error may urge a grand retrieval. (890)

He goes on, however, to offer a continued history of these young lives which it is difficult *not* to take as a coherent extension of the sample provided by the novel proper. To all appearances, promises are not broken, or opportunities found, or errors retrieved. The web of the characters' lives seems less uneven than the liminary caution would appear to warrant. Paradoxically, the reader is warned against the very conventions that make the coherence of the Finale possible.

If the Finale *had* offered radical conversions of the kind theoretically admitted by the narrator, it would have seriously compromised the novel's continually reasserted claim to representativeness, along with its ambition to totalize its materials into a cohesive narrative formation. It would have undermined what is both a traditional formal assumption and an explicitly propagated doctrine in the novel—namely, that lives develop a binding coherence ("a persistent self") through a process of moral choice and practical action. One easily imagines a hypothetical novel (not of the nineteenth century!), in which an ending realized in substantial ways the possibilities admitted, but unpursued, in the Finale of

Middlemarch. The most trustworthy promises would be broken, golden opportunities discovered, past errors utterly revoked—and all in a parody of an accelerando. The meanings and conventions of the narrative proper would be subverted into chaos, and the cohesiveness developed there would be exposed as a category of the fiction alone, its law and not its subject's. George Eliot's practice, of course, is far more traditional. Like most nineteenth-century epilogues, the Finale confirms the novel's limits by briefly extending them to show more of the same. The suggestion is that, even if narration were carried forward, its future yield has already been preempted by closure. At this level, at least, the theoretical caveat may not so much contradict what follows, as rationalize it, rather as though the narrator were saying: "The rules of my fiction are not necessarily of a piece with the processes of life; but they happily conform, in the present instance, to the lives I have happened to treat."

"L'ineptie consiste à vouloir conclure."[31] The Finale may not be an "ineptness," but it does seem to "want to conclude." It offers a last synthesis to the analysis that—*grosso modo* and if only by comparison—has dominated the rest of the novel. One of the forms of bad faith by which the novel obliquely puts in question the dispersive tendency of its own narrative is Bulstrode's. For the banker's act of ethical abdication proceeds, as a matter of strategy, by dispersion: "The fact was broken into little sequences" (666). That which it is morally imperative to see as a whole action is diffracted into its components, each below a certain threshold of moral choice and culpability, "like the subtle muscular movements which are not taken account of in the consciousness" (739-40). The Middlemarchers may speak of a "necessary 'putting of two and two together'" (772), but for Bulstrode himself there is never any summing up.

---

[31] Gustave Flaubert, in a letter to Louis Bouilhet dated September 4, 1850, rpt. from the *Correspondance* in *Préface à la vie d'écrivain*, p. 52.

By contrast, the moral necessity of a Finale is evident, as an attempt to make explicit biographical wholes out of what can seem, in the novel proper, only serial instances.

Yet if the Finale obviously wants to conclude, it also wants, in part, to dissolve its conclusiveness into something more problematic. It is an uneven tissue of discretionary ellipses and truncations, woven into a conspicuously unintegrated series of separate times. Characters are followed up to vastly different extents. Ben and Letty Garth never even get "well into their teens," their nephews never beyond childhood; but Fred and Mary Vincy may "still inhabit Stone Court," and "on sunny days the two lovers . . . may be seen in white-haired placidity" (892). Mary's sons and siblings may be fairly assumed to have grown up and settled down, but any account of this has been elided. Similarly, Dorothea's son is brought up at least to his majority (when he "might have represented Middlemarch"); but the history of his father is cut off at a much earlier point: "Will became an ardent public man, working well in those times when reforms were begun with a young hopefulness of immediate good which has been much checked in our days" (894). Will is last remembered as a young and eager reformer, well before the "fall" that has apparently separated "those times" from "our days." Did he live through it? Already, as early as what are probably the 1860s, his son declines to enter Parliament, and this may be a sign that the disillusionment of "our days" has begun. Did Will always retain his ardor and his hopefulness? or, if he did not, why are we not told so?

I indulge in such dubious speculations not because there is evidence to confirm any of them, but rather in order to approach a curious patchiness in the Finale. More is at stake than the fate of Mary's boys. What matters is not the omission of this or that sequence from the histories, but the consequent suspension of the meanings that might be attached to them. Some meanings, of course, are more or less fully yielded. Lydgate's life has been a failure, and there is little

ambiguity over the fact. But the meanings of other characters' lives are left suggestively unresolved. Poised on—and
brought no further than—the threshold of aspiration, Letty
Garth is not arbitrarily or casually eclipsed from view. We
are clearly intended to see in her a prospective image of another potentially frustrated woman (much like Dorothea,
even more like Maggie Tulliver in *The Mill on the Floss*).
Will she repeat Dorothea's career? or make a substantially
different peace? It is similarly difficult to evaluate Dorothea's son and his need to remain "out of doors." An ambiguity hints at opposing interpretations: a reenactment of
the terms of his father's life (which also began, so to speak,
out of doors), or a reversal of these terms (from outdoors
to Parliament; from Parliament to outdoors); a progressive
deliverance ("his opinions had less chance of being stifled"),
or a reactionary withdrawal (an outdoors equivalent of the
"luxurious shelter"); a history closed off by the persistence
of essential patterns, or a history whose patterns persist only
by being changed.

Even major characters like Will and Dorothea are not
fully given over to the meanings their lives may bear. Will
may have become "an ardent public man," but whether he
lived to know it or not, the meaning of his ardor and his
politics has been wrested away from him by subsequent developments. Dorothea too is undecided about the final meaning of her life: "Dorothea herself had no dreams of being
praised above other women, feeling that there was always
something better which she might have done, if she had only
been better and known better. Still, she never repented that
she had given up position and fortune to marry Will Ladislaw" (893). How much weight does one allow to the reservation implied in that disturbing "still"? The last assertion
of the Finale certainly aims to recoup Dorothea's hesitation, but it is hedged about with its own qualifications: "The
growing good of the world is *partly* dependent on unhistorical acts; and that things are not *so* ill with you and me
as they might have been, is *half* owing to the number who

lived faithfully a hidden life, and rest in unvisited tombs" (896, my italics). It is as though the novel itself ended with a version of the "view from the window," but were already regretting its insubstantiality and the incalculability of its necessary "diffusion."

The various attempts to end *Middlemarch*, then, issue in a compromise formation between a fully narrated closure and an unlimited narratability that can never be all told. The compromise takes place at several levels: psychologically, between a defensible satisfaction and an ongoing, unbound desire; ideologically, between an effective position and the persistent contradictions within it; textually, between a more or less established meaning and unending semiosis. Ultimately, like Will, the novel refers us to "the wisdom of balancing claims" (506). If it arrests desire, it also knows that desire stops nowhere; if it overcomes its ideological bind, it also shows the bind being reinstated in the same formation that resolves it; and if its signs ultimately attach to meaning, this meaning is recognized for another diffusive sign. I am not sure that this is wisdom—for it settles nothing—or that it is a balance, except in the sense of a teeter-totter or a Sartrian *tourniquet*. The exemplarity of *Middlemarch* is, precisely, its uneasiness, whereby the assumptions of traditional novelistic form are set off in ironic quotation marks— just enough to make us worry about them, and not just in *Middlemarch*.

Chapter 3

Narrative "Uncontrol"
in Stendhal

THE MORAL DESIRABILITY of closure in Jane Austen and George Eliot is inseparable from a reluctance to entertain the pleasures of narrative suspensiveness. If these pleasures are often suggested in Jane Austen, they are also thoroughly condemned. George Eliot more willingly accepts the suspensive character of narrative, but this is partly because she deeroticizes it, equating it with a state of grim process. What ensues is an anxiety at once inevitable and uninviting. Whereas Jane Austen deplores the erotics of suspensiveness, George Eliot scarcely recognizes that they exist. Accordingly, to *enjoy* being in the narrative of *Mansfield Park* is merely unprincipled, while to enjoy being in *Middlemarch* is all but impossible. Different as each novelist is in this respect, however, both exemplify the fearful attitude of the traditional novel toward its own suspensive play.

What distinguishes Stendhal from these novelists is precisely the fact that he elevates this play (in its full erotic sense) to the position of a supreme value. His consequent dislike of closure (as that which ends the possibility of play) even extends to narrative itself, insofar as it is organized in end-determined plots. Yet the traditional formal requirements of plot and ending are by no means irrelevant to Stendhal's fiction, for its cherished play is ultimately defined as the perpetually reenacted *evasion* of these requirements. Thus, Stendhal's novels must admit closural controls as part of a perverse strategy for disrupting their functioning. We can begin to explore this strategy by considering the strategist who brings it best to light, Julien Sorel.

The Man of Plots

Julien Sorel is an intriguer, and his Machiavellianism has its counterpart in his paranoid readiness to detect the intrigues of others against him. Perversely enough, this sharply developed "plot sense" ought to be a useful adaptation to the terrain, for the world of *Le Rouge et le Noir* is defined by little else than an incessant play of conspiratorial forces. Yet Julien's adaptation is strikingly dysfunctional. The paranoia is nearly always misplaced, and the progress from Verrières to Besançon to Paris depends less on Julien's actual schemes of advancement than on lateral, unforeseen developments. If the Machiavellian strategies are not very effective, it may be in part because they are executed in so careless a fashion: neglected in this or that detail, forgotten or abandoned at this or that juncture. Moreover, the moments when plots falter coincide with moments when Julien seems most closely in touch with himself, at a primary level of being. The gaffes, one begins to suspect, are slips as well: not mere inadvertencies, but—like neurotic symptoms—protests and reversions.

In an important sense, Julien's behavior in *Rouge* can be seen to turn on his anxious relationship to his own plots. The moment from which to start, however, is the moment of fantasy and daydream, before plot has been born.

Dès sa première enfance, il avait eu des moments d'exaltation. Alors il songeait avec délices qu'un jour il serait présenté aux jolies femmes de Paris, il saurait attirer leur attention par quelque action d'éclat. Pourquoi ne serait-il pas aimé de l'une d'elles, comme Bonaparte, pauvre encore, avait été aimé de la brillante Mme de Beauharnais? Depuis bien des années, Julien ne passait peut-être pas une heure sans se dire que Bonaparte, lieutenant pauvre et sans fortune, s'était fait le maître du monde avec son epée. Cette idée le consolait de ses malheurs qu'il croyait grands, et redoublait sa joie quand il en avait.[1]

By treating what are in fact countless daydreams as though they were all one, Stendhal suggests the obsessive structure of recurrence that governs them. Repetition here seems to involve no difference, and although the daydream can be inserted into historical time ("from his earliest childhood," "for several years,"), it apparently has no internal history of its own. Indeed, it tends to abolish the historical time in which it is constituted, by reinvoking the same atemporal state of beatitude at every replay. In addition, a logic of temporal "shortcircuiting" operates within the daydream itself. "He would be introduced to the pretty women of Paris; he would attract their attention by some brilliant action." Behind so compressed a syntax would seem an attempt to convert what is inevitably a diachronic sequence into what becomes virtually a synchronic list, all of whose items are present at once. Wish and fulfillment, want and satisfaction, present and future—beginnings and ends are collapsed into copresence. "Bonaparte, an unknown lieutenant without money, made himself master of the world with his sword." Poverty and mastery, although grammatically represented as successive states, seem at a deeper level to combine in a structure of flickering alternation, such as permits *both* states to be enjoyed, as it were simultaneously.

[1] *Le Rouge et le Noir*, in Stendhal, *Romans et nouvelles*, ed. Henri Martineau, 2 vols. (Paris: Pléiade, 1952-55), 1: 239. I have used this edition for *Lucien Leuwen* and *La Chartreuse de Parme* as well. Succeeding references will be indicated in the text according to the following abbreviations:

RN *Le Rouge et le Noir* (vol. 1)
LL *Lucien Leuwen* (vol. 1)
CP *La Chartreuse de Parme* (vol. 2)

A page number without accompanying letters indicates the last work specified in preceding references. Translations from the French are my own.

Poverty implies the mastery that will redeem it, mastery the poverty that is its stimulus. Julien's daydream might be taken as the ultimate retraction of plot, all its successive articulations drawn back (as far as grammar will allow) into an arrangement of simultaneous order: available all at once for purposes of consolation.

The daydream, therefore, is not narratable per se. Rather, narratability depends on the dissatisfaction that compels Julien to transpose his daydream into the mode of everyday reality. What awakens this dissatisfaction may simply be the obvious insubstantiality of daydreams, whose gratifications are "unreal"; but it may also be the erotic foreclosure of daydreams, whose gratifications leave nothing to be desired. In either case, it is significant that Julien comes to everyday reality with an awareness that "times have changed." In the place of an ideal past (idealized with the help of a little rouge), there has arisen a darkened state of affairs that will never permit his daydream to be directly pursued. The narratable does not, then, coincide with a naive decision to realize daydream, as it does for the characters of *Middlemarch*. More perversely, it coincides with a recognition that daydream cannot be realized—at least, not in straightforward ways. As a result, the inspiration of plot is less a longing to adequate fantasy and reality than a more devious desire to circumvent a given inadequation. Unlike Dorothea Brooke, Julien Sorel knows at the start that plot is radically different from daydream, and he aggressively assumes the difference.

La construction de l'église et les sentences du juge de paix l'éclairèrent tout à coup; une idée qui lui vint le rendit comme fou pendant quelques semaines, et enfin s'empara de lui avec la toute-puissance de la première idée qu'une âme passionée croit avoir inventée.

"Quand Bonaparte fit parler de lui, la France avait peur d'être envahie; le mérite militaire était nécessaire et à la mode. Aujourd'hui, on voit des prêtres de quarante ans

avoir cent mille francs d'appointements, c'est-à-dire trois
fois autant que les fameux généraux de division de Napoléon. Il leur faut des gens qui leur secondent. Voilà ce
juge de paix, si bonne tête, si honnête homme, jusqu'ici, si
vieux, qui se déshonore par crainte de déplaire à un jeune
vicaire de trente ans. Il faut être prêtre." (239)

His project of ambition will involve certain contradictions
from the first. Whereas in daydream, beginning and end
were virtually copresent to enjoyment, the end is now placed
at a distance to be traversed. Plot is to bring about the end,
but that end is now an absence, something "to be brought
about." Julien must space out the recovery of his imaginary
plenitude into successive steps. Steps toward an end? or
steps *from* an end? What on one face is plot's transitivity is
on the other its resistance. A detour recalls the direct route.
That, however, is a second problem. Is Julien's plot a detour
(that is, a circuitous route of access), or is it a pure deflection? Can the black of strategy ever hope to recover a red
of wish *and* fulfillment, available together and at once?

These ontological dilemmas might be appropriately re-
formulated in the social and historical terms provided by the
novel. Julien's movement from daydream to plot can be
seen to internalize the historical displacement that has over-
taken France: from red to black, from the original promise
of the Italian campaign ("all that [Julien] knew of history")
to the construction of the imposing church in Verrières and
the decisions made against the town liberals. Daydream is
anachronism, and plot must involve the pathos of updating.
Julien's Napoleonic urgings can only take alien and reductive forms. "J'ai gagné une bataille," he says after obtaining
a three-days' leave from M. de Rênal, and the discrepancy
between his language and what it actually describes is sourly
comic. As for the real risks of battle, the world of *Rouge*
has relocated them in the social institution of the duel, so
stylized that, as Mathilde complains, "tout est su d'avance,
même ce qu'on dit en tombant." Even the richly and dis-

turbingly undermotivated attempt to kill Mme de Rênal is implicitly absorbed into the journalistic category of the *fait divers*, like the one Julien reads about in the church at Verrières (and like, of course, the article in the *Gazette des Tribunaux* from which Stendhal got his story). In a context that translates all actions into trivial parodies of the inspiration behind them, success under the Restoration becomes a monstrous deformation of an exemplary revolutionary career. Plot tends to produce its own end, which relates to the original object of desire that it was designed to reach only as black to red.

Yet the untimeliness of Julien's desire goes beyond mere anachronism, even in social-historical terms, and must ultimately be taken in something like its root sense. It is no accident that the atemporal structure of Julien's daydream takes Napoleonic themes for its content, since an essential synchrony (be it that of daydream or that of myth)[2] governs Stendhal's treatment of the revolutionary period. Similarly, a relentlessly diachronic structure of plot—all extended arabesques of deflection and delay—orders the representation of what Stendhal might well have called Restoration comedy.

Georg Lukács has argued that the sense of history behind the historical novel—and, with a turn of the screw, behind realism itself—depended on "the French Revolution, the revolutionary wars and the rise and fall of Napoleon, which for the first time made history a *mass experience*, and moreover on a European scale."[3] The argument seems generally right, but in the case of Stendhal's novels, one wants to stand it on its head. The revolutionary verb, as it were, in Stendhal is not the insistently transitive verb of history in Lukács's

[2] For a view of mythical "time" as an abolition of historical time, see Mircea Eliade, *Le Mythe de l'éternel retour: archétypes et répétition*. See also the argument that mythical structure is independent of diachronic sequence in Claude Lévi-Strauss, "La Structure des mythes," *Anthropologie structurale*, pp. 227-56.

[3] Georg Lukács, *The Historical Novel*, p. 23.

sense (history as "an uninterrupted process of change"),
but the essentially copulative verb of wish fulfillment and
myth. In the opening chapter of *La Chartreuse de Parme*—
the entry of the French into Milan in 1796 and the exemplary career of Lieutenant Robert—the historical process
seems more like the stroke of a magical wand. Everything
yields before this unresisted march of passion and high
spirits. The Revolution would seem to have disposed of
time in a spontaneous burst of energy—if only for a time.
For while the revolutionary history can be written as the
jubilant finale of fairy tale, contested only by token dragons,
the finale of fairy tale is the beginning of novel. Much like
Emma's "perfect union" in Jane Austen or St. Theresa's
"rapturous consciousness" in George Eliot, the Revolution
in Stendhal intrinsically *has no story*. For the most part, it
is scattered across his texts in fragments of memory, or
myth, or daydream—taken up directly only when, as in the
Chartreuse, it is about to be over. The real motivation of his
fiction (in the sense given to the word by the Russian Formalists) lies elsewhere, in the black plots of reaction. It is in
the court intrigues of Parma, the electoral campaign of *Lucien Leuwen*, Julien's mission to Strasbourg, and the like,
that the novels most pointedly thematize the fact of narrative. In almost a strictly formal sense, Stendhal's novels *must*
begin at Waterloo or some version of it, for as he sees it, the
essence of revolutionary history can scarcely be narrated at
all.

Thus, two modalities of deviation appropriate Julien's
daydream at the moment it becomes plot ("il faut être
prêtre"): an ontological one, spacing out fulfillment in time
and consigning it to incompleteness at any given point; and
a social-ideological one, recasting daydream into its own
nonconvertible terms. Together they determine the drama
of what Sartre has called "counterfinality": the deflection
of the project by the very instruments it must employ. The
"terminal objectification," to use Sartre's terms, will not
correspond to the "original choice"—the end arrived at will

no longer be the end that one wanted to reach.[4] A local and easily isolated example of such counterfinality might be found in the unannounced nocturnal visit that Julien pays to Mme de Rênal after his departure from the seminary. A fresh convert to the religion of remorse, she resists his advances and so sharpens their edge. Unhappily, Julien becomes a strategist ("un froid politique"), and recounts his experience in the seminary in such a way as to exploit her pity. As his "last resource," he resolutely informs her that he is now off to Paris.

> —Oui, madame, je vous quitte pour toujours, soyez heureuse; adieu.
> Il fit quelques pas vers la fenêtre; déjà il l'ouvrait. Mme de Rênal s'élança vers lui et se précipita dans ses bras.
> Ainsi, après trois heures de dialogue, Julien obtint ce qu'il avait désiré avec tant de passion pendant les deux premières. Un peu plus tôt arrivés, le retour aux sentiments tendres, l'éclipse des remords chez Mme de Rênal eussent été un bonheur divin; ainsi obtenus avec art, ce ne fut plus qu'un plaisir. (426)

In such a framework, one needs to place Julien's curiously patchy performances. The irruption of his "passion intérieure" into his schemes forms part of an unconscious enterprise of nostalgia: a series of attempts to inscribe the full promise of daydream within the plot that frustrates it. No sooner is Julien's plot formed than it is betrayed:

> Une fois, au milieu de sa nouvelle piété, il y avait déjà deux ans que Julien étudiait la théologie, il fut trahi par une irruption soudaine du feu qui dévorait son âme. Ce fut chez M. Chelan, à un diner de prêtres auquel le bon curé l'avait présenté comme un prodige d'instruction, il lui arriva de louer Napoléon avec fureur. (239)

[4] Jean-Paul Sartre, "Question de méthode," p. 93.

Stendhal's passive constructions ("il fut trahi," "il lui arriva de parler") make it clear that Julien is not in full control of such lapses. Whether against his will or simply without his willing, the coherence of the scenario of ambition is undermined by a regressive fondness for "souvenirs" of archaic passion. Imprudently, Julien keeps now a portrait of Napoleon under his mattress, now the address of a friendly café waitress in his trunk. All at once, he decides to see Mme de Rênal a last time before leaving for Paris. In Paris, he makes a pilgrimage to Malmaison and to the tomb of Marshal Ney; in London, he visits the imprisoned radical Philip Vane. At an embassy reception in England, he can't help saying that "there are three hundred thousand young Frenchmen of twenty-five who passionately want war," and at the ball of M. de Retz, he can't stop talking to the exiled republican Altamira.

Julien's most conspicuous lapse, surely, is his decision to "avenge" himself on Mme de Rênal—because she has maligned him in a letter to the marquis de la Mole, who as a result has repudiated him. Perhaps, as Mathilde theatrically takes to saying, "all is lost"; but then again, perhaps not. Is the marquis' anger as final and irrevocable as he seeks to make it and his daughter to interpret it? Some doubt would seem at least permitted, for the marquis has been already and more than once displeased with Julien's conquest of Mathilde (on grounds, moreover, similar to those furnished in Mme de Rênal's letter), and he has each time moderated his displeasure. On the other hand, it is a certainty that the marquis will never "come round" after a murder; then, all will be lost indeed. From the standpoint of Julien's ambition, no move could be more unwise than his attempt to shoot his former mistress. Yet the initial shock of the marquis' fury reaches him, paradoxically, "in the midst of transports of the most unbridled ambition." At the very moment when he would seem most committed to the spoils of ambition, he perversely acts to despoil himself.

One might recall, however, that Julien has himself solicited Mme de Rênal's letter. The marquis writes in uncom-
prehending rage, "L'impudent m'avait engagé lui-même à
écrire à Mme de Rênal." It is as though Julien unconsciously
sought in the letter another "souvenir": a disguised remembrance of a love whose value has seemed to increase with
the distance of retrospection from which it is viewed. Yet
even souvenirs, it would now appear, have changed color.

Pauvre et avide, c'est à l'aide de l'hypocrisie la plus con-
sommée, et par la séduction d'une femme faible et mal-
heureuse, que cet homme a cherché à se faire un état et
à devenir quelque chose. C'est une partie de mon pénible
devoir d'ajouter que je suis obligée de croire que M. J. . . .
n'a aucun principe de religion. En conscience, je suis
contrainte de penser qu'un de ses moyens pour réussir
dans une maison, est de chercher à séduire la femme qui
a le principal crédit. Couvert par une apparence de dé-
sintéressement et par des phrases de roman, son grand et
unique objet est de parvenir à disposer du mâitre de la
maison et de sa fortune. (643-44)

In an obvious sense, the letter is grossly unfair, even to the
point of exaggerating Julien's tactical abilities. "The most
consummate hypocrisy" seems an extravagant formula with
which to designate the naive, clumsily enforced bluffing
that went into the seduction of Mme de Rênal and Mathilde.
Yet if the letter is not true in the sense of conforming to
the full portrait of Julien drawn by the novel, it just fits the
facts and it offers a different way in which these facts might
be seen. Muddle is erected into system, and incidental effects
treated as manifest intentions. The letter's reductiveness
drains Julien's career of his own particular relationship to
it, and so confers on it all the coherence that his depth of
feeling had tended to disperse. By significant omission, the
letter brings into question the very existence of such feeling.
This is a souvenir that refuses to function as such. It says, in

effect, that the event to which it testifies never really happened—Julien has never been there.

His attempt to destroy Mme de Rênal, then, is an extreme attempt to save what she has meant to him—to put her back in her place at the dead center of red. At the same time, it forcefully rejects the spirit of the letter, adding a new fact to the biography that the readings of hypocrisy and ambition cannot well account for. Most important, this unlawful act (in a double sense: both against the law and against the rules of his own game) brings about the final reunion of Julien and Mme de Rênal, a reunion invested with the only values that now matter. Under their pressure, Julien dismisses his past plotting as an irrelevant diversion, and with it much of the novel. Even the issues of his long-tortured examination of conscience (sincerity, immortality, and the like) give way to the cry: "Grand Dieu, Dieu bon, Dieu indulgent, rends-moi celle que j'aime!"

Figure has yielded decisively to ground, as Julien's attention redirects itself from ambition to love, and authority passes from the official performance to an affecting drama of wholly different priorities occurring in the wings. Only in the blinds of his official project, in its failure to be totally absorbing, does Julien now place the worthwhile meanings of his life. The reader, however, has been encouraged to reach such a conclusion long before Julien. Julien has practiced figure-ground reversals from the very beginning (although without surrendering to their full implications), and it is on these that Stendhal has founded his case for Julien's superior worth. The many moments in which a project is suspended, and the energies sustaining it released in irrelevant or even subversive affect, are his moments of greatest moral value and novelistic richness. Conversely, at rare moments when Julien attends wholly to the demands of plot, he seems both morally contemptible and novelistically flat, no different from all the other vicious puppets that people the world of *Rouge*.

An obvious pair of examples, one a plot-breaking lapse, the other a plot-conforming surrender, concerns the "dépôt de mendicité." When M. Valenod silences the singing in the poorhouse (which shares a wall with his dining room), it is "too much for Julien."

Il avait les manières, mais non pas encore le coeur de son état. Malgré toute son hypocrisie si souvent exercée, il sentit une grosse larme couler le long de sa joue.

Il essaya de la cacher avec le verre vert, mais il lui fut absolument impossible de faire honneur au vin du Rhin. *L'empêcher de chanter!* se disait-il à lui-même, ô mon Dieu! et tu le souffres!

Par bonheur, personne ne remarqua son attendrissement de mauvais ton. Le percepteur des contributions avait entonné une chanson royaliste. Pendant le tapage du refrain, chanté en choeur: Voilà donc, se disait la conscience de Julien, la sale fortune à laquelle tu parviendras, et tu n'en jouiras qu'à cette condition et en pareille compagnie! Tu auras peut-être une place de vingt mille francs, mais il faudra que, pendant que tu te gorges de viandes, tu empêches de chanter le pauvre prisonnier; tu donneras à dîner avec l'argent que tu auras volé sur sa misérable pitance, et pendant ton dîner il sera encore plus malheureux!—O Napoléon! qu'il était doux de ton temps de monter à la fortune par les dangers d'une bataille; mais augmenter lâchement la douleur du misérable! (348)

Later, however, confronted with Valenod's appalling success, he requests the direction of this same poorhouse for his father:

—A la bonne heure, dit le marquis en reprenant l'air gai; accordé; je m'attendais à des moralités. Vous vous formez.

M. de Valenod apprit à Julien que le titulaire du bureau de loterie de Verrières venait de mourir: Julien trouva plaisant de donner cette place à M. de Cholin, ce vieil imbécile dont jadis il avait ramassé la pétition dans la chambre de M. de la Mole. Le marquis rit de bien bon coeur de la pétition que Julien récita en lui faisant signer la lettre qui demandait cette place au ministre des finances.

A peine M. de Cholin nommé, Julien apprit que cette place avait été demandée par la députation du département pour M. Gros, le célèbre géomètre: cette homme généreux n'avait que quatorze cents francs de rente, et chaque année prêtait six cents francs au titulaire qui venait de mourir, pour l'aider à élever sa famille. (483)

The important recognition that Julien achieves in the earlier scene at the Valenods is pointedly sacrificed in the later one at the Hôtel de la Mole. Now the demands of Machiavellianism are unhesitatingly met and begin to seem like positive gratifications. (Even here, perhaps, one might see hidden messages of dissent transmitted in the very conduct of compliance—and hence, a wider interval between Julien and his role than can appear on the surface. For if he now accepts what the poorhouse stands for, it is also the case that he accepts it for his father, when he hates, as if to suggest privately that it were only fit for such a one. Moreover, to assign the lottery bureau to an acknowledged fool may be a personal comment on a system in which assignments seem no less perversely motivated. Julien's cynical amusement would then be only the guilt of an accomplice assuaging itself.) Whatever qualifications we may want to introduce, it is nevertheless clear that his response in the first episode defines something like Julien's authentic self, a residual worth as yet unadjusted to the requirements of his social career; and that what the marquis sees as Julien's formation indicates only the extent to which he has been deformed.

Implicitly, my discussion has so far remained within what might be called the novel's official view of itself. I have seen plot in *Rouge* much as Julien comes to see it: as a pure counterfinality, delaying and deflecting fulfillment, threatening to absorb the self into its own graceless arabesques.

There seems no mistaking Stendhal's official antithesis, whatever names one prefers to give the opposing terms: on the one hand, the passionate condensation of daydream, which he likes, and on the other, the postponement and aberration of plot, which he regrets. To an important extent, *Rouge* is a novel about the dilemmas of romanticism, with a demonstrable romantic bias in its own presentation of them.

As such, it is well described by theories of the novel that (albeit in chastened form) reconstitute this opposition and share these valorizations. *Rouge* may be meaningfully read according to the schema provided in Lukács's *Theory of the Novel*: as a nostalgic quest for a coincidence of life and essence, frustrated (or at least problematized) by a world that holds them separate.[5] Similarly, it may also be seen to embody the related structure elaborated by Lucien Goldmann—an anachronistic hero harkens back to a world in which unmediated value ("use value") was the dominant form of moral economy.[6] My own discussion has been an attempt to give specific content to precisely this anachronistic movement of nostalgia. Nostalgia implies that there was a home where . . . (in the epic world); anachronism, that there was a time when . . . (in a precapitalistic economy). Both are treated as holdovers from an original state of affairs; and as a result, either tends to seem authentic in ways that what frustrates it is not. At an obvious level, *Rouge* is organized along these lines. Stendhal's portrayal of the Napoleonic period presents a home par excellence, and Julien is evidently a character who has been born at the wrong time.

Suppose, however, that instead of placing the source of the nostalgia outside a system that "then" appropriates it, one sees *both* the nostalgia *and* what is perceived to threaten it interlocking in the play of a single system. Suppose one sees anachronism as a complementary version of modernity, in the same contemporary structure. Suppose, finally, one

---

[5] Georg Lukács, *The Theory of the Novel*.
[6] Lucien Goldmann, *Pour une sociologie du roman*.

begins to recognize how dependent Stendhal's romantic bias
is for its expression on what allegedly thwarts it. Figure and
ground, after all, dovetail into a single gestalt; and if plot
foils daydream, might it not also act as a foil for it? be its
very condition of possibility? Might not both the values of
individualism and the threats to it, rather than succeeding
one another (as romantic myth would have it), be con-
temporaneous, mutually dependent discoveries (as it would
seem historically the case)?

Some such recognition would seem to operate practically
in *Rouge*, if mainly under cover. A chief example might be
Julien's seduction of Mme de Rênal. Even here, of course,
it is possible to treat the scene as part of a problematic of
sheer counterfinality. From Julien's point of view, counterfinality involves the deflection of the end by the means.
"Qui veut la fin veut les moyens," he will say later to Count
Altamira, in good Machiavellian style; but here the means
seem to produce their own end, different from the one presumably desired. Strategy has evidently absorbed so much
passion that none remains for pleasure. The paramilitary
means of seduction have obtained—only a paramilitary seduction. The moment of *bonheur* is literally left blank in the
text—or, to put it in the novel's own color scheme, it has
been entirely blacked out. Only when Julien forgets his role,
on the following nights, can he begin to enjoy himself.

From the reader's point of view, counterfinality appears
in its complementary form, as what might be called "coun-
terinstrumentality." The desired end has been brought about
by means different from those that were supposed to obtain
it. When Mme de Rênal scolds Julien, who has boldly entered her bedroom, he quite simply bursts into tears. Tellingly, these unscheduled tears lubricate his victory: "Quelques heures après, quand Julien sortit de la chambre de Mme
de Rênal, on eût pu dire, en style de roman, qu'il n'avait plus
rien à désirer." Indeed, victory has been largely owing to
the love Julien had already inspired ("qu'il *avait* inspiré"—
my italics), and to the unexpected impression made on him

by feminine charms rather than to his maladroit shrewdness. Strategy would hardly have worked if unaccompanied by a redeeming counterpoint in the unguarded, the impetuous, the unforeseen.

Either way one takes it, plot would seem mainly a futile enterprise. For Julien, whose plot has failed to produce a love experience, the end has been deflected by the means. For Mme de Rênal, who is initiated by Julien's seduction into an experience of genuine passion, the end has been reached by means other than those meant to promote it. Plot either misses its mark of necessity, or hits it by accident. Yet running counter to these typically Stendhalian ironies is a rather different possibility:

> Mon Dieu! être heureux, être aimé, n'est-ce que ça? Telle fut la première pensée de Julien, en rentrant dans sa chambre. Il était dans cet état d'étonnement et de trouble inquiet où tombe l'âme qui vient d'obtenir ce qu'elle a longtemps désiré. Elle est habituée à désirer, ne trouve plus quoi désirer, et cependant n'a pas encore de souvenirs. (299)

What matters to the narrator here is not the "arrival" of fulfillment, but the "journey" of desire: the movement of traversing a distance, which constitutes desire and reconstitutes it at every turn in the road. On the one hand, plot has been seen as the consignment of fulfillment to a succession of steps and to socially given forms of alienation. Rupture, reversal, retraction were strategies whereby to escape from plot into a wholeness of fulfillment. Here, on the other hand, that wholeness is very nearly empty, and that same temporal and social adjournment of fulfillment comes to seem almost relished for the sheer charge that it confers on desire.

Very basically, it becomes a problem of having and eating one's cake. Without exactly resolving the contradiction, Julien develops an undeclared tactic of transaction that permits him to pass from one side of it to the other, in the manner of a Sartrian *tourniquet*. We might describe the *tourni-quet* in the following way. Desire treats middles as anticipations of the end; and it puts ends back into a middle, by forgetting or revising their status as ends. Ending can be accepted only as prolepsis; when it is met in its proper position (at the end!), the sequence needs to be extended to eclipse its closural finality. So, the edge of Julien's desire will be restored once his affair has become a memory, for ends remembered are already in the middle of something else.

Julien's curiously undaunted naiveté depends critically on a need to keep himself in a state of surprise: "*le besoin d'an-xiété*," as an epigraph in *Rouge* puts it, apparently referring to Mathilde but implicating as well Julien himself. The way in which anxiety works turns on the felt proximity of an ending. When an ending is sensed to be all too far removed, Julien is tempted to enjoy it in advance, borrowing against vague future expectations. Typically, this takes the form of a plot-breaking gaffe. When an ending is at hand, however, he seems to regret the fact, and to try to deprive the finale of its finality and so restore to it some of the distance of approach. The weird and pathological game that Julien and Mathilde play together might stand as an almost perfectly realized figure of a plot with a continually repostponed end point. As soon as Julien reaches the point where he can be natural, he meets afresh the need to use artifice, the end functioning merely to relay a cycle of repetitions.

In this perspective, one must return to the scene of the crime, which now becomes explicable in yet another sense. Immediately before the "thunderstorm" brought about by Mme de Rênal's letter, Julien faces the fact that he has virtually achieved the objects of his ambition:

Le soir, lorsqu[e Mathilde] apprit à Julien qu'il était lieutenant de hussards, sa joie fut sans bornes. On peut se la figurer par l'ambition de toute sa vie, et par la passion qu'il avait maintenant pour son fils. Le changement de nom le frappait d'étonnement.

> Après tout, pensait-il, mon roman est fini, et à moi seul
> tout le mérite. J'ai su me faire aimer de ce monstre d'or-
> gueil, ajoutait-il en regardant Mathilde; son père ne peut
> vivre sans elle et elle sans moi. (639)

Yet although he recognizes "the end of his novel," Julien's
tone is far from one of restored equilibrium. His sadistic
dominance seems too desperately asserted to be assured. It
is almost as though Julien couldn't think of closure without
creating new enclaves of narratable tension. Placed in such
a context, Mme de Rênal's letter would become an unad-
mitted blessing in disguise, offering a spectacular occasion
not to terminate, to spin out the plot still further. There is
no place for a *telos* in Julien's surprise tactics; there are only
displacements of it. A sliding *telos* allows plot always to
anticipate its ending but never to attain it—to thicken, one
might say, but not to congeal. Plot is thus kept in an effectively permanent state of irresolution.

At the same time, this attempt to displace the end becomes
ultimately part of an attempt to make it absolute. Julien has
refused one form of closure only to be confronted at last
with another, death being the inalienable ending par excellence. To the extent that Julien's crime, his defense plea at
the trial, and his behavior afterward contribute to "une
sorte de suicide," they are efforts to establish an ending that
cannot be cheated, and will end the very process of cheating.

Yet even here, under sentence of death, the anxiety of
coming to an end continues and at a raised pitch. There is
now an absolute ending, but what is the sequence that it can
be said to end? What does death conclude? "Life" is an inadequate answer, for Julien's death scarcely comes as an appropriate biological ending (to an internally coherent sequence of birth, maturity, decay). It closes the biological
series but is not itself produced by it. Of what is it the ending? in what series does it belong? Most simply, one might
take death as concluding a sequence of crime and punishment; but one would still be left with the gap between them,
after the one and before the other.

Occurring precisely in the gap of this *temps mort* is Julien's extended and fragmented prison soliloquy. Significantly, it enacts a meditation on modes of meeting the end, not as an arbitrary end point, but as an appropriate closure. Julien would want to personalize death as *his* death. "On meurt comme on peut; *moi je ne veux penser à la mort qu'à ma manière*. Que m'importent *les autres*? Mes relations avec *les autres* vont être tranchées brusquement" (667, first italics mine). More or less explicitly, his soliloquy attempts to prepare him for death—better put, prepare death for him. The conclusion must be made natural, internally motivated, the capstone of a meaning. Thus, under the pressure of death, Julien elaborates a philosophy meant to make him desire its coming ("de nature à faire désirer la mort") by disgusting him with things human. For example, "J'ai aimé la vérité. . . . Où est-elle? . . . Partout hypocrisie, ou du moins charlatanisme, même chez les plus vertueux, même chez le plus grands; et ses lèvres prirent l'expression du dégoût. . . . Non, l'homme ne peut pas se fier à l'homme" (690).

René Girard has called this reevaluation, in which "Julien disavows his will to power" and "breaks away from the world which fascinated him," his "conversion in death."[7] Yet it is hard to see Julien renouncing his "will to power," when his conversion is basically an attempt to *master* death, to make it a choice. Conversion is a way to inscribe the life and death opposition within life, and the death that it mimes gives a purchase on the real thing. Julien dies to his old self (to use a familiar formula for conversion), so that his actual death can do no more to him than he has already done to himself. Conversion naturalizes death, and conversely, death sanctions the validity of conversion—it makes the before and after dichotomy imposed by conversion less problematic, if only because there will not be much "after" to undermine its neatness.

Despite the device of a conversion, Julien is still unable to meet his death directly. Without engaging the Sartrian on-

[7] René Girard, *Mensonge romantique et vérité romanesque*, p. 291.

tology en bloc, one might introduce here Sartre's argument in *L'Etre et le Néant* about the impossibility of living toward one's death:

> Loin que la mort soit ma possibilité propre, elle est *un fait contingent* qui, en tant que tel, m'échappe par principe et resortit originellement à ma facticité. Je ne saurais ni découvrir ma mort, ni l'attendre, ni prendre une attitude envers elle, car elle est ce qui se révèle comme l'indécouvrable, ce qui désarme toutes les attentes, ce qui glisse dans toutes les attitudes et particulièrement dans celles qu'on prendrait vis-à-vis d'elle, pour les transformer en conduites extériorisées et figées dont le sens est pour toujours confié à d'autres qu'à nous-mêmes. La mort est un pur fait, comme la naissance; elle vient à nous du dehors et elle nous transforme en dehors.[8]

Much as in Freud the dream can never say no, the Sartrian project can never say die. *Avant la lettre*, Julien makes Sartre's point in explicitly grammatical terms, when he remembers an observation of Danton's: "C'est singulier, le verbe guillotiner ne peut pas se conjuger dans tous ses temps; on peut bien dire: Je serai guillotiné, tu seras guillotiné, mais on ne dit pas: J'ai été guillotiné" (677). A subject can never grasp his own death, because grammatically he can never "say" it. "I" cannot be the grammatical subject of a proposition that logically presupposes the abolition of the subjectivity that an "I" constitutes.

Thus, what seems a movement toward the end turns out necessarily to be a flight from it. The philosophy that "makes death desired" in fact continually elides the fact of death, whether its reflections turn toward an afterlife, toward Mme de Rênal in this life, or toward both at once, as in the following deflected syllogism:

> Ainsi la mort, la vie, l'éternité, choses fort simples pour qui aurait les organes assez vastes pour les concevoir. . . .

[8] Sartre, *L'Etre et le Néant* (Paris: Gallimard, 1943), p. 630.

Une mouche éphémère naît à neuf heures du matin
dans les grands jours d'été, pour mourir à cinq heures du
soir; comment comprendrait-elle le mot *nuit*?

Donnez-lui cinq heures d'existence de plus, elle voit et
comprend ce que c'est que la nuit.

Ainsi moi, je mourrai à 23 ans. Donnez-moi cinq années de vie de plus, pour vivre avec Mme de Rênal.

Et il se mit à rire comme Méphistophélès. Quelle folie
de discuter ces grands problèmes! (692)

Inevitably, Julien's thoughts slip back into retrospect, or
forward into plans and prophecy. Mathilde must marry the
marquis de Croisenois, or later, when he is killed, M. de Luz;
she will neglect his child; Mme de Rênal must promise to
care for it; and so on.

"What do *the others* matter to me?" Julien's anxiety
stems from a perfectly correct sense that they matter a great
deal—that finally they will be all that matters. For, in a
proper Sartrian manner, the meaning of his life proves not
to be in his control. Stendhal has already shown how the
suggestively undermotivated force of Julien's crime is made
instantly subject to a series of social appropriations: for the
Abbé de Frilair, it means a chance at a bishopric; for the
jurors, an occasion for class spite; for the town ladies, an
invitation to sentimental indulgence; for the vigilant priest,
an opportunity to make his reputation; for the hawkers, a
salable commodity. (Moreover, if we have understood the
point of the demonstration, there is every reason to extend
the sequence: for the newspapers, some hot copy; for a
novelist, a fascinating subject.) Julien's horror that "at every moment [the priest] is repeating my name" speaks for
itself. Even while alive, Julien has become public property;
death will complete the process, and its meaning can *only*
be conferred by "the others." Hence Julien's anxious attention to the scenario that Mathilde and Mme de Rênal must
follow on his death; hence also, his wish for posthumous developments that might revise the public meaning of his life.
Both come together, significantly, in a concern for his son:

—La mort de mon fils serait au fond un bonheur pour l'orgueil de votre famille [de la Mole], c'est ce que devineront les subalternes. La negligence sera le lot de cet enfant du malheur et de la honte. . . . J'espère qu'à une époque que je ne veux point fixer, mais que pourtant mon courage entrevoit, vous obéirez à mes dernières recommandations: Vous épouserez M. le Marquis de Croisenois.

—Quoi, déshonorée!

—Le déshonneur ne pourra prendre sur un nom tel que le votre. Vous serez une veuve et la veuve d'un fou, voilà tout. J'irai plus loin: mon crime n'ayant point l'argent pour moteur ne sera point déshonorant. Peut-être à cette époque, quelque législateur philosophe aura obtenu, des préjugés de ses contemporains, la suppression de la peine de mort. Alors, quelque voix amie dira comme un exemple: Tenez, le premier époux de Mlle de la Mole était un fou, mais non pas un méchant homme, un scélérat. Il fut absurde de faire tomber cette tête. . . . Alors ma mémoire ne sera point infâme; du moins après un certain temps. (665)

The possibilities that Julien elaborates and even tries to manage are, of course, indefinitely postponed by the novel. Whom does Mathilde marry? Does she marry at all? Does she eventually look back on her episode with Julien with embarrassment, as he predicts? What happens to their son, whose appointed guardian dies before he is born? It may be futile to speculate along the lines of such questions, but it is a matter of some importance to recognize that they cannot be answered, especially since far more basic questions are kept in a similar state of suspension. "Serais-je un méchant?" Julien asks himself in prison. Although the fact that he is now able to pose such a question does not go without its moral evaluation, the question itself raises a serious problem of interpretation. If one treats it as a mainly rhetorical question—that is, meant as such in the light of the reader's superior knowledge—Julien's soliloquy gets reduced to a piece

of sentimentality, in the manner of Dickens. (The scruples
that Amy Dorrit or Florence Dombey entertain about their
conduct never seriously indict it, but only invite us to feel
sorry for them.) On the other hand, if one takes it as a legitimate question, whose answer is not already given, then one
must acknowledge that it goes unanswered—or rather, that
there is evidence for either way of answering it. "Ai-je beaucoup aimé?" is another question, presenting a similar problem. Much in our interpretation of *Rouge* would seem to
hang on how we answer it, and yet it appears that we aren't
allowed to answer it at all.

One is brought back (as one always must be) to the crime,
the most crucial example of the text's own foul play. The
examples so far given might easily be explained as part of a
novelistic attempt to specify the complex density of experience, always throwing up questions that conspicuously
fail to grasp its real intricacy. The interpretation of Julien's
crime, however, necessarily stands in the position of key-
stone to any interpretation of the novel. It simply must be
explained; for if it is "inexplicable" (as the Abbé de Frilair
and Julien's Jansenist confessor both say it is), then so is
Julien himself, and so to an important extent is *Le Rouge et
le Noir*. His crime is the most spectacular and consequential
act of self-definition that Julien performs, but perversely, the
scene of the crime is the chief locus of the text's indeterminacy. One is forced to wonder whether, at the level of
interpretation, the crime be only a figure for this, the real
transgression: the signifying act par excellence has no decisively apparent signified.

Julien himself seems in some doubt about why he did it.
"Je me suis vengé" is his first statement of motive, and this
by itself would have seemed plain enough, although why he
decided to avenge himself—moreover, in so self-punishing
a way—might still have remained a puzzle. Other theories
of motivation, however, are also broached. In his defense
plea, for instance, Julien implies that the frustrations of class
have been an important source of motive. Furthermore, after

the trial, he tells himself: "Enfin j'ai voulu la tuer par ambition ou par amour de Mathilde." Ambition? It is hard to see
a public homicide as an act of ambition. Love for Mathilde?
when he will tell Mme de Rênal a little later "I have loved
only you"? The Abbé de Frilair seems at one point to suggest that the crime was motivated by jealousy—"why else
would M. Sorel have chosen the church, if not for the
reason that precisely there, at that moment, his rival was
celebrating the mass?"—and Mme de Rênal offers to say as
much to the king. Does she believe it? For as one critic has
rightly seen, there is indeed a sense in which Julien may be
motivated by jealousy—"jealousy, perhaps, at the tone of
those religious phrases [in Mme de Rênal's letter], remembering that if Napoleon was Mme de Rênal's rival, the
church was his."[9]

One cannot then agree with Gérard Genette that Stendhal
leaves Julien's crime unmotivated, in order to confer on it
"by his refusal of all explanation, the wild individuality that
characterizes the unforeseeability of great actions."[10] To assert simply that Julien's act is unintelligible, a signifier without a signified, seems at the very least to underplay the
speculation about motive and intention that occurs in the
novel. The fact that a novelist doesn't explicitly offer a motive may not mean that there is none to derive. What Genette calls an "ellipsis of intention" may often function practically as a kind of understatement in the text, the reader
being encouraged to infer what is not directly stated. (Genette, of course, recognizes this kind of ellipsis-litotes, but
he restricts its occurrence to highly conventionalized genre
literature, in which the code is too obvious to need specification.) Indeed, Genette treats Stendhal's so-called refusal of
all explanation in exactly this way. The lack of an explanation is instantly converted into an implied explanation of a
second order: the uniqueness—Genette might say the code-
lessness—of a great action. The possibility of meaning is

[9] Michael Wood, *Stendhal*, p. 89.
[10] Gérard Genette, "Vraisemblance et motivation," *Figures II*, p. 77.

barely threatened. The great refusal is no sooner posed than recouped in a familiar Stendhalian thematic of the *être supérieur*. Once this has been done, one could quite easily group Julien's inexplicable crime with those highly explicable acts of twentieth-century French literature: Lafcadio's "gratuitous" act in Gide, and Mathieu's "free" act in Sartre's *La Mort dans l'âme*.

In fact, of course, the text offers a superabundance of psychological explanations—vengeance, ambition, love for Mathilde, jealousy—and this is to ignore what other motives might result from the ingenuity of critical inference. If anything, Julien's crime is overdetermined. Yet each separate motive on its own merits is insufficient, and all the motives taken together do not command a cohesive psychological case. Genette is right to say that the crime has no obviously given signified, but he fails to recognize how Stendhal makes us pass from one possible signified to another. Motivation is not open a priori; it is only *left open*, finally, when the process of interpretation is exhausted and suspends itself, as it were, in marks of ellipsis. That process makes us aware not of an absence of meaning (quickly translated into the idiosyncrasy of the *être supérieur*), but of a suspension of meaning: its continual postponement to a tomorrow that never comes. Any attempt to discuss the crime implicitly recognizes this deferment, at least insofar as it is this lack of an immediately given meaning that makes discussion possible in the first place.

In my own analysis, I have suggested two ways in which the crime might be read: as plot renounced and as plot prolonged. Yet while each explanation seemed required by its own series of moments in the text, both explanations taken together are plainly contradictory. This fact might now be seen to define the explosive force of the act itself. Unlike other actions, which took place *within* a *tourniquet* of desire, this act wholly contains the *tourniquet*: it *is* its separate and contradictory moments in one. As such, might not Julien's crime be a parable of the *tourniquet* of interpretation that it initiates? We center our readings of *Rouge* on the crime, and then find that we cannot give our center a decisive content. We privilege this moment in the text as a moment of all-presence ("everything is here," as we like to say); but as we endeavor to make our center more than a merely formal one, we must succumb to what Roland Barthes calls "the enchantment of the signifier."[11] A formal promise and a practical disappointment make up a vicious circle.

THE PROMISE

Julien's crime necessarily focuses any reading of *Rouge*, superseding the ordinary novelistic deployment of incident and character in order to gesture toward an overriding revelation of destiny. This is so because the novel builds up to the crime—that is, it has set up a pattern of expectations, which the crime can be seen to complete. Early in the novel, for instance, Julien finds in the church at Verrières a newspaper account of the "execution and last moments of Louis Jenrel, executed at Besançon." If Julien only half-recognizes the anagram, the reader is likely to be embarrassed by the use of so obvious a device on the part of so sophisticated a novelist. (Other embarrassments of this sort in nineteenth-century fiction, of course, are not wanting—Anna Karenina's dream, Mrs. Tulliver's fears that Maggie will "tumble in" the Floss and "get drowned," Tess Durbeyfield's "prefigurative superstitions," and so on.) There are other hints about Julien's destiny as well, most notably Mathilde's piece of wit that "only sentence of death distinguishes a man; it's the only thing that can't be bought." One can deplore such crudity, or more loyally, one can say that Stendhal couldn't really have meant it; but it is best to take such heavy-handed hinting for what it is: a way to center the fiction and to guarantee its meaning.

These emphatic prolepses are only the most conspicuous

[11] Roland Barthes, *S/Z*, p. 10.

aspect of what Barthes has generally called the "complete-ness" ("la complétude") of the traditional text. "Terms and their connections are posed (invented) in such a way as to join one another, double one another, create an illusion of continuity. Fullness generates the pattern which is supposed to 'express' it, and the pattern calls forth its complement, its coloring." This completeness can also be seen as a sort of redundancy, a superfluity of signification, imposing "a dense fullness of meaning . . . a kind of semantic chatter, proper to the archaic or infantile era of modern discourse, marked by the obsessive fear of failing to communicate."[12] Barthes here would call attention to the way in which meaning in the traditional novel depends on *matching up*: answer is matched up with question, fulfillment with prophecy, end with beginning. As part of its pretension to a mastery of meaning (Barthes's "maîtrise du sens"), the traditional novel is set up like a somewhat scrambled catechism: a system of interrogations and responses that legitimize one another.

In this way, *Rouge* points to its own key as such. The echoes of prolepsis appear to have been called forth in ad-vance by an originating voice. Here, the novel would say, in the crime, is the plenum of meaning available elsewhere in the text only in dispersed fragments. The reader finds himself miming Julien's retreat from plot (temporality and syntax) to a daydreamlike moment in which everything would be present at once. For on the level of reading, the crime is the novel's transcendent precipitate, much like day-dream on the level of story. It haunts, directing and deflect-ing, whatever sequence we might establish to grasp the novel's meaning. It is the souvenir that we must always keep in mind.

THE DISAPPOINTMENT

Carrying within it its preliminaries and its consequences, the crime is formally announced as the scene of all-presence;

[12] Ibid., pp. 112 and 85-86.

yet interpretation of the crime is explicitly invited, as though this scene of presence needed to be supplemented and completed by a meaning that we must seek to find. As I have already argued, however, every meaning that one is tempted to apply seems incomplete, and one moves from one temptation to another finally (only finally) to suspend the process. Shifting explanations from one teasing suggestion to another, one engages in the process of deferring Julien's knowability. Once more, the reader reenacts a gesture of the protagonist—this time, his gesture of prolongation. One is never allowed to reach the end of interpretation, much as Julien's psychology can never constitute its own annihilation.

THE VICIOUS CIRCLE

The crime anchors the play of meanings in the text, but we are left at sea about the nature of the anchor—always drifting, always restrained by its tug. Julien's act of violence formally puts an end to our anxiety about meaning by giving meaning a location. It also, however, dooms this anxiety to repeat itself in an endless series—endless for the reason that (as Freud said about the quest for irreplaceable objects) "every surrogate . . . fails to provide the desired satisfaction."[13] We are set looking, precisely, for an irreplaceable object, the meaning that will regulate and control the novel's production of meaning, and we know the place where this meaning is to be found. Yet we find that anything we put in this place is already a replacement, never meeting the demands made on it by its station. . . .

Love Plots and Love of Plots

Lucien Leuwen is a long, patchy novel that Stendhal never finished, and my own treatment will make no pretense to cover it in its entirety. I want only to take up a few epi-

13 Freud, "A Special Type of Choice of Object Made by Men," 11: 169.

sodes where the problematic of plot might be inserted into the context developed out of our discussion of *Rouge*. Yet there are more reasons for turning to *Leuwen* than the redundancy of mere confirmation. *Rouge* presented plot as a teleological progress disappointed of its *telos*, which could only be seized in slips and souvenirs along the way. The dominant mode of this presentation was pathetic. In *Leuwen*, however, there is a tentative willingness to relish the patterns of plot for their own sake. Their "purposiveness without purpose" grounds an aesthetic potential barely suggested in *Rouge*. This view of plot as a purely artful construction, independent of the moral status of whatever end has called it into being, is both a reflection of the world of the novel, and a creative response to it, too. It reflects the bad faith of a social world in which few ends stand up to moral scrutiny, by sanctioning the irrelevance of the ethical. But it also offers a kind of compensation for participating in this world from which ethics is absent, in the possibility of salvation by stylization.

Julien Sorel felt the issues of plot with a needful urgency. Only a plot, after all, would take him from Verrières to Paris; only a scheme would make his fortune. For Lucien Leuwen, Paris is at hand, and the fortune has already been made by his father. His problem is that no end seems desirable or exigent or honest enough to justify a plot. The scenarios available under the July Monarchy do not merit the personal commitment required to realize them as genuine individual projects as well. Like *Rouge*, *Lucien Leuwen* opens with a reminder of the old and better order in which significant action was possible: the funeral of General Maximilien Lamarque, a leader of the opposition to the July Monarchy. Lucien has marched in the funeral procession, and has been expelled from the Ecole Polytechnique in consequence. *That* kind of action, then, seems hopeless from the start. Thus, a crisis of identity (Lucien says, "Je ne suis sûr de rien sur mon compte"), and a search for surrogate forms of action ("J'ai besoin d'agir et beaucoup" [LL 778]).

The first form of alternative action explored in the novel is love. The dance of approach and avoidance performed by Lucien and Mme de Chasteller should be, by now, a familiar demonstration. It has the same circular structure (seeking the natural in order to retreat from it, retreating from it by way of seeking it out once more) as that which characterized the "love" between Julien and Mathilde. Almost like textbook illustrations of the theory in *De l'Amour*, occasions that ought to facilitate the progress of love only paralyze it.[14] "On annonça madame de Chasteller. A l'instant Lucien devint emprunté dans tous ses mouvements; il essaya vainement de parler; le peu qu'il dit était à peu près inintelligible" (909).

The contradictions of an inherited male ideology are only another, less likable figure of the same dilemma. Believing the town gossip that has given Mme de Chasteller a previous lover, Lucien admits to the ridiculousness of his position: "Il aimait, sans doute avec l'envie de réussir, et cependant il était malheureux et prêt à mépriser sa maîtresse, précisément à cause de cette possibilité de réussir" (908).

Out of an inverted form of this ideology, Mme de Chasteller is caught in the same play of forces: to be a worthy object of Lucien's love, she cannot openly solicit the "object choice." (Lest too light winning make light the prize—in the prize's own eyes, too—she finally has recourse to a viciously proper "dame de compagnie," who will monitor her visits from Lucien.) With two such protagonists, it is no wonder that the history of their passion abounds in perversely insistent misunderstandings, impossible to clear up. At a soirée, for instance, Lucien tells Mme de Chasteller that he has a "frightful suspicion." She goes red from having

----

[14] "Tout ce qui est cérémonie, par son essence d'être une chose affectée et prévue d'avance, dans laquelle il s'agit de se comporter *d'une manière convenable*, paralyse l'imagination et ne la laisse éveillée que pour ce qui est contraire au but de la cérémonie, et ridicule" (Stendhal, *De l'Amour*, p. 51).

displayed her eagerness to know what it is; he goes white at not being able to tell her. If his suspicion is true, his love must die of humiliation; if false, her interest in him must give way to courtly indignation. Both lovers are kept in a permanent state of suspiciousness: he, that she is *légère*; she, that he is calculating.

Each, moreover, is likely to misread the other, turning gestures of approach into those of avoidance. In the efforts that Lucien makes to begin a love correspondence, the liability becomes literal. Mme de Chasteller's first reply, despite its appearance of reserve, is really a first step toward surrender, as indeed (Stendhal reminds us) a more vulgarly raised young man than Lucien would instantly have known. Instead, Lucien is "frightened at the severity of the language and of the deeply persuaded tone with which she exhorted him never again to speak of feelings of that nature." He thinks that he has received "un congé bien en forme." The letter of despair that he writes back will in fact overcome Mme de Chasteller by its "nearly childlike simplicity" and its "perfect, simple, effortless, hopeless devotion." But Lucien thinks that it has left him with "no means of returning to the attack," and so writes a lengthy and formal second letter, meant to redeem the helplessness and incoherence so disastrously exhibited in the first. In its way, this second letter comes from the same naive and despairing egoism that dictated the first. To Mme de Chasteller, however, it is all gross sexual politicking and Parisian fatuity, and she replies with a letter of irrevocable dismissal—"rien n'était plus sec" (960-64).

Typically, Stendhalian eros would seem to depend on love plots engendered from misjudgments and blind spots like these. Error, as it were, permits the narratable movement of errantry (wandering, elapsing, delaying) in which finally comes to lie the erotic. A love plot of this kind is a staple of Stendhalian narration, one of its chief motivations. One finds it not only in *Leuwen* and *Rouge*, but in the *Char-*

treuse as well, where the obstacles to love obviously contribute to its romantic excitement. Even those three years of
"divine happiness" that Clelia and Fabrice enjoy toward the
end of the novel contain an attenuated version of the same
structure of frustration. For Clelia can only receive Fabrice
in profound darkness: "I want you to know that, if you
should ever force me to look at you in daylight, everything
would be over between us." Moreover, the vaccination never
really allays the disease, and even here Fabrice must at last
introduce a new difficulty, compelled by "a whim of affection that changed everything" (CP 488). Other examples
are not wanting in the minor fiction. In two unfinished
novels, *Le Rose et le Vert* and *Une Position sociale*, as well
as in a short story, *Mina de Vanghel*, the narration moves
swiftly to set up a typical situation in which the lovers seem
virtually to have fetishized their own frustrations, erecting
barriers, disguising their own feelings and doubting those
of their lovers at the wrong times, and generally doing
things the hard way. Indeed, in view of the pervasiveness of
this situation in Stendhal, what strikes us as pathological in
the love between Julien and Mathilde has probably less to
do with its dependence on what obstructs it (which is, we
see, perfectly normal) than with the fact that this dependence is conscious and its unfolding accelerated. Pathology
may only be parody.

Two points may be made here about Stendhal's love plot.
The first is that it is rather difficult to take it fully on its
own professed terms. In general, the minds of the characters
seem genuinely tortured by what stands between them and
fulfillment. Doubts are real doubts that they want to clear
up, and obstacles real obstacles that they want to strike
down. One is always tempted to say, however, that while
their minds do not recognize the contradiction of desire
(which wants both to fulfill itself and to keep itself going),
their behavior takes it practically into account. "The psychical value of erotic needs is reduced as soon as their satisfaction becomes easy. An obstacle is required to heighten li-

bido."[15] This observation of Freud's may not describe the deliberate strategies of Stendhal's lovers, but it does characterize the implicit logic that these strategies display. For what Freud knew, Stendhal knew before him, as *De l'Amour* bears witness: "Toujours un petit doute à calmer, voilà ce qui fait la soif de tous les instants, voilà ce qui fait la vie de l'amour heureux. Comme la crainte ne l'abandonne jamais, ses plaisirs ne peuvent jamais ennuyer. Le caractère de ce bonheur, c'est l'extrême sérieux."[16]

Yet if Stendhal knows this, why does he rarely allow his characters to admit as much? They know the truth only "unconsciously," as if Stendhal meant to say that ignorance makes part of the bliss. Once deferment becomes a mainly conscious strategy (as in the case of Julien with Mathilde), most of the fun goes. There is also probably a further distinction to be drawn, between obstacles imposed by the lovers themselves and obstacles imposed by "the others." It is not hard to judge which kind of imposition is invested with more romance. Mina de Vanghel, for instance, creates most of her difficulties; Fabrice in the Farnese Tower has his created by others. If the *Chartreuse* (rather than *Mina de Vanghel*) seems the supreme Stendhalian love story toward which all the others aspire, it is probably because the necessity of interference *within* the movement of desire is more camouflaged, and the sincerity of desire less in question, when the function of interference can be assigned to a manifestly external reality.

There is at least one exception, among Stendhal's characters, to this rule of enforced unawareness. In the middle-aged hero of *Une Position sociale*, we find an untypical recognition.

> Il se rappelait tous les moments heureux qu'il avait dus, dans sa vie, à l'amour.

[15] Freud, "On the Universal Tendency to Debasement in the Sphere of Love," 11: 187.
[16] *De l'Amour*, p. 101.

Toujours c'était faute d'art et en se laissant entraîner
par le bonheur à être tout à fait *naturel* qu'il avait eu la
maladresse de laisser éteindre l'amour de ses maîtresses.
Faute d'art, il avait quitté plusieurs fois et à la suite de
ces accidents, il avait perdu plusieurs années de sa jeunesse
à être triste.[17]

His melancholy tone barely disguises the shock of revalua-
tion. Most of the time, Stendhal's lovers lament the fact that
they cannot be natural with their loves, as if this were the
only value that mattered. Stendhal himself can even neutralize the amatory art by assimilating it to nature. "Tout l'art
d'aimer se réduit, ce me semble, à dire exactement ce que le
degré d'ivresse du moment comporte, c'est-à-dire, en d'autres termes, à écouter son âme."[18] Now, however, the secret
dependence of nature on art (no longer absorbed into nature,
but asserted in opposition to it) is given less oblique expression. If love can fail by lack of naturalness (as in Julien's
seduction of Mme de Rênal), it can also falter through lack
of art ("faute d'art"). The vicissitudes of a love plot in
Stendhal articulate this contradictory exigency—for a plot-
less nature found only in the lapses of a highly plotted art.
Desire must always be double, moving toward a desired
object and perpetuating its own movement.

The second point to be made about Stendhal's love plot is
a narratological one. Such a plot is, optimally, never ending,
because an ending would put an end to eros. By way of cheating fulfillment, the love plot either produces new obstacles
out of its own dynamics or has them imported from other
domains. This point has already been made in the context
of the general problematic of desire in Stendhal, but in the
case of the love plot (the novels' most obvious thematization
of desire), it has a special pertinence. The two novels that
depend exclusively on this kind of plot, *Le Rose et le Vert*
and *Une Position sociale*, are unfinished, and as we have
them, there seems a logic to the incompletion. Even in the

---

[17] *Une Position sociale*, p. 468.   [18] *De l'Amour*, p. 96.

Chartreuse, the love plot does not so much finish as it is
finished off by death. There is, perhaps, a genuine resolution achieved by Julien and Mme de Rênal in *Rouge*, but it
has everything to do with Julien's approaching execution, as
though only with the knowledge of an inescapable end
could he begin to tie up his love plot as well.

As for *Lucien Leuwen*, its love plot too is left in suspense,
dismissed from center stage as the novel turns to approach
political solutions to the problem of action. But whereas the
love plot at least commanded a full commitment, political
plots in the novel require detachment. As a mode of performance, erotic involvement has been replaced by aesthetic
appreciation. The necessity of an aesthetic performance,
when the plots are political, is not difficult to determine. For
a morally sensitive young man like Lucien, or a person with
the refined irony of his father, the political plots available
for performance under the July Monarchy must be—on
their own terms—either scurrilous or coarse. What is wanted to engage in such plots is a suppression of purpose that
would allow them to be treated as largely gratuitous elaborations—sheer proofs of artfulness whose practical applica-
tions needn't be posed. Intrigue would become an aesthetic
construction, producing its own accompanying emotions,
and these would be ironically sampled rather than felt.

Between father and son, however, there is an important
contrast in both the attitude and the ability with which such
an enterprise is undertaken. Lucien only *tries* to achieve the
moral detachment of the aesthetic, and his attempts are
sabotaged in the end by the insistence of a moral conscience
that can never be definitively bracketed. Leuwen *père*, on
the other hand, begins with this detachment already acquired. His political arabesques are aestheticized easily
enough, but these then tend to impose their own motivation,
and so to be reinvested with the commitment that it was
their virtue to flout. Two kinds of moral recuperation
threaten to discredit the ambitions of the purely artful plot:
a commitment preceding it, or a commitment proceeding

from it, a moral stance outside the game, or generated from the game's own play.

We might first take up these issues where they concern Lucien: in the major political intrigue that engages him in the novel. This is his electoral mission in two *départements* (the Cher and the Calvados) to secure the election of governmental candidates. Since the Cher election is demonstrated to be already safe, the intrigue really involves only the campaigning at Caen, against the republican candidate M. Mairobert. An important liminary incident provides the relevant moral perspective. On their way to Cher, Lucien and his secretary, the ironical Coffe, make a stop at Blois. The libelous pamphlets that they are to distribute against M. Mairobert, having fallen from the roof of their carriage, are discovered by an irate mob. Denounced as a "spy" and a "police commissioner," Lucien flees from the inn to his carriage: "Comme il ouvrait la portière, une énorme pelletée de boue tomba sur sa figure, et de là sur sa cravate. Comme il parlait à M. Coffe dans ce moment, la boue entra même dans sa bouche." As if the moral implications of the scene were not already sufficiently clear,

> Un grand commis aux favoris rouges, qui fumait tranquillement au balcon du premier étage chargé de tous les voyageurs qui se trouvaient dans l'hôtel et qui dominait la scène de fort près, dit en criant au peuple:
> —Voyez comme il est sale; vous avez mis son âme sur sa figure! (LL 1189-90)

Two days later, although the carriage has been "washed, brushed, etc., etc., two separate times," Lucien reaches into one of its pouches for a notebook and finds the pouch "filled with mud still wet, and the book ruined." The mud, evidently, won't go away, and its memory recurs throughout the campaign at Caen, either explicitly or in the form of nagging moral scruples. Entering the town, he asks, "What new infamy shall I commit here?" He is shocked by the pamphlet written against Mairobert by the prefect, and

the tone of his protest is "more that of a wounded respecta-
bility than that of a commissioner of elections shocked by a
false maneuver." When confronted with the cynicism and
servility of public officials, he cries in despair: "Grand Dieu!
. . . il faut donner ma démission de tout et aller voyager en
Amérique. Ah! ce voyage-ci fera époque dans ma vie. Ceci
est bien autrement décisif que les cris de mépris et l'avanie
de Blois" (1241). Finally, in the middle of the campaign,
Lucien receives a letter from his mother. It is, of course, a
wryly understated version of what letters from mother can
be in nineteenth-century fiction; but when Mme Leuwen,
abandoned in Paris by both her husband and her son, objects
to the risks Lucien is taking "for so dirty a business," the
moral and sentimental reminder is plain enough.

The imagery of maculation always threatens to reduce
the electoral intrigue to the primal slime from which, in
moral terms, it has emerged. Why, however, does it never do
so? Why does Lucien continue to spin out the plot, elaborat-
ing it far beyond the bureaucratic requirements of the situation? An answer would seem implicitly to lie in the possibility of an aesthetic performance, retrieving "the highly
dubious justice" of Lucien's enterprise in a game compelling
on its own terms. One might compare this possibility to that,
in film theory, opened up by the concept of the *auteur*. The
materials offered to the *auteur* can be banal, shoddy, even
immoral; but under his signature, they are manipulated in
the service of higher, less immediately visible values of
style and *sprezzatura*. The space in which parodic comment, ironical reservation, and subterraneous gratification
can take place is kept hidden from all but the connoisseurs,
curtained by the very obviousness with which the materials
are displayed. The *auteur* takes the genre on its own terms,
so that these terms can be covertly overdetermined by his
own, as though personality were only discovered indirectly,
at a distance. Similarly, rather than resisting his role, Lucien
responds to its suggestiveness. Leo Bersani has placed the
Stendhalian novel in a tension between "center" and "cir-

cumference."[19] Here, the center of self is not allowed to
hold—nor to hold Lucien back from exploring the circum-
ferential possibilities that might make this center richer in
content than a "brilliant perhaps."

In another sense, however, the center is meant indeed to
hold: at the point of mental reservation. What is always kept
hors jeu, and what permits the *jeu* to take place, is the distinction between earnest and game, reality and mere play. In
order to play, Lucien must convince himself that he is *only*
playing, and playing only for low stakes. When he meets
the reputedly formidable head of the legitimist faction at
Caen, M. Le Canu, he needs to notice that "the man has the
tone of an old provincial prosecutor."

> Cette observation soulagea fort l'attention de Leuwen.
> D'après les ouvrages de M. de Chateaubriand et la haute
> idée qu'on a des jésuites, l'imagination encore jeune de
> Leuwen s'était figuré un trompeur aussi habile que le
> cardinal Mazarin, avec les manières nobles de M. de Nar-
> bonne qu'il avait entrevu dans sa première jeunesse. La
> vulgarité du ton et de la voix de M. Le Canu le rendit
> bien vite à son rôle. "Je suis un jeune homme qui mar-
> chande une terre de cent mille francs qu'un vieux pro-
> cureur ne veut pas me vendre, attendu qu'un voisin lui a
> promis un pot de vin de cent louis s'il veut la réserver
> pour lui." (1245)

Le Canu has implicitly threatened to become too real for
Lucien, so that his role is in danger of disappearing, and his
real self runs the risk of becoming part of the stakes. Satiric
commentary restores limits to the role, as if to suggest that
the self-consciousness of role playing were a way of keeping the liabilities of selfhood safely in reserve, a way of insisting that this secret selfhood actually exists.

One remarks, in passing, the perversity of the conjunc-
tion: where shady dealings are concerned, art—the supreme

---

[19] Leo Bersani, *Balzac to Beckett: Center and Circumference in
French Fiction.*

alibi—is never far away. The ambivalent value of Machiavellianism for Stendhal would seem always to contain the
prospect of an internal reorientation such as Lucien embraces, from political-ethical categories to political-aesthetic
ones. Precisely because Lucien needn't feel—mustn't let himself feel—personally at stake in the electoral maneuvering,
he can enjoy its ins and outs with a pleasure that was never
available to him in his affair with Mme de Chasteller. He
can get caught up in its demands, delighting in the stylization of events that he is instrumental in imposing. He begins, for instance, to be satisfied "that he was behaving just
as he should with this cavilling little prefect, and that he was
giving his full attention to the piece of knavery in which he
had accepted a role." At the end of the same scene: "the
consciousness of having played his role well put the incident of Blois into the background for the first time." His
dilemma is not mainly whether or not he ought to have accepted the role of commissioner of elections, so much as
how he ought to play it. "Let's see if, despite my youth, I
can manage my role properly." Once he has arranged, or
purchased, an alliance with the legitimists, he enjoys "a
store of perfect satisfaction; he felt that he had done all
that he could for a cause whose justice was in truth highly
debatable" (1222-23, 1246, 1251).

As Henry James might say, Lucien's mission is perfectly
"done." He hasn't held himself back or skimped in his commitment. Indeed, his full involvement in the mission suggests
an excessive energy, which the bureaucrats of Paris will
disapprovingly call "zeal." To some extent, Lucien has
meant his zeal to be, precisely, an oblique affront to the
Paris office. The moral objection that he entertains toward
his conduct, Stendhal tells us, is "more than compensated for
by the consciousness of having had the courage to risk without prudence the growing consideration that he was beginning to enjoy at the ministry" (1251-52). Yet we are also
allowed to see this zeal as a willingness to engage in plot for
the sake of the sheer process of plotting. Plot offers a se-

quence of dangers to circumvent, risks to take, forces to keep in balance; it asks, in a word, to be invented, composed, made interesting. If not exclusively, these are artistic concerns, and one seems fairly entitled to wonder what, as such, their bearing might be on Stendhal's own narration. Might not the "compositional" temptation to which Lucien succumbs during the campaign be a figure for the formal devices and procedures whereby the campaign is represented?

I have mainly in mind the ironic detachment assumed here by the narration toward its own motivation. For while the story of Lucien's maneuverings to defeat Mairobert is, by common consent, one of the most compelling pieces of narration in the novel, its power would not seem to depend on its being especially charged with high seriousness or deep meaning in the ordinary senses. To be sure, if we ask our habitual question, Why is such an episode in the novel?, we can, in reply, establish familiar cognitive connections in terms of theme, character, and world, some of which have already been suggested. Yet another answer, less orthodox and more frivolous, imposes itself: "because, simply, it is fun." One can't help feeling that what we most basically respond to as readers has less to do with episode's cognitive consistency with the rest of the novel than it ought. We respond chiefly, I think, to the intricate disposition of forces in the episode, and to their complicating play. How will the election go? we wonder, and we don't much care what the outcome will mean, except as a resolution of the mounting suspense. Stendhal's treatment opens up an insistent gap between cognitive and ludic functions in the episode, no longer comfortably doubling one another. The cognitive function is made to seem tenuous and peripheral, and what is vigorous and central belongs primarily to the function of game. In beautifully low-comic style, Stendhal brackets the episode from the rest of the novel. It begins when Lucien enters Caen and a man tells him "to go f... himself" ("faire f... en termes fort clairs"); and it ends when the returns have come in and General Fari tells Lucien, "We are f..."

("Nous sommes f..."), to which the narrator adds a deadpan "en effet" (1218, 1264-65). These verbal echoes enclose the episode like a pair of parentheses. For symbolically, it has only reached the point from which it started: beginning has already contained ending, and middle—that is, the campaign itself—becomes a supererogatory arabesque. We may not, then, have much to learn from the episode, and the very outrageousness of the language here suggests that the novel has taken leave of its better, more serious self, to indulge in gratuitous play.

In a more pointed demonstration than this, the elaborateness of the intrigue is developed out of proportion to the trivial and inconsequential *telos* that has called it into being. Stendhal barely bothers to canvass our interest in the candidates, the issues of the campaign, the political fate of France. How much, after all, is at stake in this election? Mairobert is practically no threat. Even after his victory—the event so feared by the government—the corruption of the July Monarchy would seem to continue unabated in the subsequent sections of the novel. What narrative connections *does* this intrigue have to the rest of the novel? One might adduce the ministerial rebuff received by Lucien in consequence of the campaign as, precisely, a seed from which more novel can grow. What would seem to grow from it, specifically, are François Leuwen's machinations in the Chambre des députés; but as one may hope to show, the extent to which Lucien's snubbing motivates his father's plots in the Chambre is problematical at the very least. Moreover, as Coffe tells Lucien, a rebuff would be incurred even if Lucien's maneuvers had succeeded in defeating Mairobert. All that matters to the rest of the novel is that Lucien display a reprehensible amount of zealousness. To speak strictly in terms of later novelistic production, the ins and outs of the campaign, its mounting suspense and complication, are sterile.

Although the outcome of the electoral campaign could not be less important for the novel as a whole, Stendhal perversely takes some trouble to develop a suspense about it—

most notably, in his temporal notations deployed so that the entire episode is watched with a sense of *time running out*: "time presses"; "and the election is the day after tomorrow"; "it is too late"; "M. Leuwen will reply immediately"; "dispatch this at once"; "I'd give a hundred louis to see M. Le Canu one hour sooner"; "if I had only forty-eight hours, the election would be mine"; "the General's spies brought them news every quarter-hour"; "every quarter-hour Lucien sent Coffe to check the telegraph"; "two o'clock struck . . . half past two—the telegraph did not move." A major structuring device, such suspense is plainly undermotivated in the novel's cognitive terms. Reasons for its being in the novel derived from these terms (such as, for instance, that it sets up an appreciation of Lucien's cool under fire) never adequately meet the case. The case is only met once we take the episode for a game, well played and sufficiently complicated to merit our interest. Suspense is there so that the game may exploit suspenseful effects.

As this example indicates, Stendhal's treatment of the episode would seem implicitly to assume a formalistic reversal of the normal priorities of nineteenth-century fiction. It is not that his narration tries to be pure in the modern French direction pointed to by a Robbe-Grillet or a Roland Barthes —that is, free from the alibis of motivation and the *vraisemblance* of prefabricated ideology. The rich texture of the traditional novel (Barthes's "babil du sens") is less unraveled by the episode than it is parodically overwoven. Character presentations have a classical fullness; and General Fari, de Séranville, Mairobert, Donis d'Angel, Le Canu, and the others are rotated into view each equipped with a plausible and operative psychology. But what must strike us as making the difference here is the conspicuously ad hoc nature of the novelistic, the way in which characters, descriptions, motivations all seem pulled from a hat so that the narration can keep going. None of these characters has appeared before in the novel, and none (except for General Fari, in a

later, vaguely placed fragment) will appear again. All that
the traditional novel tends generally to privilege—character
and its attendant issues—are here transparently put into the
service of plot. With most traditional fiction, it is a perfectly easy proposition to say that a scene exists in order to tell
us this or that about a character, thus and such about a
theme. Action serves to embody a point, a meaning. Here
the reader is slyly invited to entertain the contrary perspective: that characters, motivations, meanings exist only to
assure a desired narrative complexity. The novelistic signifiers are not in the text simply to be defined and arrested by
their meanings, but these meanings contribute to motivating
the signifying process itself.

We need to pursue the analogy established between Lucien's conduct and Stendhal's text. Lucien's willingness to
take on a role for the purely internal challenges posed by it
has its counterpart in the novelist's arbitrary display, drained
of the urgency of meaning, of what technique can do. Just
as Lucien suspends his constant self in order to produce a
provisional self out of the requirements of the situation, so
Stendhal's text sets aside ultimate questions of purpose to indulge in an episode that can sustain itself on its own terms.
So far, the analogy can seem mechanical enough; but there
is a loose screw: Lucien's relapse into ethical modes.

I have already pointed out a hint in the text that, if Lucien's "real" self is eclipsed in the electoral campaign, it remains the governing sun, ensuring the distinction between
permanent and provisional, workaday and holiday selves. As
if this distinction weren't firm enough to protect him against
the temptations of playful inventiveness, Lucien reintroduces into his adventure the self-consistency that he had
apparently abandoned on its threshold. In addition to the
moral scruples that threaten to inhibit play (the memories
of Blois), come moral scruples that allow play to proceed,
now controlled by an ethical code. When the prefect, de
Séranville, refuses to turn over the government's votes to

support the legitimist candidate against Mairobert, Lucien
fears that the legitimists (whose assistance has been purchased outright) will think him false.

> Il expliqua [to Disjonval and Le Canu] le malheur nou-
> veau avec tant de simplicité et de sincérité évidente que
> ces messieurs, qui connaissaient le génie du préfet, finirent
> par croire que Leuwen n'avait pas voulu leur tendre un
> piège. . . .
> Le pauvre Leuwen était tellement emporté par l'envie
> de ne pas passer pour un coquin, qu'il supplia M. Disjon-
> val d'accepter de sa bourse le remboursement des frais de
> messager et autres qu'avait pu entraîner la convocation
> extraordinaire des électeurs légitimistes. M. Disjonval re-
> fusa, mais, avant de quitter la ville de Caen, Leuwen lui
> fit remettre cinq cent francs par M. le président Donis
> d'Angel. (1262-63)

Such anxiety, coming when the maneuver has already been
doomed to failure, betrays a personal investment in excess
of what the role would demand. The prefect's betrayal has
risked more than the merely practical matter of diplomatic
credibility. A whole personal creed is at stake, which has
surreptitiously converted free play into fair.

How Lucien's role might be ethically salvaged had already been envisioned in a conversation between him and
Coffe, after the incident at Blois:

> —Je ne puis être plus contrarié que je ne le suis. Jetons
> la dernière ancre de salut qui reste au misérable, faisons
> notre devoir.
> —Vous avez raison, dit froidement Coffe. Dans l'ex-
> trémité du malheur, et surtout du pire des malheurs, de
> celui qui a pour cause le mépris de soi-même, faire son
> devoir et agir est en effet la seule ressource. (1196-97)

This sternly enunciated morality of duty will scarcely account for the pleasure that Lucien comes to find in his role,

but it is a way of recomposing the self-divisions that the role has opened up.

To bolster this position seems a main function of the military metaphors used by Lucien—"strategic naming," in Kenneth Burke's phrase, if ever there were. The standard themes of a military code of honor (the cowardice of desertion, the fight to the finish, and the like) recur throughout the campaign, as spurs to action. "I didn't want to see a battle lost before my very eyes without sending in our troops." And after the battle, this consolation: "Although the battle was lost, I sent in my regiment." It is obviously helpful to this way of seeing that Lucien is assisted in his maneuvers by an actual general, Fari, who speaks of Mairobert "as he would have done of a Prussian general commanding the town that he was besieging" (1250, 1263, 1225). Typically, these metaphors evoke a losing, or lost, battle which must in honor be fought out. Lucien's situation, in fact, does not entirely justify this perspective on it—suspense depends on a possibility that the "battle" might be won. The military metaphors, however, reintroduce into the situation the possibility of honorable action, which the alternative imagery of "un bourbier sans issue" threatened to foreclose. Moreover, if the battle can be perceived as already lost, then the ethical status of the losing cause, powerless in any case to impose itself, need not be an overriding concern. Indeed, to accept defeat in advance may well be a moral strategy for recouping the dubious justice of this cause.

These ethical guarantees, then, are perhaps so many ways of permitting play to proceed, by masking, or doubling, or neutralizing its amoral inventiveness. A system of military metaphors nicely expresses the double nature of Lucien's enterprise. For the military field is one in which ethics and tactics can comfortably coexist: the games of war, as it were, are played on the field of honor. Lucien's conduct thus strikes a compromise between the modalities of game and earnest, continually negotiating between the appeal of a self that would be free to be reconstituted by the roles that traverse it, and the demand of a self that would adhere to a central character or personality. In this way, self-consistency is readmitted into a role initially defined by its eccentric relationship to self. The *auteur*'s style, so to speak, has recovered the diversity of his *oeuvre*, providing a fund of repetitions with which to neutralize the differences.

This is the ultimate function of military metaphors in the episode: to assimilate new experience into an older, established problematic of self. As always in Stendhal, military metaphors, by their very status as metaphors, define the situation of the latecomer. Their pathos stems from the fact that their source, in the Napoleonic campaigns, is now available only as a figurative vehicle—in electoral ones, for instance. Earlier in the novel, Lucien has been a lieutenant in a real regiment, called out in a policing action against organizing workers. For seven hours or so under a hot summer sun, the soldiers stand about in a public square, without food or drink. Someone eventually fires a shot, but no one is hurt. On this listless instance of repression, Stendhal comments, "Such was Leuwen's first campaign" (993). Military metaphors put Lucien's electoral mission in the same ironical series as his first campaign: a series of so many variations on Lucien's position when the novel opens, defined in the symbolism of the funeral of General Lamarque.

Lucien may always be a "brilliant perhaps," in the sense that neither he nor his narrator knows what will become of him; but the brilliant perhaps tends to display more regularity than the formula by itself suggests: always attached, at least, to a core of social-psychological insistencies. Yet if Lucien is always slipping back to a consistent self, even when he would appear to be slipping away from it, what of Stendhal's novel? Does the text have the equivalent of a consistent self—a fixed center, or an overall meaning, to which elements can be referred? In what might its consistency consist? To an important extent, *Lucien Leuwen* makes these questions hard ones. For apparently, the recurring themes and attitudes that anchor Lucien as a character only propel the narration endlessly onward, from one episode to the next. The point of the exercise is located on an ever-receding horizon, as though Stendhal were trying, and failing, to surprise himself into a revelation of what his story was all about.

The relatively closed and centered form of the other major novels provides a significant contrast. Both *Rouge* and the *Chartreuse* build up to a major event (Julien's crime, Fabrice's imprisonment in the Farnese Tower), which can serve as a central reference for questions of form and meaning. In both novels, moreover, the protagonist dies—narratologically, a consummation much to be wished, for his death can motivate the curtailment of narration, and ensure the minimal narrative coherence of biography. Not only does *Lucien Leuwen* lack these resources; it also lacks a source. *Rouge* and the *Chartreuse* could amplify and alter their sources (respectively, the newspaper account of Antoine Berthet's trial and the Farnese manuscript); but these sources remained to limit, shape, and sanction the novelistic production. One is even tempted to say that they could be made to bear the burden of meaning, much as a model ensures the meaning of its copy, or as a proper term validates the figurative substitutions for it. To be sure, Stendhal began *Leuwen* as a revision of *Le Lieutenant* by Madame Gaulthier; as Henri Martineau points out, however, "from the mass of notes, instructions, alterations, and successive plans with which Stendhal overloads the margins of his manuscript, one can deduce that the work of his lady-friend was barely more than a springboard on which to take flight" (737). "Springboard" is one way of putting it; but what the notes would seem to prove is that Stendhal's source had failed him, requiring him to go out on his own.

The problems of a central controlling meaning are clearly related to the text's unfinished state. An ending, at least, would have invoked a retrospective illusion, organizing what had gone before into a meaningful pattern. Indeed, twentieth-century narrative theory usually assumes that *telos* produces the meaningfulness of narrative in the first place. If all else fails, a minimal meaning for every narrative unit can be found in the ways in which it allows an ending to come about. In my readings of Jane Austen and George Eliot, I have argued that this assumption hides the profound discrepancy between the narrative movement and the claims of closure. In *Lucien Leuwen*, such an assumption simply becomes untenable, for there is not even a *telos* of which the work can be read as a function.

Moreover, the incompleteness of *Leuwen* seems a more intrinsically determined matter than, say, the incompleteness of Dickens's *Edwin Drood*. Had Dickens lived to complete his mystery story, one can be certain that nearly all the elements in the text as it now stands would have been fitted into an overall design, like those that govern his other mature works. If one has had no such certainty in the case of *Leuwen*, it is in part because its incompleteness seems only to radicalize a compositional principle found even in Stendhal's completed novels. This principle might be named "resistance to closure." Critics have noticed, in *Rouge*, the abruptness with which Julien comes to crime, and the formal resolution that the crime guarantees seems undercut by its sudden, insufficiently motivated appearance. Julien's subsequent failure to resolve internally the novel's own closure baffles one's sense of an ending even further. If the closure of *Rouge* is suspiciously emphatic, that of the *Chartreuse* is perhaps not emphatic enough: it is, really, an enforced fade-out, although the editor who made Stendhal shorten the work into two volumes may be partly to blame.

Despite his great admiration for *Tom Jones*, Stendhal never displays Fielding's kind of care in his own constructions. *Rouge* can seem to be the best articulated of Stendhal's plots. Julien's rise is divided into three major stages (tutor in Verrières, seminarian in Besançon, secretary in Paris), each of which is prefaced by an important threshold scene. Yet what propels Julien from one stage to the next is rather a lateral development than the main one. Brilliance and hard work don't move him from Verrières to Besançon—only the fear of scandal that his affair with Mme de Rênal has put into her husband, who wants to get him out of town in a socially plausible fashion. Similarly, it is not his academic success at the seminary that procures him his appointment as secretary to the marquis de la Mole; simply, the Abbé Pirard accepts a benefice in Paris and decides to rescue Julien along with himself. Even Julien's title and commission do not result directly from his schemes of advancement, but from the unforeseen pregnancy of Mathilde, who now wants to marry him. It is always as though the direct channels established for a linear progression from one stage to another were being deliberately ignored in favor of an expansion of peripheral possibilities.

There is nothing even so organic as this in *Leuwen*. New exfoliations of plot are introduced with all their arbitrariness left uncovered. For instance, the transition between the provincial part of the novel and the Parisian one could not be a clumsier or more conspicuous display of novelistic sleight of hand. A comically malevolent doctor, M. Du Poirier, counterfeits Mme de Chasteller's illness into an apparent childbirth, which Lucien has been secretly placed to witness. He is so disgusted at this "proof" of betrayal that he leaves almost at once for Paris. The child is grossly overdeveloped for a newborn infant, but if the narrator flaunts the fact, Lucien does not notice it. A realistic verisimilitude has been openly sacrificed on the altar of proliferating story.

If *Leuwen* is internally doomed to incompleteness, it is not on account of a poverty of imagination, but on account of an inability to restrict it. The textual production is too fertile, the "digressive" intrigues too ready to insert themselves, for the narrative not to seem *all* digression, all local effect. The manuscript trails off with Lucien accepting a diplomatic post abroad. Here is its last, unconcluding paragraph: "Enfin, en arrivant à son poste, à Capel [Stendhal's code name for Rome], il eut besoin de se sermonner pour prendre envers les gens qu'il allait voir le degré de sécheresse convenable" (1384). It is a stunning piece of impudence that, after seven hundred or so pages, the narrative should so shed its skin. The accumulated foundation of the fiction is coolly dismissed; and the novel will apparently move on to drive new pilings ("pilotis," as Stendhal called them), on which a new world ("Capel"), new characters ("les gens qu'il allait voir"), and new intrigues (requiring a "degré de sécheresse convenable") can be fabricated. We know that Stendhal eventually decided to suppress this third, Roman section of his novel; but the decision seems to have involved not so much questions of artistic form, as a fear that the reader's capacity to absorb new material had been exhausted. "Je supprime le troisième volume, par la raison que ce n'est que dans la première chaleur de la jeunesse et de l'amour que l'on peut avaler une exposition et de nombreux personnages. Arrivé à un certain âge, cela est impossible" (740).

Martineau says that when Stendhal abandoned the third volume, he realized, as an unforeseen consequence of his decision, that his novel was in fact finished, wanting only some revisions and its ending. Unless the revisions were to be more considerable than Martineau implies, however, it is hard to imagine an ending that could tidy up so many loose threads. Various "plans pour la fin" suggest concluding with a marriage between Lucien and Mme de Chasteller; but if this nicely ties up the love plot, it turns the political sections into excessively prolonged digressions. It is perhaps significant that the plans remained at the level of plans—even when Stendhal, having liquidated his third volume, was according to Martineau in a position to execute them. We might look at a suggestive pair of these plans, to see how Stendhal imagined placing the marriage in the narrative.

PLAN *for the end.*—Une brouille vraiment sérieuse sépare Mme de Chasteller de Lucien. Elle a raison d'être en colère (par la fourberie et scélératesse de Mme Grandet, à laquelle, dès qu'elle a une passion, le chagrin

d'amour-propre d'être laissée, les crimes ne coûtent plus rien). Lucien, croyant tout fini, va à Omar. Là, quelque sage lui dit: "Vous ne parviendrez à oublier Mme de Chasteller que par une nouvelle liaison." Il s'attache à Mme la duchesse qui le fait destituer et le jette dans la pauvreté. Alors, Mme de Chasteller sent renaître toute sa tendresse et l'épouse en lui donnant ce qu'elle a, 15 ou 20.000 livres de rente. Mme Grandet devient un diable quand elle est quittée. Modèle: lady Menti. Extrêmement folle et passionnée. Civita-Vecchia, 5 février 1835.
[This plan was written before Stendhal abandoned the third part; Martineau notes that the line evoking Lucien's departure for Rome (Omar) has written over it "supprimé." The rest would seem to stand.] (1589)

Plan pour la fin.—Madame de Chasteller se fait épouser, Leuwen croyant qu'elle a fait un enfant. A Paris, après la noce: "Tu es à moi, lui dit-elle en le couvrant de baisers. Pars pour Nancy. Tout de suite, monsieur, tout de suite! Tu sais malheureusement combien mon père me hait. Interroge-le, interroge tout le monde. Et écris-moi. Quand tes lettres montreront la conviction (et tu sais que je suis bon juge), alors tu reviendras, mais seulement alors. Je saurai fort bien distinguer la philosophie d'un homme de bon sens qui pardonne une erreur antérieure à son bail, ou l'impatience de l'amour que tu as naturellement pour moi, de la conviction sincère de ce coeur que j'adore." Leuwen revient au bout de huit jours.—"Fin du roman."
[Martineau claims that this plan dates very probably from the first months of the novel's composition, that is, the summer of 1834.] (740)

In the plan I have put first, the marriage of Lucien and Mme de Chasteller concludes an elaborate and extensive spiraling of plot. Quasi-automatically, Stendhal ends the plan on an unresolved note (Mme Grandet's fury at being scorned), when he could easily have placed it before the marriage resolution. In the plan I have put second, it is the marriage

resolution itself that provokes an oddly anticlimactic arabesque. Enveloped, and nearly eclipsed by the intrigues sur-
rounding it on either side, the marriage resolution seems in
danger of disappearing—at least, qua resolution. Even at the
level of planning, Stendhal's imagination would seem invariably to veer away from the finality conferred by closure.

Why were the plans not used? One might note that both
of those cited would entail a rather more considerable addition to the text than the mere "mise au point" of Martineau's
argument begins to suggest. Perhaps Stendhal was exhausted
in advance by the prospect of carrying his story to the
lengths presupposed in his plans for ending it. Perhaps too,
as I have already suggested, the marriage resolution didn't
seem to conclude enough of his story. Yet when the plans
themselves exhibit a tendency to redissolve the final chord
into an extended cadenza, one has grounds for suspecting
that their very status *as plans*—holding out an unrealized
prospect of resolution—may have been preserved according to a logic. A plan that remains a plan is in effect a strategy for having and not having one's ending. In a sense,
Lucien Leuwen is the only major novel by Stendhal in which
love conquers all, for the logic of his love plots—desire's
double movement—is here wholly absorbed into the novel's
structural program.

A last example of plot in *Leuwen*, embracing all the issues
attendant on it, is the legislative intriguing of Leuwen *père*.
Here, plot is at once an indirection—desire's wily detour on
the road to gratification; a deflection, away from the motivation generating it; an autonomous structure controlled at
an aesthetic distance; and finally, an autonomous structure
controlling the very agent who was apparently mastering it.
All these incongruous, even contradictory possibilities are
plotted against one another, in a half-exuberant, half-pa-
thetic tension that is left, typically, unresolved.

François Leuwen's legislative career is, at its beginning,
archly undermotivated. He puts himself up as a candidate in

Aveyron, out of what his wife calls "une velléité d'ambition," and wins the election. Mme Leuwen's phrase already
suggests somewhat conflicting motives that tend to cancel
one another out. Ambition is generally taken for a more exacting passion (think of Julien's) than can be expressed by
a mere *velléité*. M. Leuwen's own report of the electoral
campaign could not be more worldly in tone. "The air was
warm, the partridges excellent and full of flavor, and the
men amusing." The trivial provincial issues that he has been
made to engage are presented with parodic seriousness:

> Un de mes honorables commettants m'a chargé de lui en-
> voyer quatre paires de bottes bien confectionnées; je dois
> commencer par étudier le mérite des bottiers de Paris, il
> faut un *ouvrage* élégant, mais qui pourtant ne soit pas
> dépourvu de solidité. Quand enfin j'aurai trouvé ce bottier
> parfait, je lui remettrai la vielle botte que M. de Malpas a
> bien voulu me confier. J'ai aussi un embranchement de
> route royale de cinq quarts de lieue de longueur pour con-
> duire à la maison de campagne de M. Castanet, que j'ai
> juré d'obtenir de M. le ministre de l'Intérieur; en tout
> cinquante-trois commissions, outre celles qu'on m'a pro-
> mis par lettre. (1274)

His pleasure can seem perverse. Was he bored or wasn't he?
a literal-minded reader might ask of the following passage:

> —Enfin, je ne me suis pas ennuyé un instant dans ce
> département, et si j'y avais eu ma femme, j'aurais été par-
> faitement heureux. Il y a bien des années que je n'avais
> parlé aussi longtemps à un aussi grand nombre d'ennu-
> yeux, aussi suis-je saturé d'ennui officiel et de platitude à
> dire ou à entendre sur le gouvernement. Aucun de ces
> bênets du juste milieu, répétant sans les comprendre les
> phrases de Guizot ou de Thiers, ne peut me donner en
> écus le prix de l'ennui mortel que sa présence m'inspire.
> Quand je quitte ces gens-là, je suis encore bête pour une
> heure ou deux, je m'ennuie moi-même. (1274-75)

Much like Jane Austen's Mr. Bennet, who is pleased that "his cousin was as absurd as he had hoped," M. Leuwen takes ironical delight in the display of folly. He is a more active ironist than Mr. Bennet, however, actually working to stage the exhibitions on which his irony can be exercised. Here, his enjoyment would seem to come not only from his deep sense of detachment from the comedy, but also from his gratification at having shaped its scenes. The *telos* of his political plot would be plotting itself: interesting enough to keep him from boredom, not so interesting that it tricks him into commitment, the worst bore of all.

When he hears how Lucien's zeal in Caen has gone unrewarded, he forms a project of revenge against the ministry. Yet if there is now a passion behind his political plots, it is kept well harnessed. It doesn't irrupt inopportunely into his schemes, like Julien's passion; nor does it inspire them with a mad bravura like Sanseverina's, in her scene before the prince ("elle avait agi par hasard"). In Leuwen's case, plot stores up passion, like a venom to be discharged only at strategic moments. For all his cool, however, he is not meant to be chilling; and when passion is released, what emerges is more sharply felt than a merely worldly *velléité*: "Son discours était le débondement d'un coeur ulcéré qui s'est retenu deux mois de suite et qui, pour parvenir à la vengeance, s'est dévoué à l'ennui le plus plat" (1283). Stendhal's favorite way of redeeming his intriguers is to endow them with a passion of this kind: proof that they are superior to the intrigues that engage them. A Mosca or a Julien Sorel has conceived his schemes out of motives transcending them; and like them, François Leuwen can display a mad daring. The minister of finance says of him, "—C'est un homme d'humeur. . . . Quelquefois il a les vues les plus nettes des choses, en d'autres moments, pour satisfaire à un caprice, il sacrifierait sa fortune et lui avec" (1289). What gives scandal to the world's good sense edifies the happy few.

Between Leuwen's actions and his declared motivation, however, there obtains a curiously oblique relationship. Although we are told that "M. Leuwen n'admettait jamais la périphrase parlementaire," what is true of his diction is less true of his conduct as a whole. What else is his legislative style, in one sense, but a periphrasis—a longer phrasing in place of a shorter, more direct one? As the "Talleyrand of the Stock Exchange" in a society whose king and ministers alike speculate on the market, he has an obvious and direct means of asserting power. Deliberately, he takes a longer and less sure way about. "Comme banquier, je ne puis sacrifier un iota sur la probité." Despite how the novel has defined probity in financial transaction, he is probably sincere. In effect, however, probity functions as an ethical alibi, much as duty did for Lucien, permitting M. Leuwen to pass from an old game at which he is already expert to a new, more challenging one.

For it is hard to justify his legislative intriguing entirely with reference to a project of personal revenge. At what point would vengeance be satisfied? After his devastating speeches in the Chambre? after Lucien's promotion, his cross, his expected government post? after the replacement of M. Vaize? after Mme Grandet's surrender? Far from being premeditated, these projects are largely improvised according to the possibilities opened up by the play of the political situation. Significantly, the text bothers to relate the plot to its declared motivation only once or twice; and if, at a certain distance, a desire for vengeance stands behind the construction of a plot, it does not immediately, in specific ways, determine its successive articulations. To a large extent, the elaborations to which periphrasis gives voice are irreducible. Suppose, even, that the plot reached the provisional end point to which it seems to aspire: the moronic M. Grandet made minister, his wife made Lucien's mistress, and everybody made to see "that it is really Lucien who is minister in his person." Could plot come to a halt even here? In conversation with his wife, M. Leuwen already envisions the challenges of an extended scenario:

—A la Chambre, [M. Grandet] parlera comme vous savez. Il lira comme un laquais les excellents discours que je commanderai aux meilleurs faiseurs, à cent louis par discours *réussi*. Je parlerai. Aurai-je du succès pour la défense comme j'en ai eu pour l'attaque? C'est ce que je suis curieux de voir, et cette incertitude m'amuse. (1331)

To avenge Lucien seems only a necessary pretext for a plot that stops nowhere.

If the skewed relationship between plot and motivation didn't exist, something like it would have to be invented, for it is this that ensures the possibility of ironical participation. On the one hand, irony is protected against the risks of participation. The terms of plot can never be taken with the seriousness of full commitment, because motivation has been placed elsewhere, outside its domain. On the other hand, participation is secured against the threat of irony. Precisely because it *isn't* clear at every step how plot relates to the motivation inspiring it, its arabesques can be enjoyed and developed for their own sake, without being reduced to their source. Paradoxically, it is passion, placed at a distance, that allows plot to have its maximal aesthetic interest as an assertion of control and controlling style.

These formal conditions, framing plot in a structure of detached engagement, reappear at the level of content: in the specific maneuvers of the plot framed. M. Leuwen's plot is programatically outrageous, as though the fact that it *could* be imposed justified the attitude behind its imposition. In its very cynicism, there is an almost ethical guarantee against the loss of detachment. For if Leuwen's plot can give proof that men are stupid, venal, and boringly knowable, why then shouldn't he, a master plotter confronted with such preposterously fixed human counters, move them about in his own game? Yet why play at all? Were the cynical vision instituted by the plot a matter of plain fact, there would be little point to engaging it. Peter Brooks has compared M. Leuwen to Valmont, in *Les Liaisons dange-*

reuses;[20] and just as Valmont never wanted much to seduce "easy" women, Leuwen's amusement—almost his excitement —depends not on characters whose freedom has been already scaled down to a mechanical fixity, but on those whose asserted independence of his pattern offers a challenge. One recalls the importance of the episode, seemingly oversized in terms of strict relevance, in which two deputies in his Légion du Midi start to rebel. They are evidently more interesting to him than his twenty-six faithful "goslings," for what engages him is rather the process of reduction than an already reduced product.

A single example in which the text makes this explicit is the scene of Leuwen's preliminary bargaining with Mme Grandet: a portfolio for her husband, against a mistress— herself—for Lucien. The interview begins with some mechanical posturing on her part—"protestations infinies," "circonlocutions bien longues," "louanges de sa propre sincérité"—and Leuwen counts the minutes on the clock. His fun begins only when she has the temerity to think that she is free of his control. She suggests, for instance, that her husband has credit of his own at the Château.

> A ces mots, M. Leuwen prit un air extrêmement froid. La scène commencait à l'amuser, il valait la peine de jouer la comédie. Madame Grandet, alarmée et presque déconcertée, malgré la tenacité de son esprit qui ne s'effarouchait pas pour peu de chose, se mit à parler de l'amitié de lui, Leuwen, pour elle. . . .
>
> A ces phrases d'amitié qui demandaient un signe d'assentiment, M. Leuwen restait silencieux et presque absorbé. Madame Grandet vit que sa tentative échouait.
>
> "J'aurai gâté nos affaires," se dit-elle. Cette idée la prépara aux partis extrêmes et augmenta son degré d'esprit.
>
> Sa position empirait rapidement: M. Leuwen était loin d'être pour elle le même homme qu'au commencement

---

[20] Peter Brooks, *The Novel of Worldliness: Crébillon, Marivaux, Laclos, Stendhal*, p. 241.

de l'entrevue. D'abord, elle fut inquiète, puis effrayée.
Cette expression lui allait bien et lui donnait de la physio-
nomie. M. Leuwen fortifia cette peur.

La chose en vint au point de gravité que madame Grandet prit le parti de lui demander ce qu'il pouvait avoir
contre elle. M. Leuwen, qui depuis trois quarts d'heure
gardait un silence presque morne, de mauvais présage,
avait toutes les peines du monde en ce moment à ne pas
éclater de rire. (1322)

The moment of maximal aesthetic interest ("the scene began to amuse him," "the expression of fear suited her well
and gave her face character") coincides with the moment
of asserted control. Later, in the same scene, when Mme
Grandet's pleading has itself become routinized, Leuwen is
bored again: "Elle se laisse traiter comme un conscrit qu'on
mène au duel." Yet as he delivers his parting shot—the conditions of the bargain—amusement triumphs once more over
boredom, almost as if he could foresee the *Phèdre*-like struggles that will begin when he leaves. "Il se sentit saisi d'un tel
besoin d'éclater de rire qu'il s'enfuit."

Infernal laughter, instantaneous disappearance—this
sounds Mephistophelian; and indeed, at moments like these,
Leuwen's plot can look like a successful power fantasy entertained by a diabolically comic playwright. His perfect
control of plot and—what this tends to mean—his perfect
control of meaning are not the least fantastical aspects of his
success, in the context of Stendhal's fiction. The meaning
of Mme Grandet's surrender has been waiting all along, before she even surrendered, to reclaim her momentary resistance. By reducing herself to her own manipulable ambition, she confirms the "worldly" vision. This worldly
vision functions to provide meaning in advance: whatever
happens in the plot is intended to be easily recovered into
Leuwen's sense of men as meretricious puppets on a string.
So, meaning is already in place at the start; and for a time,
although it may be deliciously teased by the resistance of a

Mme Grandet, nothing happens really to threaten it. Although in one sense, then, Leuwen's plot would seem to consign itself to the metonymical (sliding from one situation to another) and the diachronic (consenting to temporal incompleteness), in another sense, his plot neither veers nor even has a course, always returning to an already arrested sense. To this extent, it is almost not a plot at all: what appears a series of sequential moves into contiguous squares defines in fact repeated statements of an already appointed theme.

The necessity of repetition, however, may betray an anxiety about the continuing presence of meaning, as though its temporary disappearance and return had always to be restaged, much as in the child's game of *Fort!/Da!* reported by Freud. More simply, it may testify to a gambler's need to play his system for ever higher stakes. The logic of either case wouldn't be much different. Leuwen's later faux pas are not departures from his program, but perfectly consistent with it. To back the stupid Grandet (so stupid that even the other ministers won't have him) and to tell Lucian the truth of his affair with Mme Grandet are both gestures that hubristically flaunt his confidence in an always-being-reconfirmed worldliness. He has merely raised the ante, as it were—only widened the gap between the *Fort!* and the *Da!* If these two moves begin to subvert his control of meaning, it is because they demonstrate a dangerous fixity. Leuwen has become less the plotter, governing his plot by responding to its own suggestiveness, than the neurotic fantasist, repeating a once gratifying meaning in contexts that no longer sustain it.

Leuwen has controlled reality, but he has never really believed in its authority:

Comme son succès à la Chambre ne lui avait coûté aucun travail, il ne pouvait croire à sa durée, ni presque à sa réalité. Là était l'illusion, là était le coin de folie, là était la preuve du plaisir extrême produit par ce succès et

la position incroyable qu'il avait créée en trois mois.
(1328)

He is thus unprepared for the counterfinality by which, as
Sartre might put it, he becomes "the product of his product." The worldly plot cannot be kept at the proper worldly distance. The whim of ambition becomes a full-scale attack of it ("un accès d'ambition"), and the legislative in-
triguings induce motives that will sustain them on their own
terms.

> *Que puis-je demander?* Si je ne prends rien de substantiel,
> au bout de deux mois le ministère que j'aurai aidé à naître
> se moque de moi, et je suis dans une *position ridicule*. Me
> faire receveur général, cela ne signifie rien pour moi
> comme argent et d'ailleurs c'est un avantage trop subal-
> terne pour ma position actuelle à la Chambre. Faire Lu-
> cien préfet malgré lui, c'est ménager à celui de mes amis
> qui sera ministre de l'Intérieur le moyen de me jeter dans
> la boue en le destituant, ce qui arriverait avant trois mois.
> —Mais ne serait-ce pas un beau rôle que de faire le bien
> et de ne rien prendre? dit madame Leuwen.
> —C'est ce que notre public ne croira jamais. M. de
> Lafayette a joué ce rôle pendant quarante ans, et a tou-
> jours été sur le point d'être ridicule. Ce peuple-ci est trop
> gangrené pour comprendre ces choses-là. Pour les trois
> quarts de gens de Paris, M. de Lafayette eût été un homme
> admirable s'il eût volé quatre millions. Si je refusais le mi-
> nistère et montais ma maison de façon à dépenser cent mille
> écus par an, tout en achetant des terres (ce qui montrerait
> que je ne me ruine pas), on ajouterait foi à mon génie, et
> je garderai la supériorité sur tous ces demi-fripons qui
> vont se disputer le ministère. (1312)

This plot must go someplace, then, to a place where it is not
ridiculous to be. "What can I ask for?" It is a question that
need not have been addressed, if the pretexted motivation in
paternal feeling retained any authority. Moreover, the ques-

tion is not put in terms of a worldly project, such as we have defined it: Leuwen is not seeking out new occasions on which to practice his reductionism. It becomes, really, a matter of verisimilitude turning into truth. The social surface no longer merely cloaks, or doubles for, private passions and fantasies; it actually begins to define what these passions and fantasies shall be.

One might invoke, very imperfectly, a linguistic analogy. The relationship in a word between its signifier and its signified is theoretically arbitrary. There is no reason why, say, the sound "sister" should impose the concept "sister." Yet in the actual practice of speech, the relationship changes from an arbitrary to a necessary one. " 'Sister' and the signified sister are not actually divisible for a speaker of English: the word comes to him already defined by a collective context."[21] By analogy, then, a master of worldliness might be seen to exploit the "arbitrariness of the signifier." Like Valmont, he can mime all the social signs of love, without feeling any; his naive victims will never suspect until too late that outward signs do not necessarily constitute inward graces. However, the transcendental viewpoint is less easily maintained than worldly masters like to assume. Valmont's end is exemplary in this regard. Whether or not one can safely say that he is in love with the Présidente, the cynical distance between the actor and his role has been disturbingly reduced. Worldly masters tend to ignore the force of the context in which they operate, and hence the extent to which signifiers can produce their conventionally given signifieds in those who would wield them. As if in proof of Pascal's claim that a gesture of genuflection helps to impose the belief that it signifies, Machiavellians typically fall prey to belief, or sincerity, or more than *mondain* involvement in their schemes.

It is as though meaning needs always to be anchored. The

[21] Anthony Wilden, *The Language of the Self*, p. 215. Wilden is following here the argument of Emile Benveniste, in "Nature du signe linguistique," *Problèmes de linguistique générale*, pp. 49-55.

signifying chain cannot proliferate endlessly or pointlessly; but it must be appropriated in what, following Jacques Lacan, can be called *points de capiton*: "points like the buttons on a mattress or the intersections in quilting, where there is a 'pinning down' (*capitonnage*) of meaning, not to an object, but rather by 'reference back' to a symbolic function."[22] I have already discussed several anchoring points outside the plot proper, which permit it to take place in a precharted terrain and install it within a symbolic function: the pretexted motivation of a project of revenge; the ultimate reference of worldliness; the ethical alibis. These do not evidently suffice to resist "the enchantment of the signifier," and a new anchoring point is now sought out within the plot's own signifying chain: in a project of political ambition, to which characters and events could be referred, and which could police the multiplying possibilities of meaning. The number and the variety of such anchoring points, taken all together, attest the intensity of the need to arrest the play of meaning. Yet is the spell of the signifier broken in this way, or is it rebound? The very multiplicity of these anchoring points suggests that they can be played off against one another, like the various motives for Julien's crime; and it reintroduces the indeterminacy that each of them individually seemed meant to forestall.

The novel abandons the plot, whose agent entertains so many different schemes of appropriating its play, precisely when the play seems to have escaped his control and things get interesting. Chapter 68 begins with an outrage that we have learned almost to expect: "after the sudden death of M. Leuwen." Presumably, in the piece of missing narration, which Stendhal never chose to write, the "sudden death" would be more directly announced; but the suddenness would remain. Much as a sudden death violates our estab-

[22] Wilden, *Language of Self*, p. 273. See Jacques Lacan, "L'Instance de la lettre dans l'inconscient ou la raison depuis Freud," *Ecrits*, pp. 493-528.

lished patterns of expected meanings in life, so in the novel, a fortiori, it forcibly introduces disorder. Deaths that are prepared for, waited upon, even lingered over, are extremely common in the traditional realistic novel—not, however, sudden deaths. (Even in the twentieth century, E. M. Forster can shock us when he abruptly kills off a character before *The Longest Journey* has barely begun: "Gerald died that afternoon. He was broken up in the football match.") Sudden death would seem to impugn the novelist's control—his comforting omniscience. If life is as arbitrary as that, if what is to be represented does not conform to the laws of novelistic consistency, then what are the grounds of representation? In the arbitrary turns of the representation, the novel must implicitly glance at the arbitrariness of its own construction. Leuwen's death would be almost an allegory of Stendhalian ending, as we have come to see it: no ending at all. Meaning is not concluded, but kept in a state of becoming (or, what comes to the same, in a state of dispersion).

Is Leuwen punished, precisely, for presuming to control meaning? More than any other of Stendhal's characteristically deficient fathers (old Sorel, the marquis del Dongo), he has commanded the destiny of his son. Lucien has willingly acceded to nearly all his father's impositions; but a startling revelation is made late in the novel: he doesn't love him. "Lucien avait un grand remords à propos de son père. Il n'avait pas d'amitié pour lui, c'est ce qu'il se reprochait souvent sinon comme un crime, du moins comme un manquement de coeur" (1315). And in the wake of his father's telling him the truth about Mme Grandet, he thinks:

> Mon père est comme tous les pères, ce que je n'avais pas su voir jusqu'ici; avec infiniment plus d'esprit et même de sentiment qu'un autre, il n'en veut pas moins me rendre heureux *à sa façon* et non à la mienne. Et c'est pour servir cette passion d'un autre que je m'hébète depuis huit mois par le travail de bureau le plus excessif, et dans le fait le plus stupide (1355)

In a sense, by arranging a sudden death for M. Leuwen, the narrative assumes and acts out this latent Oedipal aggressiveness on Lucien's behalf. To kill the father, however, means also to supplant him: to assume the father's symbolic functions. The function of manipulation passes from Leuwen to be taken up directly by the novelist himself, who must ostentatiously play the role of arch-puppeteer in order to reduce Leuwen to a puppet. Yet in another sense, of course, Leuwen's schemes have always been just as much the novelist's work as his sudden death and Lucien's liberation. Of the Oedipal contest that the plots of Stendhal's novels notoriously feature (in the relationship of Julien to old Sorel, Abbé Pirard, the marquis de la Mole, of Lucien to Leuwen *père*, of Fabrice to Mosca), it may be asked, whose side, father's or son's, is taken by the narrative itself?

The Oedipal struggle in Stendhal might be seen as the novelist's most congenial representation of the logic of his narration: its double postulation of authority and subversion. The paternal imposition coincides with the demands of ending, or (what depends on it) meaning: definitive, already in place, requiring only to be reconfirmed. The filial challenge in turn motivates the anxious strategies for delaying, evading, and eliding this fixture. Actual fathers and sons and their relationships may thematize the Oedipal figure, but it is not confined to such literal enactments. The functions of Father, Son migrate in devious, paradoxical ways. Leuwen, for instance, functions mainly like a father, but when he is imposed upon by his own plot, he is in a position like that of his son. In like manner, when Lucien chooses for himself (as at Caen) the roles that have been chosen for him, he becomes his own father. In a still more extended sense, we have seen how Stendhalian narrative always constitutes itself as a prolonged act of resisting authority, as an evasion from the incompletely sealed space of its immobilizing domination. Temperamentally, we know, Stendhal is partial to this movement of evasion. Yet the filial challenge inevitably occurs within a paternal relationship, and it is sustained only by

upholding as well, in however spectral a fashion, the authority that its value comes from threatening. So, Stendhalian narration must always chase after its own tail. whether one prefers to see that tail as a phallic power of control,
or simply, in more purely narratological terms, as a tail *end*.

The End: Conversation on the Way

In Chapter 6 of the second book of *Le Rouge et le Noir*,
Julien Sorel fights a duel, and the episode is one contretemps
after another. In the first place, Julien is eager to challenge
a man who has merely looked at him crosswise, mainly because he failed to challenge another man who looked at him
crosswise earlier in the story. The duel is already a surrogate
for a lost opportunity, another black parody of red originals;
and in a wider sense, dueling in general is only a travesty of
the Napoleonic military engagement. In the second place,
there is some difficulty in actually imposing the scenario of
the duel. Julien must repeat his challenge "from minute to
minute," until his "constancy" attracts the attention of a
crowd of onlookers, who presumedly shame the "tall man
in a beaver-trimmed coat" into responding. Stendhal itali-
cizes the challenge—"*Monsieur, votre adresse? je vous mé-
prise*"—in part to render Julien's desperate insistence, in part
to indicate its formulaic, prescribed nature. The man thus
provoked flings some visiting cards into Julien's face, and a
duel it seems to be. On the following day, having secured a
second, Julien presents himself at the address written on the
cards, only to find that he has the wrong man. The chevalier
de Beauvoisis is not "son homme de la veille." Julien begins
to leave, but discovers in the person of M. de Beauvoisis's
coachman the man who had insulted him. Instantly, he begins to whip him, offending his master, and finally "il y a
là matière à duel!" in truth, although the *matière* has
changed entirely and the duel is now with someone else.

The scenario has been already subjected to a process of
metonymic displacement, or distraction. The appearance

of Beauvoisis himself, for instance, is unexpectedly striking
—Julien's second even suspects that he kept them waiting
to have his hair done. Similarly, Julien's own appearance
astonishes the dandified chevalier. His black suit, worn at
seven in the morning, seems distinctly in bad taste, although
later he notices that the cut is good—it is from the fashionable Staub's—the boots are fine—still, at seven in the morning! The major distraction, however, occurs when the two
combatants leave together for the dueling place.

> On ouvrit la portière de la voiture: le chevalier voulut ab-
> solument en faire les honneurs à Julien et à son temoin.
> On alla chercher un ami de M. de Beauvoisis, qui indiqua
> une place tranquille. La conversation en allant fut vrai-
> ment bien. Il n'y avait de singulier que le diplomate en
> robe de chambre.
>   Ces messieurs, quoique très nobles, pensa Julien, ne
> sont pas ennuyeux comme les personnes qui viennent
> dîner chez M. de la Mole; et je vois pourquoi, ajouta-t-il
> un instant après, ils se permettent d'être indécents. On
> parlait des danseuses que le public avait distinguées dans
> un ballet donné la veille. Ces messieurs faisaient allusion
> à des anecdotes piquantes que Julien et son temoin, le
> lieutenant du 96ᵉ, ignoraient absolument. Julien n'eut
> point la sottise de prétendre les savoir; il avoua de bonne
> grâce son ignorance. Cette franchise plut à l'ami du cheva-
> lier; il lui raconta ces anecdotes dans les plus grands dé-
> tails, et fort bien. (RN 474)

As for the duel, it is cursorily picked up by the narration
after it is over:

> Le duel fut fini en un instant: Julien eut une balle dans
> le bras; on le lui serra avec des mouchoirs; on les mouilla
> avec de l'eau-de-vie, et le chevalier de Beauvoisis pria Ju-
> lien très poliment de lui permettre de le reconduire chez
> lui, dans la même voiture qui l'avait amené. (474)

If the prospect of a duel had parodic overtones before, the actual duel becomes pure farce and what it is supposed to express virtually nonexistent. The characters and the narrator seem to have forgotten the point of the exercise, which is described as if there weren't one, stripped of the cultural and emotional halo that is meant to attach to it. Julien is more fascinated by the elegant wit of "the conversation on the way" than filled with hostility or fear; and the chevalier has no more than a dandy's respect for protocol and good manners. What began with such urgency ends on Stendhal's favorite discrediting interrogation, as Julien wonders: "un duel, n'est-ce que ça?"

The sequence is a brilliant example of Stendhal's method at its most typical, and it may help us to describe the method more precisely. There is, on one hand, something like a scenario: a sequence of actions whose order is presumed to be known in advance. Logical expectations are invoked: it is hard to imagine any telling of a duel (qua duel) in which the actual shooting would not be the logical climax or ending of the account. Cultural expectations are aroused as well: semantically, a duel would seem naturally to involve motifs of honor, risk, fear, shame, and so forth. On the other hand, narrative attention is distracted from what logically and culturally "ought" to happen; and it is instead focused on what retards or frustrates the articulation of the scenario, on peripheral details and incidents that the scenario neither demands nor accounts for. The very contours of the scenario run the risk of dissolving under the pressure of so much "irrelevant" material. Finally, there is an almost inevitable peripeteia: the scenario yields to the surprise, the prescribed to the unforeseen.

The units of any narrative sequence would seem intuitively to have a variable degree of importance to the sequence as a whole. Some seem less dispensable than others. At opposite ends of the range of relevance might be placed the terms of Boris Tomashevsky: the "bound" motif, absolutely essential to any telling of the story, and the "free" motif, whose omission would affect nothing else in the story.[23] What Stendhal has done in his treatment of the duel, then, is to have redistributed his accents. The bound motif becomes secondary to our sense of the episode as a whole: it becomes perfunctory and peripheral. Conversely, the relatively free motifs (Beauvoisis's curls, the cut of Julien's coat, the conversation on the way) become primary and essential.

In the best contemporary discussion of Stendhal's method, Gérard Genette has written of an "elision of downbeats" accompanied by an "accentuation of accessory circumstances," and this is a congenial way of describing Stendhal's syncopated rhythms.[24] Genette tends to view this double dislocation, however, as a conventional metonymy: the amplified accessories are figures for the elided main event indirectly represented by them. In other words, accents are redistributed only by a rhetorical feint whose ultimate purpose is to preserve them in their "proper" places. By accommodating Stendhal's method to this conventional rhetorical operation, Genette seems to me to be surrendering the specificity of his argument altogether. All novelists (including of course Stendhal) rely heavily on this sort of metonymy: accessory circumstances, or objects, stand in for other more central and less explicit concerns. The Balzacian room is a character study, and the Dickensian house a comment on those who dwell in it. Fanny Price's Maltese cross *is* her piety, much as the crack in the golden bowl *is* Maggie's flawed marriage. In the last analysis, Genette leaves the primacy of the main event (over the accessory), the scenario (over the surprise), the name (over the metonym), unchallenged. Yet it is on attempted overthrows of these hierarchies that Stendhal's method depends. The conversation on the way does not really stand in for the duel; it genuinely supplants it as a center of interest and value.

[23] Boris Tomashevsky, "Thematics," in Lee T. Lemon and Marion J. Reis, eds., *Russian Formalist Criticism: Four Essays*.
[24] Genette, " 'Stendhal,' " *Figures II*, p. 181.

Stendhal's text is always flirting with the possibility of resisting strict metonymy, and it frequently enacts (as here)
a quasi-emancipation of the metonymical moment. The peri-
phrastic sliding from detail to detail is only minimally, per-
functorily brought back to the prescribed formula.

Insofar as the conversation does supplant the duel as a
center of interest, of course, it is a way of passing implicit
comment on it. The conversation's wit and elegance have
sparked some of the excitement that ought to have been
generated by the prospect of a duel. The validity of dueling
as an authentic form of action would seem thoroughly discredited. Yet even this meaning is not left in a settled state,
any more than the logical and cultural expectations initially
invoked by the episode. Having trivialized the institution of
the duel, which would no longer seem able to incite or express much passion, the text undoes itself once more and
rehabilitates it:

> Mademoiselle de la Mole apprit la mort du marquis de
> Croisenois. M. de Thaler, cet homme si riche, s'était per-
> mis des propos désagréables sur la disparition de Mathilde;
> M. de Croisenois alla le prier de les démentir: M. de
> Thaler lui montra des lettres anonymes à lui adressées, et
> remplies de détails rapprochés avec tant d'art qu'il fut im-
> possible au pauvre marquis de ne pas entrevoir la vérité.
>
> M. de Thaler se permit des plaisanteries denuées de
> finesse. Ivre de colère et de malheur, M. de Croisenois
> exigea des réparations tellement fortes, que le million-
> naire préféra un duel. La sottise triompha; et l'un des
> hommes de Paris les plus dignes d'être aimés trouva la
> mort à moins de vingt-quatre ans.
>
> Cette mort fit une impression étrange et maladive sur
> l'âme affaiblie de Julien.
>
> —Le pauvre Croisenois, disait-il à Mathilde, a été ré-
> ellement bien raisonnable et bien honnête homme envers
> nous; il eût dû me haïr lors de vos imprudences dans le
> salon de madame votre mère, et me chercher querelle; car

la haine qui succède au mépris est ordinairement furieuse. (694)

The marquis de Croisenois has not been an especially lovable character in *Rouge*. Here, however, he suddenly becomes noble, in more than a nominal sense; and the nobility is conferred, precisely, by dueling, which has apparently recovered its genuine dangers and its possibilities of authenticity. No wonder his death makes "a strange and morbid impression" on Julien.

Stendhal had a horror of fixity in all its narrative forms: the cliché, the foreordained meaning, the ending that locks everything into place. Yet he needs to invoke a form of such fixity, so that he can call forth from the borders his own "freedom": in surprises, indeterminacies, inconclusions. It is odd, in a way, that the trivial, frivolous conversation between Beauvoisis and his second should be invested by Stendhal with so much value. (For it is not just Julien gaping in awe—"La conversation en allant fut vraiment bien"!) Of course, Stendhal's worldliness would naturally put a high estimation on elegant conversation. One suspects, however, a deeper source of joy: in the very marginality of the conversation, unassuming but thoroughly composed, slyly inscribing itself within the text and finally absorbing the text within itself. Also: conversations on the way are supremely inconclusive.

Afterword

IN THE LAST ANALYSIS, what discontents the traditional novel is its own condition of possibility. For the production of narrative—what we called the narratable—is possible only within a logic of insufficiency, disequilibrium, and deferral, and traditional novelists typically desire worlds of greater stability and wholeness than such a logic can intrinsically provide. Moreover, the suspense that constitutes the narratable inevitably comes to imply a suspensiveness of signification, so that what is ultimately threatened is no less than the possibility of a full or definitive meaning. Thus, novelists such as Jane Austen and George Eliot need to situate their texts within a controlling perspective of narrative closure, which would restore the world (and with it, the word) to a state of transparency, once for all released from errancy and equivocation.

One might say, of course, that this merely reformulates a truth generally acknowledged in every manual for aspiring writers—namely, that there must be conflict to generate a story and resolution to end it. Less simplistically, one might say that the traditional novelist gives play to his discontent only to assuage it in the end, much as the child in Freud makes his toy temporarily disappear the better to enjoy its reinstated presence. Charles Grivel has even argued that the novel's whole reason for being is precisely to *negate* the negativity that is its narrative.[1] The traditional novel

---

[1] Grivel accepts Derrida's position that there is no full meaning in a text, but only "différance" (difference, deferment). Yet for him the novel is precisely the mode in which "la différence existe pour faire cesser la différence." Difference in the novel is always mastered from the closure of a "being present," and thus, Grivel claims, it no longer

would therefore work on the principle of vaccination: incorporating the narratable in safe doses to prevent it from breaking out.

There is no need to deny the novel's attempt to master the narratable. The only real question is whether we can take it for granted that such an attempt perfectly succeeds. The novel may be a game of *Fort!/ Da!*, turning on the disappearance and return of a full meaning, but in the cases we have considered, the game seems to have gone beyond this simple ground rule and begins to look like a symptom of the anxiety that its purpose was to master. In a sense, this is the case even in Freud. The seeming binary opposition on which the child's game is founded is in fact radically asymmetrical. The anxiety of disappearance is intrinsically stronger than the gratification of return, for the former is not merely a moment in the game, it is the underlying inspiration for the game itself. Even the gratification of return belongs to the logic of disappearance, since the toy stands in place of a primary, but irrevocably lost satisfaction (total possession of the mother).

Similarly, I have implied, the narratable is stronger than the closure to which it is opposed in an apparent binarity. For the narratable is the very evidence of the narrative text, while closure (as, precisely, the nonnarratable) is only the sign that this text is over. It is significant that closure in Jane Austen takes the form of a dramatic conversion, a total abandonment of a narratable world. In George Eliot, it takes the form of a mystical, quasi-miraculous experience of whose reality the novelist herself can hardly be sure. The otherness of closure suggests one of the unwelcome implications of the narratable—that it can never generate the

---

deserves the name. See Chapter 3 of his *Production de l'intérêt romanesque*.

A more orthodox criticism found no better compliment to pay to a literary work than to say that "it fully mastered its materials." It should be clear that Grivel's perspective hardly alters the assumptions under which the novel is usually studied.

terms for its own arrest. These must be imported from elsewhere, from a world untouched by the conditions of narratability. Yet as soon as such a world is invoked in the novels —its appearance is necessarily brief—its authority is put into doubt by the system of narrative itself. The closural world seems less like the absence of the narratable than its strategic denial or expedient repression. The problems of closure (suppression in Jane Austen, ambiguity in George Eliot) testify to the difficulty of ridding the text of all traces of the narratable, even—especially—at the moment when it is supposed to be superseded. Furthermore, just as the child's toy does not answer to what has really been lost, so too, closure, though it implies resolution, never really resolves the dilemmas raised by the narratable. In essence, closure is an act of "make-believe," a postulation that closure is possible. Although we have tried to make clear the moral advantages of this postulation, we have also been concerned to show its self-betraying inadequacy.

There is no more fundamental assumption of the traditional novel than this opposition between the narratable and closure. Even the devious endgames in which Stendhal defers or displaces the moment of closure are played within the orthodoxy of this assumption. The "perversity" we have found in his novels should not mislead us into thinking that they represent a radical break with the "normality" of Jane Austen or George Eliot. Perversity is no less dependent than normality upon the sanction of the law, with the difference, of course, that what the law in this case sanctions are the deliberate infractions on which perversity is founded. Though Stendhal overturns the opposition between the narratable and closure, one cannot say that he overthrows it, and the narrative regime organized by its polar terms proves just as relevant to an understanding of his fiction as it is to Jane Austen's. The appealingly libertarian ways in which Stendhal resists coming to closure, far from breaking this opposition down, may be the most subtle and persuasive means of keeping it in place. Sustained by the sheer insistence of Stendhal's dislike, closure ceases to be a positive ideal without ever surrendering its ideality per se, which is, moreover, rather enhanced than impugned by his attempts to render it unreachable. Yet if the regime of the traditional novel commands even the obedience of so evidently rebellious a subject as Stendhal, then the attractiveness of its governing opposition—between the narratable and closure—needs to be accounted for. To what advantage, we must finally ask, does such an opposition function in the novel? In the end, it may only be that it functions to prove its own possibility. For the most unwelcome implication of all carried by the narratable may well be that *there is nothing to oppose to it.* In this light, Stendhal's notorious resistance to closure would in fact only help him to believe—perversely —in the validity of its claims. His deepest strategy in evading closure would be to conceal the possibility that there is no closure to evade. Instead of the "freedom" that must always be won, there would only be a less joyful instability that could never be *lost.* The texts of all three of the novelists we have considered, then, would display a similar anxiety toward the narratable—an anxiety that Stendhal can turn into positive excitement only because he too believes in quiescence.

Jane Austen would say that conclusion is the moment when we should "have done with all the rest," but George Eliot would tell us instead that this is the moment for reflecting on the inadequacy of our "sample," which like any other risks being mistaken for an all-inclusive paradigm. I have implied, of course, precisely that Jane Austen, George Eliot, and Stendhal triangulate the field of the traditional novel in far more comprehensive ways than their interest as individual cases suggests. Psychoanalytically, the respective corners of the general topography that they typify may be conceived of as the normal, the neurotic, and the perverse; and ideologically, as the conservative, the liberal, and the libertarian. In terms, too, of the narratable and its closure, the three novelists project a triangular generalization, with the value emphases we have associated with Jane Austen reversed in those represented by Stendhal, and both mediated under the name of George Eliot. In defense of the schema, I should point out that the possibilities it fails to admit—psychotic desire, revolutionary politics, a fully effaced closure—are absent from the traditional novel as well. Yet lest, as triangles tend to do, this one persuade us that all the bases have been neatly covered, some cautions may be in order. For one thing, if I have proposed such divisions, I have also suggested that they divide each *oeuvre* from within itself as much as from one another. The triangle formed by Austen, Eliot, and Stendhal is ultimately only the most developed version of the triangle found in Austen, Eliot, *or* Stendhal. For another, I hope each case we have undertaken to study has been argued differently enough to warrant the inference that other novelists might have been included here with more profit than redundancy. In particular, I regret the absence of a few cases exemplifying special problems that might have complicated our geometry.

The narrative model we have derived from Jane Austen, for example, need not be confined within the small space and domestic scale of her "little bit (two Inches wide) of Ivory." On a far grander historical stage, the novels of Sir Walter Scott display a similar ambivalence toward narrative. On one hand, of course, the historical novel is based on a valorization of history and historical processes, and it might seem as if its attitude to narrative would be more positive. Yet on the other hand, it would be possible to show that the historical novel—at least as practiced by Scott—exists to deprive the course of history, as well as the course of narrative thus motivated, of its necessity. In a novel like *Old Mortality*, the narratable typically coincides with civil discord, which Scott not only deplores, but sees as ideally uncalled for. His reasonable narrator and his reasonable hero, Henry Morton, together offer a perspective in which, if sufficiently stressed, the entire conflict that has generated the novel must be seen as senseless waste. It is telling that Morton, the spokesman of reason, is neither corrupted nor transformed by his participation in the struggle of the novel. The balanced compromise that obtains at the end of the novel does not—*pace* Lukács—emerge from a dialectical process as the result of a conflict of social forces. Rather it is postulated a priori as a principle that allows us to see the narrative as at least theoretically dispensable. People make history in Scott only because people make mistakes: both can and should be avoided. Although one might well argue that such an ideology is contested and exposed by the narrative, Scott is Jane Austen's contemporary in a deeper sense than is usually recognized. In a similarly blinded dialectic, narrative remains a "development of every thing most unwelcome."

While the epic implications of this unwelcome development are most fully drawn in the novels of Scott, its erotic consequences are most extremely realized in the work of another, somewhat older contemporary, the marquis de Sade. Sade's reputation as the novelist of an endlessly inventive erotic excess may not seem to promise much in common with the more restrained libidinal economy that operates in Jane Austen. Yet when, as we have seen, desire in Jane Austen is consistently subject to a "repression" that not only intensifies its transgressive and dangerous character, but also (as in the cases of Elinor Dashwood and Fanny Price) positively *maintains* desire as such, then a rapprochement between her kind of fiction and Sadean pornography can no longer be thought outrageous. Moreover, if our reading of Jane Austen has brought her closer to Sade, it would also be possible to broach a reading of Sade that would place him nearer to Jane Austen. Specifically, such a reading would turn on the curious moralism that accompanies the portrayal of Sade's most egregious "crimes of love."

Instruire l'homme et corriger ses moeurs, tel est le seul motif que nous nous proposons dans cette anecdote. Que l'on se pénètre, en la lisant, de la grandeur du péril, toujours sur les pas de ceux qui se permettent tout pour satis-

faire leurs désirs. Puissent-ils se convaincre que la bonne
education, les richesses, les talents, les dons de la nature, ne
sont susceptibles que d'égarer, quand la retenue, la bonne
conduite, la sagesse, la modestie ne les étayent, ou ne les
font valoir: voilà les vérités que nous allons mettre en action. Qu'on nous pardonne les monstrueux détails du
crime affreux dont nous sommes contraints de parler:
est-il possible de faire détester de semblables écarts, si l'on
n'a pas le courage de les offrir à nu?[2]

This is the opening paragraph of *Eugénie de Franval*, a short
novel in which the eponymous heroine, seduced by her father, goes on at his instigation to murder her mother.
Though the details of the "hideous crime" to which the
narrator alludes will thus prove "monstrous" enough, they
are apparently not so monstrous as to perturb the confidence with which he here installs his narration *dans le vrai*.
Too moral not to have to be "constrained" to speak of such
horrors, he is also too moral to need to fear that his laudable
task of instructing man and reforming his morals might be
undermined by the libidinal force of its own cautionary examples. Announced as a gross violation of natural order, the
story is simultaneously kept from bringing the "truth" of
this order into question. As matters turn out, moreover, the
closure thus positioned at the start is perfectly confirmed at
the end, both in Eugénie's self-punishing attack of conscience and in her father's contrite repentance.

If one is still likely to feel that *Eugénie de Franval* is more
equivocal than the moral pretensions of its narrator, this is
partly because a very different version of his situation occurs
within the narrative itself. M. de Clervil, the spiritual direc-

---

[2] *Les Crimes de l'amour*, in *Oeuvres complètes du marquis de Sade*,
ed. Gilbert Lély, 16 vols. in 8 (Paris: Cercle du livre précieux, 1966-
68), 10: 425. My subsequent comments on this passage are partly in-
formed by Pierre Klossowski, preface to vol. 10 of the *Oeuvres complètes*, and *Sade, mon prochain* (Paris: Seuil, 1945); and by Georges
Bataille, *L'Erotisme* (Paris: Minuit, 1957).

tor of Eugénie's much-abused mother, is at least as moral as
the narrator, but when he is asked to publicize the incest, he
declines on the grounds that "le récit qu'on en fait réveille
les passions de ceux qui sont enclins au même genre de dé-
lits." In his eyes, the narration of incest would give not a
negative "leçon," as the narrator contends, but a positive
"conseil" (440). This seems closer to our intuitions about
the pandemically contagious nature of desire in pornography, but why Sade's narrator would wish to deny this here
remains to be explained. Possibly his opening remarks merely make provision for the "redeeming social value" that permits the censorious reader to think he is reading a more edi-
fying text than the one actually before him. Yet the outside
evidence goes to show that Sade himself was convinced by
the moral force of his story.[3] More plausibly, then, these
lines offer only the purest statement of intention. Sade writes
them as *an absolute moralist*, for only as such can he become
the supreme pornographer, who invokes the law persuasive-
ly at every step and so secures for desire the full delectation
of its flagrant delicta. The pornographic effect of *Eugénie
de Franval* depends crucially on the eagerness of the text to
retain all the closural sanctions of the law in the midst of the
infractions that constitute it as a narrative. Thus, Sade's
pornographic narrator is no less obliged to moralize than,
from the other side of the mirror, a moralist like Jane Austen
is compelled to narrate the dangerous course of erotic excitement. A radical incompatibility between desire (desire
for narrative) and the law (the law of closure) determines
the narrative structure that, for different reasons, accommodates both novelists. Jane Austen lets all the evidence of the
incompatibility stand, knowing that her text will eventually
pass over to the side of the law, where the rest doesn't count.
Faced with the same incompatibility, Sade is profoundly

[3] Sade's claim that "il n'y a ni conte ni roman dans toute la littérature
de l'europe où les dangers du libertinage soient exposés avec plus de
force" may be found in his "Catalogue raisonné des oeuvres de M. de
S*** à l'époque du 1ᵉʳ octobre 1788," *Oeuvres complètes*, 2: 269.

more "co-operative": willing to inhabit permanently the (cruel? monstrous? sadistic?) universe in which desire and the law, narrative and closure, are as radically inseparable as they are absolutely at odds.

The limiting prestige of Jane Austen as a miniaturist does not encourage comparisons with Scott or Sade, but the typical character of George Eliot's closural practice in the nineteenth century will be more easily recognized. Balzac is a less persuasive intellect than the translator of Strauss and Feuerbach, but his work similarly exemplifies a closure at once enforced and effaced. Each novel in *La Comédie humaine* has a traditional enough ending (though often, as Roland Barthes points out in what is only the most literal case, taking the form of a mere cutting off of desire[4]), but what is left over is demonstrably capable of producing further narrative. Indeed, these further narratives are our best evidence that something *has* been left over. What better way of having, and not having, one's closure than the device of the *retour des personnages*, where what is most importantly "returned" are not the characters, but the narratable desires they have sponsored. Closure coexists with the possibility of going beyond it in Trollope's Barsetshire and Palliser novels as well. In both novelists, the double vision of closure projected by *Middlemarch* has simply been displaced into the structure of the novel *series*.

Displaced in still another way, the double vision determines the two endings of Dickens's *Great Expectations*. From our perspective, the chief interest of the endings—the first forever parting Pip and Estella, the second forever joining them—lies in the sheer fact that they both were possible. For if either ending wholly regulated the narrative leading

---

[4] According to Barthes, the castration in *Sarrasine* cuts with a double edge. Traditionally, it provides the "final nomination" that ends narrative discourse (*S/Z*, pp. 193-94 and pp. 215-16). Less traditionally, however, it also threatens to unmask the "repleteness" of the classical text, whose seemingly full forms in fact only reproduce the central deficiency of the castrato (pp. 204-6).

up to it, Dickens would simply have been *unable* to change the original without substantially revising the rest of his novel. That the text can issue in either of two opposite resolutions points up the indeterminacy with which, in particular, the function of Estella has been invested. If, as there is reason to suppose, Estella embodies merely the most seductive of Pip's neurotic expectations, then his cure requires she be relinquished along with the others. But if, as there are also grounds for thinking, Estella represents a fairy princess whose worth is only temporarily and superficially obscured, then she is clearly destined to be Pip's reward for his mature self-understanding. The appropriateness of each ending is thus bound to bespeak a certain inappropriateness as well. Pip's sense of recovery in the original ending cannot allay the disappointment that the Estella for whom he was surely meant has married someone else. Neither, in the revised ending, can his happier vision of "no shadow of another parting from her" exclude the history of his blatantly obsessive attachment. One might, of course, dismiss such observations by arguing that, while each ending resolves opposite sides of a textual ambivalence, what counts—and what renders the text perfectly "readerly"—is the mere fact of resolution itself. Whether Pip loses or gains Estella must considerably affect the emphases of our reading, but not its fundamental stability. In either case, the narrative of Pip's cure (involving, as we should by now suspect, his being cured of narrative itself) would stand complete. Such memories of an unrealized "otherwise" as each ending seems to induce would only belong to what Barthes has called the "pensivity" of the traditional novel: the token gesture it makes, *once closure has taken place*, to imply that there may be more to tell.[5]

⁵ *S/Z*, pp. 222-23. In a recent reading of *Great Expectations*, where the plot of Pip's cure is powerfully conceived as an attempt to "bind" (in Freud's sense) the mobile psychic energies behind it, Peter Brooks makes a similar point: "We may . . . feel that choice between the two endings is somewhat arbitrary and unimportant in that the de-

Yet while the anecdotal opposition between the two endings can be easily collapsed, a structural oscillation operates less vulnerably within each: between the signs of Pip's cure, ensuring resolution, and the symptoms of his disease, requiring—if not providing—further development. In both endings, evidence of closure coexists, overlaps, and often coincides undecidably with counterevidence of the narratable. The conspicuous notice that the original ending takes of "little Pip," for instance, holds open the prospect of an irrecuperable process of repetition and difference. It is as though the text were underlining, by doubling, the self-contradictory name whose semantic content promises maturation even as its palindromic form threatens endless reversals. And when Estella wrongly takes little Pip for Pip's own child, her uncorrected error not only alludes (like the many other mistaken identities in the novel) to the mistaken *nature* of identity; it brings the allusion forward at the very moment when Pip may be most safely supposed to "know himself." The oscillation between cure and disease persists in the final sentence:

> I was very glad afterwards to have had the interview [with Estella]; for, in her face and in her voice, and in her touch, she gave me the assurance, that suffering had been stronger than Miss Havisham's teaching, and had given her a heart to understand what my heart used to be.[6]

Much as in the Finale of *Middlemarch,* the lines are filled

---

cisive moment has already occurred before either of these finales begins. The real ending may take place with Pip's recognition and acceptance of Magwitch after his recapture—this is certainly the ethical denouement—and his acceptance of a continuing existence without plot, as celibate clerk for Clarriker. The pages that follow may simply be *obiter dicta*" ("Repetition, Repression, and Return: *Great Expectations* and the Study of Plot," p. 521).

[6] Charles Dickens, *Great Expectations* (London: Oxford University Press, 1953), p. 461.

by what they leave untold, as Pip skips from his melancholy last interview with Estella to a time "afterwards" when he can gladly assess it. The ambiguity of his heart as well as of his cure is perfectly maintained by the linguistic discretion of "used to be," which may be considered either a preterite ("used to be but is no longer") or an imperfect ("used to be and continues being"). In addition, this declaration of finality is what most immediately motivates a *further* narrative development, taking place even later than "afterwards": I mean Pip's decision, omitted but fully presupposed by the text, to write his autobiography. The end of narrative thus proves only its rebeginning, as the life concludes in a desire for the life story.

The revised ending deploys a more emphatic closural vocabulary, to which the act of autobiography, together with the need for narrative it implies, may appear irrelevant. Yet even here the details that lay stress on wholeness and quiescence are left ambiguous. "As the morning mists had risen long ago when I first left the forge, so the evening mists were rising now" (460). If we suppose that the evening inverts the morning, the text would clearly be suggesting that the forces of narratability have been turned back upon closure. But if, alternatively, we suppose that one rising simply repeats another, then the text would be telling a different story whose end is not in sight. In support of such a possibility, Estella's last words to Pip, telling him that they "will continue friends apart," bear the same burden as her language has always done; and Pip, who sees "no shadow of another parting from her," once more confers on her text the convenient legibility of his desires. Although one might bridge the gap between Estella's text and Pip's enraptured interpretation by reading the scene as a piece of romantic understatement, it remains the case that the romantic understatement takes the same form as the erotic delusion it ought to leave behind. In the oscillating perspective thus opened up, it becomes clear why Pip, repeating earlier projects, needs to embark on the autobiographical conquest of authority and control—and also why his passage (like the two I have been discussing) will not be altogether smooth.

The work of many other novelists could be adduced to suport the claims we have made for the typicality of closure in Austen and Eliot, but the sheer embarrassment of examples raises a more general question which is perhaps better addressed. For while no doubt the problematic of closure could be profitably located even in prenovelistic fiction (such as Chaucer's, for instance), it enjoys unique prominence and pertinence in the novel—particularly, in that epoch of the novel that finds its center of gravity in the nineteenth century. What is it about the novel that has especially qualified it to be the site of our discussion? A sociological answer might well emphasize the general nineteenth-century tendency to elevate the categories of process and production—mainly negative or neutral in the preceding period—to the status of positive values. The tendency would be most obviously provoked by the emergence of an industrial economy, but it would surface in an "expansionist" fiction as well, whose inherited attempts to bring its processes to a position of arrest or synthesis must fail or be only half-hearted.[7] It is certainly the case that the novel is peculiarly obliged to take notice of its textual productivity, even when it seems most committed to neutralizing it. It is not just that the novel is a *long* form, but also that the form dramatizes its length serially, in the regularly broken line between letters, chapters, installments, and even whole works. One readily grants that the conditions of the literary marketplace are most immediately responsible for determining this lengthiness.[8] But I am less concerned here with its

[7] The sociology of literary language in the nineteenth century has been impressively advanced along these lines in Paola Colaiacomo, "Sul linguaggio poetico dei romantici," *Calibano* 3 (Rome: Savelli, 1979), pp. 13-37.

[8] In England, for instance, the profitability of novels that the lending libraries could distribute to several readers at once established the "three-decker" as the normative form. On this basis, Terry Eagleton

efficient causes than with one of its formal effects: namely, the question of totality that it raises. The issue has not been better put since Edgar Allan Poe first broached it, in his comparison of the novel with the short story:

> The ordinary novel is objectionable, from its length, for reasons analogous in those which render length objectionable in the poem. As the novel cannot be read at one sitting, it cannot avail itself of the immense benefit of *totality*. Worldly interests, intervening during the pauses of perusal, modify, counteract and annul the impressions intended. But simple cessation in reading would, of itself, be sufficient to destroy the true unity. In the brief tale, however, the author is enabled to carry out his full design without interruption. During the hour of perusal, the soul of the reader is at the writer's control.[9]

Interrupted, discontinuous, our reading of a novel necessarily puts in jeopardy the virtues of organic unity that Poe prizes. If, moreover, as Poe suggests in "The Philosophy of Composition," "It is only with the *dénouement* constantly in view that we can give a plot its indispensable air of consequence, of causation, by making the incidents, and especially the tone at all points, tend to the development of the inten-

---

has argued that "the multiple complicated plots, elaborate digressions and gratuitous interludes of such works were the effect of producers ingeniously elongating their material to meet the requirements of the form" (*Criticism and Ideology*, p. 52). The matter, however, is much more overdetermined than this account must suggest. The producers' attempts to generate the required length are too congenial to be merely ingenious. A novelist like Trollope, whose cynical awareness of market conditions is notorious, writes under them with the opposite of constraint. Not only did major novelists easily accept these conditions, they sometimes even reconstituted them, as Dickens did when he published his novels serially in his own magazines.

[9] "Tale-Writing—Nathaniel Hawthorne," in *The Complete Works of Edgar Allan Poe*, ed. James A. Harrison, 17 vols. (New York: George D. Sproul, 1902), 13: 152-53. The subsequent quotation from "The Philosophy of Composition" may be found in 14: 193.

tion," then the length of the nineteenth-century novel, elaborated as it is in subplots and digressions, runs the risk of detotalizing the form at the level of writing as well as of reading. For both writer and reader, the novel must promote a discomforting awareness that totality is not yet available, the threads not yet gathered or the pieces fitted. If only by virtue of its sheer length, therefore, the novel is particularly implicated in the anxieties about closure we have canvassed.

Yet it would be a mistake to conclude that, because the novel insistently thematizes such anxieties, it is any less attached to the *prospect* of being released from them. Carefully cultivating our desire for a next installment or a future volume, the novel continually *promises* the totality it cannot, at any single moment, deliver. It seems strange that Poe should consider the novel a weaker form than the short story or the lyric, during the very period when the novel was achieving literary and cultural dominance. It is less likely that the novel's inherent discontinuities remove the reader from its control of his soul than that, distributed within a series of worldly interests, they allow this control to be broadened: beyond the temporal limits of the hours of perusal, and outside the spatial boundaries of library or study. In realist fiction, for example, the imbrication of literary and worldly interests that Poe laments ministers to a highly powerful confusion between the two. The intervention of worldly interests has already, so to speak, been foreseen and exploited by a novel that persistently *invites* us to turn our attention to the world as a means of verifying its portrayal. In that turn, moreover, the world is correspondingly reduced to its novelistic model, so that, as Leo Bersani has put it, "society is behind the novel, and the novel tells us what is behind society."[10]

It is doubtful whether we escape from the postulation of closure even on the advent of modernism. The work of

[10] Leo Bersani, *Balzac to Beckett: Center and Circumference in French Fiction*, p. 7.

Stendhal, anticipating the modernist tendency to formal openness and psychological mobility, suggests some of the difficulties inherent in it. We have already seen how, reversing the priorities of the traditional novel, Stendhal preserves the system they mutually determine. Even when rendered unavailable by Stendhal's strategies of ellipsis—especially then—closure remains a powerful ideal. Yet the paradoxes of his perversity do not stop even here. For as Stendhal deconstructs specific acts of closure, making them once again narratable, the position of closure—that is, of an ultimate signified to which everything in the text eventually speaks—comes to be occupied by narratability itself. We are thus led to confront the possibility, oxymoronic but far from frivolous, of being enclosed in openness.

The contradictions of Stendhal's fiction—retaining the traditional ideal of closure while eliding it, reinstalling this ideal in the guise of its opposite—are only more explicit in the work of an early modernist like Gide. At the level of character psychology, Gide's openness is represented by the supreme virtue he assigns to *disponibilité*, the ability to entertain experience freshly and without prescriptions. Yet, as with Michel in *L'Immoraliste* or Lafcadio in *Les Caves du Vatican*, this liberating availability is consistently expressed in flagrant violations of a moral order whose claims Gide appears reluctant to abandon entirely. Similarly, the structural playfulness of the Gidean novel is doubled by a thematic pathos. On one hand, following the example of Stendhal, the narrative moves toward a valorization of narrative per se. The principle of "pourrait être continué" comes precisely from a willingness to keep narrative open, to preserve its pockets of suspensiveness and indeterminacy—for future reference, so to speak. Closure would only be equivalent to the statement: "Ici commence un nouveau livre." Yet on the other hand, rather like George Eliot, Gide has an acute sense that narrative must always be trying to track down a prey (be it the gay wisdom of *L'Immoraliste* or the saintly transcendence of *La Porte étroite*) that inherently eludes it. It is evidently the nature of narrative to *monnayer* —to break up wholes into "small change," and the conversion irrevocably puts in question all totalizing ambitions, including those Gide has most sympathy for. Despite his frequent delight in the coinages thus produced, he never lets us forget that they are counterfeit. In the traditional epistemological and moral perspective that haunts it, narrative can never be more than a *faux*-monnayeur. At the same time, this may be enough. For when the processes of narrative become "all there is," then they easily ground the text in a new truth that, albeit less pleasant, seems far more solid than the one they call into question. Accordingly, the transcendent signified that Gide thematically mourns and formally undercuts is, by means of these very acts, recovered. Despite its new bleakness, as well as on account of it, an old parable of transcendence ("si le grain ne meurt") may be successfully retold.

Even, therefore, when one thinks closure impossible, one may never be able to think it away. On sociological grounds, moreover, the very attempt to do so must inspire wariness. It is no doubt true, as both Sartre and Barthes have maintained, that the end-orientation of the traditional novel serves the repressive order of the nineteenth-century bourgeoisie; and also that modernist fiction, relatively disabused of teleological illusions, registers an implicit protest against this repression. Yet even in the traditional novel, as we have seen, closure is fraught with self-betraying contradictions; and conversely, modernist fiction is sometimes suspiciously consonant, not to say complicitous, with aspects of the social order that provides its own context.[11] The way we live now is certainly less repressed than in the nineteenth century, but it may be equally disciplined. In our first example of the narratable, we saw Harriet Smith hanging over the

[11] Of recent critics, Fredric Jameson has best helped us to recognize this consonance in "The Ideology of the Text," *Salmagundi* (Fall 1975-Winter 1976): 204-46; and "Reification and Utopia in Mass Culture," *Social Text* (Winter 1979): 130-48.

muslins on the counter at Ford's and torn by an indecision that Jane Austen's text moved quickly to suppress. One easily imagines a Gidean rendering of *Emma* in which much greater justice would be done to the claims of the counter, and a far higher premium set on Harriet's willingness to entertain its seductively multiple possibilities. Yet it is perhaps no more coercive to move Harriet away from the "interesting counter" than to detain her there indefinitely. So, at least, it must seem in a *société de consommation* that increasingly positions us *in front of a counter*: immobilizing us as it enjoins our mobility and reducing the dimensions of our lives as it recommends the variousness of our lifestyles.

We must perversely conclude on a note of prudence. For Stendhal's problems, or Gide's, are also those of this study, which has reversed the priorities of the traditional novel, but not escaped from them. It too has been obliged to postulate closure, if only to define and make visible its opposite in the narratable. We are thus in the paradoxical position of casting doubt on the primacy of a closure to which it is not at all clear we have ceased to adhere. Nor is it more certain that a case for the constitutive unrest of narrative is ultimately any less closural than the narrative closure it deconstructs. Inevitably, it seems, the work of deconstruction comes to *re-construct* the dissonances by which it proceeds into a new truth, which reasserts all the stability denied to the old. Though the impasse does not render useless the work that has allowed us to reach it, it may possibly prevent us from concluding that, more than any other story, narratology has (to) come to an end.

According to Jane Austen, this is the moment to conclude; according to George Eliot, the moment to worry about concluding; according to Stendhal, the moment to do *something else*. Before we do so, however, we might recall this prayer from *Le Voyage d'Urien*: "Nous avons remercié Dieu de nous avoir caché le but, et de l'avoir à ce point reculé que les efforts faits pour l'atteindre nous donnassent déjà quelque joie, seule sûre."[12] Gide wrote these lines, as Stendhal might have done; and, bound as we are to the paradoxes of both writers, we are certainly entitled to cite them in valedictory thanksgiving for "the conversation on the way."

[12] André Gide, *Le Voyage d'Urien*, in *Oeuvres complètes*, ed. L. Martin-Chauffier, 15 vols. (Paris: Nouvelle Revue Française, 1932-39), 1: 362-63.

Bibliography

Texts

Austen, Jane. *Minor Works*. Edited by R. W. Chapman. London: Oxford University Press, 1954.
————. *The Novels of Jane Austen*. Edited by R. W. Chapman, 5 vols. Third edition. London: Oxford University Press, 1932-34.
Eliot, George [Mary Ann Evans]. *The George Eliot Letters*. Edited by Gordon S. Haight, 7 vols. New Haven: Yale University Press, 1954-55.
————. *Middlemarch*. Edited by W. J. Harvey. Penguin, 1965.
Stendhal [Marie Henri Beyle]. *De l'Amour*. Edited by Henri Martineau. Paris: Garnier, 1959.
————. *Une Position sociale*. In *Oeuvres complètes*, edited by Georges Eudes, 25 vols. 14: 439-69. Paris: P. Larrive, 1946-56.
————. *Romans et nouvelles*. Edited by Henri Martineau, 2 vols. Paris: Pléiade, 1952-55.

Critical Studies of Jane Austen

Babb, Howard S. *Jane Austen's Novels: The Fabric of Dialogue*. Hamden, Conn.: Archon Books, 1967.
Lodge, David, ed. *Emma: A Casebook*. London: Macmillan, 1965.
Moler, Kenneth L. *Jane Austen's Art of Allusion*. Lincoln: University of Nebraska Press, 1968.
Mudrick, Marvin. *Jane Austen: Irony as Defense and Discovery*. Princeton: Princeton University Press, 1952.

[285]

Price, Martin. "Manners, Morals, and Jane Austen," *Nineteenth-Century Fiction* 30 (December 1975): 261-80.
Southam, B. C., ed. *Critical Essays on Jane Austen.* London: Routledge & Kegan Paul, 1968.
————, ed. *Jane Austen: The Critical Heritage.* London: Routledge & Kegan Paul, 1968.
Tanner, Tony. Introduction to *Mansfield Park*, by Jane Austen. Penguin, 1966.
————. Introduction to *Pride and Prejudice*, by Jane Austen. Penguin, 1972.
————. Introduction to *Sense and Sensibility*, by Jane Austen. Penguin, 1972.
Tave, Stuart M. *Some Words of Jane Austen.* Chicago and London: University of Chicago Press, 1973.
Trilling, Lionel. "Mansfield Park." In *The Opposing Self*, pp. 206-30. New York: Viking, 1955.
————. *Sincerity and Authenticity.* Cambridge, Mass.: Harvard University Press, 1972.
Watt, Ian. *Jane Austen: A Collection of Critical Essays.* Englewood Cliffs, N.J.: Prentice-Hall, 1963.

Critical Studies of George Eliot

Carroll, David, ed. *George Eliot: The Critical Heritage.* London: Routledge & Kegan Paul, 1971.
Creeger, George R., ed. *George Eliot: A Collection of Critical Essays.* Englewood Cliffs, N.J.: Prentice-Hall, 1970.
Haight, Gordon S. *George Eliot: A Biography.* New York and Oxford: Oxford University Press, 1968.
Hardy, Barbara, ed. *"Middlemarch": Critical Approaches to the Novel.* London: University of London, The Athlone Press, 1967.
————. *The Novels of George Eliot: A Study in Form.* London: University of London, The Athlone Press, 1959.
Harvey, W. J. *The Art of George Eliot.* London: Chatto and Windus, 1961.

Miller, J. Hillis. "Narrative and History." *ELH* 41 (Fall 1974): 455-73.

――――. "Optic and Semiotic in *Middlemarch*." *Harvard English Studies* 6 (1975): 125-45.

Paris, Bernard. *Experiments in Life: George Eliot's Quest for Values*. Detroit: Wayne State University Press, 1965.

Critical Studies of Stendhal

Adams, Robert M. *Stendhal: Notes on a Novelist*. New York: Funk & Wagnalls, 1968.

Blin, Georges. *Stendhal et les problèmes du roman*. Paris: Corti, 1954.

Brombert, Victor. *Stendhal et la voie oblique*. Paris: Presses Universitaires Françaises, 1954.

Brooks, Peter. *The Novel of Worldiness: Crébillon, Marivaux, Laclos, Stendhal*. Princeton: Princeton University Press, 1969.

Genette, Gérard. " 'Stendhal.' " In *Figures II*, pp. 155-93. Paris: Seuil, 1969.

Hemmings, F.W.J. *Stendhal: A Study of His Novels*. Oxford: The Clarendon Press, 1964.

Prévost, Jean. *La Création chez Stendhal*. Paris: Mercure de France, 1951.

Valéry, Paul. "Stendhal." In *Variétés II*, pp. 77-139. Paris: Gallimard, 1930.

Wood, Michael. *Stendhal*. Ithaca: Cornell University Press, 1971.

General Works Relevant to This Study

Althusser, Louis. *Lénine et la philosophie*. Paris: Maspéro, 1969.

――――. *Lire le Capital*. 2 vols. Paris: Maspéro, 1968.

Auerbach, Erich. *Mimesis: The Representation of Reality in Western Literature*. Translated by Willard R. Trask. Princeton: Princeton University Press, 1953.

Bakhtin, Mikhail. *Problems of Dostoevsky's Poetics.* Translated by R. W. Rotsel. [Ann Arbor, Mich.]: Ardis, 1973.

Barthes, Roland. "Analyse textuelle d'un conte d'Edgar Poe." In *Sémiotique narrative et textuelle,* edited by Claude Chabrol. Paris: Larousse, 1971.

————. *Le Degré zéro de l'écriture.* Paris: Seuil, 1953.

————. "L'effet de réel." *Communications* 11 (1968): 84-89.

————. *Essais critiques.* Paris: Seuil, 1964.

————. "Introduction à l'analyse structurale des récits." *Communications* 8 (1966): 1-27.

————. *Mythologies.* Paris: Seuil, 1957.

————. "Par où commencer?" *Poétique* 1 (1970): 3-9.

————. *Le Plaisir du texte.* Paris: Seuil, 1973.

————. *Sade, Fourier, Loyola.* Paris: Seuil, 1971.

————. *Sur Racine.* Paris: Seuil, 1963.

————. *S/Z.* Paris: Seuil, 1970.

Becker, George J., ed. *Documents of Modern Literary Realism.* Princeton: Princeton University Press, 1963.

Benjamin, Walter. *Illuminations.* Edited by Hannah Arendt. Translated by Harry Zohn. New York: Harcourt, Brace & World, 1968.

Benveniste, Emile. *Problèmes de linguistique générale.* Paris: Gallimard, 1966.

Berger, Peter L. *Invitation to Sociology: A Humanist Perspective.* Garden City, N.Y.: Doubleday, Anchor Books, 1963.

Bersani, Leo. *Balzac to Beckett: Center and Circumference in French Fiction.* New York: Oxford University Press, 1970.

————. *A Future for Astyanax: Character and Desire in Literature.* Boston: Little, Brown & Co., 1976.

Bettelheim, Bruno. *The Uses of Enchantment.* New York: Alfred A. Knopf, 1976.

Blanchot, Maurice. *La Part du feu.* Paris: Gallimard, 1949.

Booth, Wayne C. *The Rhetoric of Fiction.* Chicago: University of Chicago Press, 1961.

————. *A Rhetoric of Irony*. Chicago: University of Chicago Press, 1974.

Brooks, Peter. "Freud's Masterplot." *Yale French Studies* 55-56 (1977): 280-300.

————. *The Melodramatic Imagination: Balzac, Henry James, Melodrama, and the Mode of Excess*. New Haven: Yale University Press, 1976.

————. "Repetition, Repression, and Return: *Great Expectations* and the Study of Plot." *New Literary History* 2 (Spring 1980): 503-536.

Burke, Kenneth. *Language as Symbolic Action: Essays on Life, Literature, and Method*. Berkeley and Los Angeles: University of California Press, 1966.

————. *The Philosophy of Literary Form: Studies in Symbolic Action*. Third edition. Berkeley and Los Angeles: University of California Press, 1973.

Culler, Jonathan. *Flaubert: The Uses of Uncertainty*. Ithaca: Cornell University Press, 1974.

————. *Structuralist Poetics: Structuralism, Linguistics, and the Study of Literature*. Ithaca: Cornell University Press, 1975.

Della Volpe, Galvano. *Critica del gusto*. Third edition, revised and expanded. Milan: Feltrinelli, 1966.

De Man, Paul. *Blindness and Insight: Essays in the Rhetoric of Contemporary Criticism*. New York: Oxford University Press, 1971.

Derrida, Jacques. *De la grammatologie*. Paris: Minuit, 1967.

————. *La Dissémination*. Paris: Seuil, 1972.

————. *L'Ecriture et la différence*. Paris: Seuil, 1967.

Eagleton, Terry. *Criticism and Ideology: A Study in Marxist Literary Theory*. London: New Left Books, Humanities Press, 1976.

Eco, Umberto. *Apocalittici e integrati*. Milan: Bompiani, 1964.

————. *Opera aperta*. Milan: Bompiani, 1962.

Ehrmann, Jacques, ed. *Structuralism*. Garden City, N.Y.: Doubleday, Anchor Books, 1970.

Eliade, Mircea. *Le Mythe de l'éternel retour: archétypes et répétition*. Paris: Gallimard, 1949.

Erlich, Victor. *Russian Formalism*. The Hague: Mouton, 1955.

Flaubert, Gustave. *Préface à la vie d'écrivain*. Edited by Geneviève Bollème. Paris: Seuil, 1963.

Forster, E. M. *Aspects of the Novel*. New York: Harcourt, Brace & World, 1927.

Foucault, Michel. *Les Mots et les choses*. Paris: Gallimard, 1966.

Freud, Anna. *The Ego and the Mechanisms of Defense*. Translated by Cecil Baines. Revised edition. New York: International Universities Press, 1966.

Freud, Sigmund. [All studies from *The Standard Edition of the Complete Works of Sigmund Freud*, edited by James Strachey, 24 vols. London: The Hogarth Press and the Institute of Psycho-Analysis, 1953-74.]

————. "Analysis Terminable and Interminable." 23:209-53.

————. "The Antithetical Meaning of Primal Words." 11: 155-62.

————. *Beyond the Pleasure Principle*. 18: 3-64.

————. *Civilization and Its Discontents*. 21: 59-146.

————. " 'Civilized' Sexual Morality and Modern Nervous Illness." 9: 179-204.

————. "The Dynamics of Transference." 12: 99-108.

————. "Fausse Reconnaissance (Déjà Raconté) in Psycho-Analytic Treatment." 13: 201-7.

————. *Inhibitions, Symptoms and Anxiety*. 20: 77-174.

————. *The Interpretation of Dreams*. 4 and 5.

————. *Jokes and Their Relation to the Unconscious*. 8.

————. "Mourning and Melancholia." 14: 243-58.

————. "Negation." 19: 235-40.

————. "On Narcissism: An Introduction." 14: 73-102.

————. "On the Psychical Mechanism of Hysterical Phenomena: Preliminary Communication" (Breuer and Freud). 2: 3-17.

————. "On the Universal Tendency to Debasement in the Sphere of Love." 11: 179-90.

————. *The Psychopathology of Everyday Life.* 6.

————. "Remembering, Repeating and Working-Through." 12: 147-56.

————. "Repression." 14: 143-58.

————. "Some Neurotic Mechanisms in Jealousy, Paranoia and Homosexuality." 18: 223-32.

————. "A Special Type of Choice of Object Made by Men." 11: 165-76.

————. "The Theme of the Three Caskets." 12: 291-301.

————. *Three Essays on the Theory of Sexuality.* 7: 125-243.

————. *Totem and Taboo.* 13: 1-161.

————. "The Uncanny." 17: 219-56.

Frye, Northrop. *Anatomy of Criticism: Four Essays.* Princeton: Princeton University Press, 1957.

Genette, Gérard. *Figures.* Paris: Seuil, 1966.

————. *Figures II.* Paris: Seuil, 1969.

————. *Figures III.* Paris: Seuil, 1972.

Gide, André. *Journal: 1889-1939.* Paris: Pléiade, 1951.

Girard, René. *Mensonge romantique et vérité romanesque.* Paris: Grasset, 1961.

————. *La Violence et le sacré.* Paris: Grasset, 1972.

Goldmann, Lucien. *Le Dieu caché.* Paris: Gallimard, 1959.

————. *Pour une sociologie du roman.* Paris: Gallimard, 1964.

Gombrich, E. H. *Art and Illusion.* Princeton: Princeton University Press, 1960.

Greimas, A. J. *Sémantique structurale.* Paris: Larousse, 1966.

————. *Du Sens.* Paris: Seuil, 1970.

Grivel, Charles. *Production de l'intérêt romanesque.* The Hague: Mouton, 1974.

Hardy, Barbara. *The Appropriate Form: An Essay on the Novel.* London: University of London, The Athlone Press, 1964.

Hartman, Geoffrey H. *Beyond Formalism: Literary Essays 1958-1970.* New Haven: Yale University Press, 1970.

Iser, Wolfgang. *The Implied Reader: Patterns of Communication in Prose Fiction from Bunyan to Beckett.* Baltimore and London: The Johns Hopkins University Press, 1974.

————. "Indeterminacy and the Reader's Response in Prose Fiction." In *Aspects of Narrative*, edited by J. Hillis Miller, pp. 1-45. New York and London: Columbia University Press, 1971.

————. "The Reading Process: A Phenomenological Approach." *New Literary History* 3 (1972): 279-99.

Jakobson, Roman. *Questions de poétique.* Paris: Seuil, 1973.

————. "Two Aspects of Language and Two Types of Aphasic Disturbances." In R. Jakobson and M. Halle, *Fundamentals of Language*, pp. 55-82. The Hague: Mouton, 1956.

James, Henry. *The Art of the Novel.* Edited by R. P. Blackmur. New York: Scribner's, 1934.

————. *French Poets and Novelists.* New York: Grosset & Dunlap, 1964.

————. *Notes on Novelists.* New York: Scribner's, 1914.

Jameson, Fredric. *Marxism and Form.* Princeton: Princeton University Press, 1971.

————. *The Prison-House of Language.* Princeton: Princeton University Press, 1972.

Kermode, Frank. *The Sense of an Ending.* London: Oxford University Press, 1966.

Kettle, Arnold. *An Introduction to the English Novel: Defoe to the Present.* Revised edition. 2 vols. in 1. New York: Harper & Row, Perennial Library, 1968.

Kierkegaard, Søren. *The Concept of Irony.* Translated by Lee M. Capel. Bloomington and London: University of Indiana Press, 1965.

Kristeva, Julia. *Semiotike: Recherches pour une sémanalyse.* Paris: Seuil, 1969.

Lacan, Jacques. *Ecrits.* Paris: Seuil, 1966.

Leavis, F. R. *The Great Tradition*. Fourth edition. London: Chatto and Windus, 1960.

Lemon, Lee T., and Reis, Marion J., eds. and trans. *Russian Formalist Criticism: Four Essays*. Lincoln: University of Nebraska Press, 1965.

Lévi-Strauss, Claude. "L'analyse morphologique des contes russes." *International Journal of Slavic Linguistics and Poetics* 3: 122-49.

————. *Anthropologie structurale*. Paris: Plon, 1958.

————. "La geste d'Asdiwal." *L'Annuaire de l'Ecole Pratique des Hautes Etudes* (Section des sciences religieuses), 1958-59, pp. 2-43.

Lewes, George Henry. *Literary Criticism of George Henry Lewes*. Edited by Alice R. Kaminsky. Lincoln: University of Nebraska Press, 1964.

Lubbock, Percy. *The Craft of Fiction*. London: Jonathan Cape, 1965.

Lukács, Georg. *The Historical Novel*. Translated by Hannah and Stanley Mitchell. London: Merlin, 1962.

————. *History and Class Consciousness*. Translated by Rodney Livingstone. Cambridge, Mass.: MIT Press, 1971.

————. *Studies in European Realism*. New York: Grosset & Dunlap, 1964.

————. *The Theory of the Novel*. Translated by Anna Bostock. Cambridge, Mass.: MIT Press, 1971.

————. *Writer and Critic and Other Essays*. Translated by Arthur D. Kahn. New York: Grosset & Dunlap, 1971.

Macherey, Pierre. *Pour une théorie de la production littéraire*. Paris: Maspéro, 1970.

Macksey, Richard, and Donato, Eugenio, eds. *The Languages of Criticism and the Sciences of Man*. Baltimore: The Johns Hopkins University Press, 1970.

Matejka, Ladislav, and Pomorska, Krystyna, eds. *Readings in Russian Poetics: Formalist and Structuralist Views*. Cambridge, Mass.: MIT Press, 1971.

Metz, Christian. *Essais sur la signification au cinéma*. Vol. 1. Paris: Klincksieck, 1968.

Miller, J. Hillis. *The Disappearance of God: Five Nineteenth-Century Writers.* Cambridge, Mass.: Harvard University Press, 1963.

————. *The Form of Victorian Fiction.* Notre Dame and London: University of Notre Dame Press, 1968.

Price, Martin. "The Fictional Contract." In *Literary Theory and Structure*, edited by Frank Brady, John Palmer, and Martin Price, pp. 151-78. New Haven: Yale University Press, 1973.

————. "The Irrelevant Detail and the Emergence of Form." In *Aspects of Narrative*, edited by J. Hillis Miller, pp. 69-91. New York and London: Columbia University Press, 1971.

————. "People of the Book: Character in Forster's *A Passage to India.*" *Critical Inquiry* 1 (March 1975): 605-22.

Propp, Vladimir. *Morphology of the Folktale.* Translated by Laurence Scott. Austin: University of Texas Press, 1968.

Robbe-Grillet, Alain. *Pour un nouveau roman.* Paris: Minuit, 1963.

Robey, David, ed. *Structuralism: An Introduction.* London: Oxford University Press, 1973.

Sartre, Jean-Paul. *L'Idiot de la famille.* 3 vols. Paris: Gallimard, 1971.

————. *La Nausée.* Paris: Gallimard, 1938.

————. "Question de méthode." Preface to *Critique de la raison dialectique*, 1: 13-111. Paris: Gallimard, 1960.

————. *Saint Genet, comédien et martyr.* Paris: Gallimard, 1952.

————. *Situations I.* Paris: Gallimard, 1947.

————. *Situations II (Qu'est-ce que la littérature?).* Paris: Gallimard, 1948.

Saussure, Ferdinand de. *Cours de linguistique générale.* Edited by Tullio de Mauro. Paris: Payot, 1972.

Scheler, Max. *Ressentiment.* Translated by William W. Holdheim. New York: Schocken Books, 1972.

Scholes, Robert. *Structuralism in Literature: An Introduction*. New Haven: Yale University Press, 1974.

Scholes, Robert, and Kellogg, Robert. *The Nature of Narrative*. New York: Oxford University Press, 1966.

Smith, Barbara H. *Poetic Closure: A Study of How Poems End*. Chicago: University of Chicago Press, 1968.

Todorov, Tzvetan. *Introduction à la littérature fantastique*. Paris: Seuil, 1970.

————. *Poétique de la prose*. Paris: Seuil, 1971.

————, ed. and trans. *Théorie de la littérature*. Paris: Seuil, 1965.

Wellek, René, and Warren, Austin. *Theory of Literature*. Third edition. New York: Harcourt, Brace & World, 1956.

Wilden, Anthony. *The Language of the Self*. Baltimore: The Johns Hopkins University Press, 1968.

Williams, Raymond. *The Country and the City*. New York: Oxford University Press, 1973.

————. *Culture and Society: 1780-1950*. New York: Harper and Row, 1958.

————. *The English Novel: From Dickens to Lawrence*. London: Chatto and Windus, 1970.

————. Introduction to *The Pelican Book of English Prose*, vol. 2, pp. 19-55. Penguin, 1969.

Wimsatt, W. K. *The Verbal Icon: Studies in the Meaning of Poetry*. Lexington: University of Kentucky Press, 1954.

Index

Anderson, Quentin, 158

Austen, Jane, ix-xv passim, 3-106, 107, 108n2, 109, 122, 151, 189, 195, 201, 242, 248, 262, 265-83 passim; chatter, 33-41; closure, 66-106; closure as censorship, 66-76, 89-98; closure as intervention, 8, 12, 19-20, 25; closure as the production of knowledge, 77-89; equivocal status of narrative, 99-106; equivocation of heroines, 54-63; "etc principle," 26-27, 41, 43-44; fear of play, 98-99n31; heroines' mania for explanation, 51-53; ideology, 40-41, 50, 54, 63; indirect discourse, 28-31; irony, 27-33, 83-85, 87-89; marriage plot, 43-44; mistaken identities, 67-68; narrative bonus, 104-106; negation, 63-66; nomination, 24-26, 44-51; nonobjectal desire, 8-15, 20-24, 91-97, 100n; "novelism," 15-19; perfect conditional, 99-101; social intercourse, 42-44, 102; suspense, 46-51.

Bakhtin, Mikhail, 153
Balzac, Honoré de, 111, 146, 159, 262, 273
Barthes, Roland, xii, xiii, 4n, 39, 43, 46, 53n, 78, 151n, 220, 221, 236, 273, 274, 281
Bataille, Georges, 271n
Benveniste, Emile, 156, 255n
Berger, Peter, 119n
Bersani, Leo, 144n, 231-32, 279
Bettelheim, Bruno, 187n
Blythe, Ronald, 101n
Bossuet, Jacques Bénigne, 132
Bray, Charles, 162
Brooks, Peter, 132, 133n, 170, 250, 251n, 274-75n5
Burke, Kenneth, 239

Chaucer, Geoffrey, 227
closure: use of the term, xi n; in twentieth-century narratology, xii-xiii, 241-42, 281; impossibility of, xiv, 188-90, 265-68; versus the narratable, xi-xv, 65, 89, 97-98, 149-50, 179,

-·--∘·{ *Index* }∘·--

Library of Congress Cataloging in Publication Data

Miller, D A   1948-
  Narrative and its discontents.

  Bibliography: p.
  Includes index.
    1. Fiction—Technique.   2. Narration (Rhetoric)
  I. Title.
  PN3383.N35M54   809.3'923   80-8565
  ISBN 0-691-06459-8
  ISBN 0-691-01458-2 (pbk.)